Thomas Conlon, Shaen Corbet

Global Health Crises and Financial Resilience

De Gruyter Studies in Finance

Edited by
Shaen Corbet

Thomas Conlon, Shaen Corbet

Global Health Crises and Financial Resilience

Analysing Market Responses

DE GRUYTER

ISBN 978-3-11-170780-8
e-ISBN (PDF) 978-3-11-170799-0
e-ISBN (EPUB) 978-3-11-170815-7
ISSN 2941-3303

Library of Congress Control Number: 2025943001

Bibliographic information published by the Deutsche Nationalbibliothek
The Deutsche Nationalbibliothek lists this publication in the Deutsche Nationalbibliografie; detailed bibliographic data are available on the Internet at http://dnb.dnb.de.

Cover image: Cemile Bingol/DigitalVision Vectors/Getty Images
Typesetting: VTeX UAB, Lithuania
Printing and binding: CPI books GmbH, Leck

www.degruyter.com
Questions about General Product Safety Regulation:
productsafety@degruyterbrill.com

MIX
Papier | Fördert gute Waldnutzung
FSC® C083411

Contents

1 Introduction

The COVID-19 pandemic represents a profound black swan event, unprecedented in living memory, generating an exceptional challenge for the global economy, not to mention broader society at large. While substantial experience exists with regard to dealing with localised pandemics, the lack of associated experience regarding pandemics of a global scale was quickly evidenced as investors failed to immediately and adequately identify the exceptional risks with which they were confronted. Further challenges, such as information asymmetry and misinformation, exacerbated by social media, played a significant role in provoking market volatility. The global governmental response to the pandemic, albeit somewhat delayed, was exceptional, matching the severity and scale of the challenge confronted. Government policies, such as lockdowns, induced abrupt economic disruptions, particularly in industries reliant on close physical interactions, accelerating digital transformation across various sectors, including retail, healthcare, and remote work, to stave off economic and social collapse. Furthermore, the pandemic's evolution showcases society's capacity for exceptional innovation in the face of extreme crisis, as seen in the development and rollout of vaccines, as well as the rapid deployment of technological solutions to maintain various aspects of daily life. In the following chapters, we examine the many impacts that the pandemic had on various aspects of society and the global economy.

To begin, in Chapter 2, we examine the early responses of financial markets to the emerging COVID-19 pandemic, focusing on how underestimations of the pandemic's severity, combined with delays in clear information dissemination, contributed to a buildup of extreme market stress. Investors' response to the pandemic is particularly interesting as it provides an excellent event study surrounding the profound impact that lagged information and miscommunication can have on global financial stability. Such influence is particularly interesting during unprecedented black-swan events. Compared to other previous crises, information flow was further muddied by the global usage and saturation of social media, which acted as an exceptional catalyst for pandemic-related information and misinformation alike.

Primarily, the chapter examines the early response of financial markets to the first realisation of the true severity of the pandemic, where, more specifically, we discuss key detection points and the crisis's impact on financial assets. Such discussion highlights the importance of clear, accurate and transparent communication when attempting to mitigate financial turmoil. Further, we consider the role of information asymmetry and risk valuation, discussing how delays and underestimation influenced investor behaviour and, for the most part, sharply elevated financial market volatility. We briefly discuss the interconnectedness of global financial markets and the speed at which liquidity disappeared, largely as a result of investors' cautious approach to severity evaluation, but also when quantifying the effects that government support structures could have in their attempts to mitigate the potential sharp negative effects. In some cases, prudent investors identified clear buying opportunities, such as those identified in the pharmaceutical and

https://doi.org/10.1515/9783111707990-001

technological sectors, for example, as demand shifted as a result of government policy. The importance of regional signals was also undervalued, where evidence of posts on Chinese media and social media discussed the presence of an “unknown pneumonia”. However, few truly obtained the important signals that were contained therein.

Accurate measurement underpins much of the medical sciences and, similarly, economics. When the COVID-19 crisis emerged in early 2020, policymakers globally found themselves on the back foot, unable to quantify the extent to which the disease was spreading in the community or, for that matter, the effects of the virus. This resulted in a reliance on heuristics in the early stages of the pandemic, the outcome being relatively blunt tools such as lockdowns, closure of schools (despite early evidence that children were relatively unaffected by the disease), and work from home. These restrictions, although not necessarily supported by accurate data, brought about substantial economic pain in a very short period.

In Chapter 3, some of the more commonly watched measures of COVID-19 are examined, namely positive COVID-19 cases, hospitalisations, numbers in intensive care and deaths. Each of these reflects a different facet of the virus, but all are impeded in some way by inaccuracies. For example, case load data is impeded by a lack of testing, restrictions that count only PCR tests in the early stages of the pandemic, and changing criteria for counting cases. Deaths from COVID-19 seem like a reasonable measure of the severity of the disease, but these are a lagging indicator and may be under-reported.

The interrelationship between these different measures is quantified using a DCC-GARCH approach to understand commonalities in information flow. This indicates the degree to which these measures provide an alternative perspective on the transmission and extent of the virus. Correlations between the metrics and changes in the S&P 500 are then quantified to determine whether any of the commonly used measurement approaches provide timely information to investors. If the measures are particularly noisy, financial markets, which are inherently forward-looking, may actually be a better indicator as to the extent to which the pandemic will impact the economy.

During the COVID-19 pandemic, the implementation of social distancing regulations resulted in profound economic disruptions, particularly in industries reliant on physical interaction. While theoretically supported, issues surrounding their implementation mostly surrounded ambiguity, a lack of clarity, and, in some cases, a lack of clear governance authority, much of which we examine in Chapter 4. More specifically, we discuss the economic impacts of social distancing measures implemented during the COVID-19 pandemic, focusing on how these measures disrupted various global economic sectors while considering the long-term effects of such regulations on industries heavily reliant on physical interactions, such as retail, hospitality, and manufacturing. Specifically, we attempt to further our understanding while considering the dilemma that governments face when attempting to balance public health measures and economic stability. However, such regulatory implementation induced structural changes and several additional economic consequences, accelerating digital transformation and shifting consumer behaviours toward remote work and the incredible growth of both online shopping and entertainment usage, much of which had secondary impacts upon businesses and the population through a variety of mechanisms, some of which result in disproportionate benefits and increased societal inequality, but often represented the best option when considering the circumstances to which governments were confronted.

Chapter 5 provides a concise overview of how the financial impacts of COVID-19 compare with those of other similar global catastrophes, while Chapter 6 discusses the exceptional financial and operational impact of the COVID-19 pandemic on the global sports industry. The pandemic, while affecting every aspect of daily life, led to the suspension of many international sports worldwide, resulting in complete revenue losses from ticket sales, broadcasting rights, and sponsorships, all of which represent critical income streams for the industry. In this chapter, we analyse the immediate effects on the broader sporting ecosystem, directly considering the widespread financial distress and operational challenges faced, while highlighting the fundamental importance of government support in maintaining hopes of continued stability when the negative effects of the pandemic eventually moderate. The rapid shift towards digital and virtual technological engagement represented a watershed moment in response to exceptional challenges to generate revenues from which stability and corporate resilience could be generated, not to mention the maintenance of a central societal node with incredible importance towards societal health and well-being. We also consider key related aspects such as workers' rights, as short-term employment contracts ended abruptly, along with delays and the stalling of some progress regarding gender equality, mental health and racial justice in sports.

In keeping with previous pandemics, the spread of the COVID-19 virus was characterised by multiple waves, with transmission volumes increasing and waning over time. This created further economic uncertainty, with restrictions being eased and reintroduced depending on the extent of transmission. This economic uncertainty, in turn, affected financial markets where investors tried to extrapolate future cash flows based on available information. The effect of this is that markets were subject to short- and medium-term volatility brought about by the transmission and severity of the virus. Chapter 7 quantifies the relationship between COVID-19 and a series of financial markets at the height of the pandemic. The extent of the COVID-19 pandemic is measured in three ways: the change in positive cases, the change in the number of patient hospitalisations and the change in deaths. Financial markets are represented by four different asset classes: Treasury bonds, corporate bonds, commodities and stocks. The analysis allows us to evaluate the impact of different facets of the COVID-19 virus on a series of distinct financial asset classes.

The continuous wavelet transformation (CWT) is employed to estimate the interrelationships. This approach is particularly appropriate for a number of reasons. First, it allows us to estimate the coherency, analogous to correlation, at various points in calendar time. The benefit here is that we can quantify how interrelationships change over time. Second, the CWT has the benefit of providing a scale-dependent relationship, allowing us to quantify the coherency at different time horizons. By disentangling the different horizons, we can get a sense of the short- and medium-term effects. Finally, the CWT also provides an indication of the lead-lag relationships between the time series, allowing us to determine whether market information flow leads to the transmission of the virus. This chapter thus sheds light on the question as to whether financial markets reacted directly to information on the extent of COVID-19 or implicitly on other signals such as government restrictions or support.

A central tenet of finance is that diversification will reduce specific risk, be that at the company-level, industry-level or country-level. The COVID-19 crisis provided a stern test of the ability of diversification to limit losses for investors. The virus was a global exogenous shock, impacting the majority of companies and sectors to various degrees. Even in cases where companies ostensibly benefited from the crisis, such as pharmaceutical firms developing vaccines, supply lines were initially damaged by restrictions placed upon them by governments. Chapter 8 focuses on the ability of diversification to assist equity investors in limiting losses during the crisis.

Using global data from MSCI, three different perspectives are examined. Regional performance allows us to isolate the extent to which investing across multiple countries helped in reducing losses versus holding equity stakes in individual regions. An analysis of various sectors helps to determine whether some sectors provided relative protection from the worst of the crisis. Finally, factor portfolios, which are often claimed to provide exposure to unrelated corporate characteristics, are examined. The performance of each of these portfolio types is quantified during the COVID-19 bear market to assess the scope for equity diversification during the crisis. Furthermore, the performance during the recovery period is assessed. While the downturn might have affected all companies, the subsequent recovery may have been focused on particular countries, sectors and factors. From the perspective of investors, this is particularly challenging if they suffer wide-ranging losses during the downturn and the recovery is not homogeneous.

The following Chapter builds further on this analysis, examining the downside risk diversification capacity of a range of assets. During periods of substantial equity losses, investors often turn to safe-haven assets, characterised by low or even negative correlations during market turmoil. By allocating a small proportion of their wealth to such assets, risk-averse investors hope to reduce the extent of losses on their portfolios. The COVID-19 equity bear market, featuring a swift and deep fall in equity prices, provides a sturdy test of the capacity of such assets to retain value.

While the literature is awash with research that considers the hedging and safe haven properties of a range of assets, only a small number of articles assess the associated costs. In other words, if an investor holds a safe haven asset in their portfolio, does this have the effect of decreasing expected returns? A trade-off may exist between the willingness of a risk-averse investor to allocate capital to a safe haven asset, the impact on long-term expected returns and the performance benefits realised during periods of extreme downside risk. This trade-off is the second research question examined in Chapter 9.

To address these research questions, five possible safe haven assets are investigated. Gold, frequently proposed as a hedge and a safe haven for equity markets, is a natural candidate asset. Treasury bonds, a favoured asset during periods of flight to safety, are also considered. Crude oil and commodities, more generally, have appealing portfolio diversification properties and their safe haven properties are assessed. Finally, Bitcoin, sometimes considered the 'digital gold', has recently been proposed as a safe haven asset, and its downside risk properties are examined. While the recent literature has indicated some ambiguity with respect to which assets acted as safe havens during the crisis, this Chapter sets out to affirm the level of downside risk reduction achieved and the cost underpinning it.

The next chapter investigates how the COVID-19 pandemic influenced and reshaped the risk appetite and risk assessment practices of firms across various industries and regions, where certain sectors, such as technology and pharmaceutical, exhibit sharply contrasting reactions. Issues regarding a lack of adequate preparation, or more specifically, a sense of false security with regard to Black Swan events, was exposed across many sectors, propagating significant uncertainty and negatively affecting both investor and corporate sentiment. Further, we consider how companies and investors quantified and responded to a pandemic of unknown duration and severity but with fluid information dynamics directly influencing almost all aspects of daily life. Such decision-making had to consider the dangers inherent within over- and under-reaction, while preeminently understanding external influences such as those from government support and additional regulatory challenges. Quite simply, while the initial shock relating to the early contagion of the pandemic was profound; the next stage of development also incorporated the growth of additional risks, such as those contained in cybersecurity risks as a result of shifts to remote working. Further risks were identified across international supply chains, requiring further risk management practices with regard to inventory management and both supplier and regional diversification in an attempt to mitigate future reoccurrence of such extraordinary challenges.

The COVID-19 pandemic has fundamentally changed some aspects of our understanding of traditional financial theories. This extreme black swan event has exposed several vulnerabilities within established financial frameworks, and this chapter critically examines some of these challenges, highlighting how unprecedented market volatility and the rapid adoption of digital financial solutions during the pandemic necessitate some reevaluation of financial stability mechanisms. Further, we analyse the unprecedented market volatility experienced during the pandemic, highlighting how exceptional geopolitical and sectoral uncertainties challenged conventional financial systems, necessitating unprecedented fiscal and monetary responses to provide financial stability. We further discuss how these interventions were crucial in stabilising economies and financial markets amid the crisis. The chapter also briefly discusses the role of artificial intelligence and advanced technologies in finance, much of which has developed incredibly since the beginning of the COVID-19 pandemic, highlighting the need for robust digital infrastructure and adaptive regulatory frameworks.

The immediate effects of the COVID-19 pandemic are now becoming clear. Millions of people lost their lives, the virus infected hundreds of millions, economies were badly impaired, inflation returned for the first time in over 40 years, and financial markets were heavily impacted. Chapter 12 takes stock of some of these implications and discusses some of the long-run effects on financial markets. Chapter 12 begins with an analysis of the short-term macroeconomic effects and the monetary stimulus required. The substantial increase in prices which occurred and the policymakers' reaction to this are then discussed. This is followed by an assessment of whether policymakers have backed themselves into a corner, leaving the market fully dependent on stimulus to buttress all forms of economic shocks. The rise of digitisation is then appraised, with a focus on the financial winners and losers from the significant pandemic upheaval. A particular focus is the real estate industry, which bore a heavy brunt during the crisis and is subject to long-run uncertainty from the societal changes brought about by the pandemic.

The demise and rebirth of digital assets during the COVID-19 pandemic is further assessed. Long-run implications for non-fungible assets (NFTs) and central bank digital currencies (CBDC) are outlined, and the necessity for stronger regulation of the cryptocurrency landscape is outlined. Finally, the prospects for a more stakeholder-friendly capitalism were at the forefront during the crisis. The chapter closes out with an appraisal of whether this has been borne out in the medium-term and surmises on whether the pandemic has acted as a catalyst for longer-term sustainability.

Bear equity markets, colloquially thought of as occasions when the stock market drops by 20 percent or more, are nothing new, with 65 reported since 1800. In Chapter 13, the equity bear market brought about by the COVID-19 pandemic is compared with a series of other crises occurring over the last 50 years. Specifically, the extent and duration of the drawdown, along with the time taken to recover all losses, is quantified for the seven equity bear markets since the early 1970s.

This is followed by an analysis of the performance of a series of other assets during the bear markets to ascertain whether diversification would have been helpful to investors. Similar to earlier chapters, gold, Treasury bonds, crude oil and the broad commodity asset class are considered. By aligning the performance of the assets with the equity bear market, we get a sense of the diversification and hedging capacity of each. Furthermore, the analysis provides investors with a sense as to which asset class best holds their value, conditional upon the driver of the loss in value during the bear market.

We continue by focusing on the effects of the pandemic on the continued growth of the green finance industry during the challenge to its continued evolution from the COVID-19 pandemic, which has acted as a disruptor but also as a catalyst for sustainable investment growth, given its addition to several unconventional monetary support systems that have been created to underpin economic systems, including the incorporation of green finance into economic recovery plans, such as the European Union's Green Deal and the United States Clean Energy Initiatives, highlighting how these strategies aim to foster a green-driven recovery. Further, we emphasise the role of central banks and their tailored interventions, such as Green Quantitative Easing, in influencing investor behaviour towards more sustainable assets during times of crisis. Fundamentally, it is important that the pandemic does not detract from the significant progress that has been made across all aspects of green finance investment. Further, the continued growth of green finance in the face of such incredible challenges represents strong evidence of the maturity exhibited in this maturing sector, albeit issues surrounding exceptional upfront costs persist and become pronounced when economic conditions dictate that companies should moderate exceptional spending.

Finally, the pandemic has necessitated significant global innovation, acting as a catalyst for accelerated technological advancements and creative solutions to many issues directly related to the pandemic across several diverse sectors. In the final chapter, we examine how the unprecedented challenges contained within the pandemic generated incredibly innovative responses, highlighting the essential role of innovation in addressing global crises, providing an important layer of defence when protecting areas such as public health, education and employment. We highlight the urgency and unconventional approaches required to address severe uncertainty and destabilisation, such as rapid advancements in healthcare innovation, rapid vaccine development and telemedicine, demonstrating how the pandemic accelerated progress in medical technologies. Innovative solutions were also required to respond to border closures, supply chain slowdowns, increased competition for limited resources, and global collaboration in vaccine development, showcasing how unprecedented partnerships led to many incredible scientific breakthroughs.

The COVID-19 pandemic presents a unique convergence of health and economic crises, testing both economic resilience and government capabilities, while presenting a unique opportunity to develop our understanding of the societal and financial issues that unfolded. The unprecedented nature of the crisis emphasised the need for greater adaptability and innovation in both economic policies and corporate strategies in the face of extreme uncertainty. Particularly, the role of, and both the expectations and demands of central banks in future crises, is now under scrutiny, with several questions persisting surrounding the continued use of quantitative easing and its direct and secondary impacts on financial markets and the global economy. The pandemic has highlighted the critical role of government and institutional support in maintaining economic stability during extreme events, setting new precedents, and expectations for future policy interventions. The fiscal support provided during the pandemic, while essential, it has raised concerns about the long-term viability of zombie firms and the potential misallocation of resources when maintaining their continued operations despite such an exceptionally elevated probability of default. As the global economy continues to recover, and as we investigate in the forthcoming chapters, there is a need for a balanced approach that addresses both immediate economic challenges and long-term sustainability goals. The lessons learned from the COVID-19 pandemic will shape future economic strategies, particularly in preparing for and mitigating the impacts of similar global crises.

2 Measuring COVID-19

An assortment of COVID-19 metrics were closely watched by the media and the public during the pandemic. The number of positive cases, hospitalisations, intensive care cases and deaths all indicate different facets of the extent and severity of the disease. This chapter describes the strengths and limitations of each measure, quantifies their links with one another and determines their correlation with financial market returns. Using a DCC-GARCH model, dynamic intra-correlations between the different metrics are estimated. The correlation between positive cases and deaths is highest, with changes in hospitalisation having the lowest correlation with other measures. Assessing links with the returns of the S&P 500, deaths from COVID-19 have the expected negative correlation with the market. As deaths are the strongest signal for policymakers to act in response to the virus, this highlights the relevance of social distancing and restrictions on commercial activity to financial markets.

2.1 Introduction

The severe acute respiratory syndrome coronavirus 2 (SARS-CoV-2) was first identified in late 2019 in Wuhan, China, following a cluster of atypical pneumonia cases. While the exact origins remain unconfirmed, the initial human transmission is likely to have come from contact with a live animal market. The rapid spread and high transmissibility of the virus led the WHO to declare it a public health emergency on January 30, 2020 and a pandemic on March 11, 2020. By August 31, 2020, over 25 million confirmed cases were registered globally (Menkir et al., 2021).

The province of Wuhan introduced public health restrictions on January 23, 2020, setting the tone for similar subsequent measures globally. Studies estimate that up to 86 percent of cases were not detected in China up to this point (Singh et al., 2021). The WHO acknowledged on January 30, 2020 that international contagion was active, with 98 known cases in 18 countries (Singh et al., 2021). This spread quickly to 5,304 acknowledged cases across 53 countries by late February. Asymptomatic and pre-symptomatic transmission, limited testing capacity and rapid testing, alongside inconsistent reporting, mean that there is substantial uncertainty about the actual level of viral transmission at this point.

The spread and impact of the COVID-19 virus were measured in many different ways. First, testing for the virus was carried out using rapid antigen testing, antibody tests and the gold standard, molecular or PCR tests. In the initial stages of the COVID-19 pandemic, many countries only included PCR-confirmed cases in the official counts underestimates the true prevalence of transmission. Criteria for counting COVID-19 cases evolved over time. For example, in the USA, the Centres for Disease Control and Prevention (CDC) updated their case definition several times throughout the pandemic to reflect a changing understanding of the virus and the availability of testing methods.

https://doi.org/10.1515/9783111707990-002

This evolving approach to measuring the prevalence of COVID-19 in the community, this means that any time series capturing infection rates is subject to structural breaks, such that the statistical properties change significantly.

Given the challenges with consistent measurement of infection, hospitalisations may be a useful proxy to understand the spread of COVID-19. This presents several advantages over community-level testing. Hospitalisation numbers do not rely on self-reporting or unreported cases; they provide an indication of the severity of cases and have reduced reporting bias. Hospitalisation numbers are not without problems, however. They are generally considered to be a lagging indicator, with delays between the time of infection and development of symptoms serious enough to warrant hospitalisation. They are also dependent on testing rates and clinical practice, which may vary dependent on guidelines in different jurisdictions. Over time the incidence of hospitalisation was also reduced by a massive global vaccination program. Finally, hospitalisations may be impacted by the capacity of the healthcare system, alongside comorbidities and risk factors.

Intensive care (ICU) cases are a further way to proxy for the spread of the COVID-19 virus. ICU cases tend to be better tracked and reported than overall hospitalisations and may be more consistently reported over time. They also provide a strong indicator of the severity of the pandemic and the impact on the healthcare system. They are, however, subject to some of the same biases as hospitalisations. They are a lagging indicator, can be impacted by capacity and may be heavily influenced by changes in best clinical practice.

A further closely watched metric from the pandemic was attributed deaths. Representing the most serious outcome from the virus, these acted as a severity measure. They tend to be consistently reported, are not subject to changes in testing protocols and are not influenced by the availability of testing. Similar to hospitalisation, they are a lagging indicator, are significantly influenced by demographic considerations and may be under-reported. The latter is particularly the case when an underlying condition is present.

The strengths and weaknesses of these reporting measures are reviewed in this chapter, focusing on data from the USA. Even within a single country, substantial state-by-state differences were evident during the pandemic (Galaitsi et al., 2021). Some states relied only on confirmed positive cases, while others included probable cases. Testing availability was mixed, especially in the early stages of the pandemic. Differences in reporting lags mean that aggregate country-level data may not accurately reflect the extent of infection over time. Finally, different criteria were employed in defining metrics, especially in classifying whether a death was due to COVID-19 or not.

The effect of COVID-19 transmission on financial markets was rapid and substantial. Comparing the response of US equity markets in the early stages to previous downturns, Gormsen and Koijen (2023) show that the 34 % decline was steeper and more rapid than any previous downturn. Furthermore, the market recovered all losses within 116 trading days, vastly quicker than in any previous market drawdown. The speed with which the market recovered is of particular note, given that initial vaccine approval was still more than six months away. This extended lag indicates that the market was impounding other information, perhaps related to trends in COVID-19 spread and severity.

This powerful effect on financial markets is in strong contrast to previous pandemics, and has been attributed to government restrictions and social distancing impacting a service-based economy (Baker et al., 2020). These findings are echoed by Szczygielski et al. (2023), where government response stringency, uncertainty and median attention are found to be linked with changes in global stock prices. The impacts of the pandemic were, however, unevenly distributed across sectors, with sectors such as tourism, energy and retail disproportionately impacted. This is borne out by increased tail risk of less resilient sectors prior to the market drawdown (Breugem et al., 2024).

The specific response of stock markets to metrics capturing the spread and severity of COVID-19 has, surprisingly, received limited attention. Over a short period to April 2020, Ashraf (2020b) finds a strong negative response to confirmed cases, but a more limited reaction to data capturing growth in deaths. Many confounding factors, such as changes in short-term discount rates, shown to account for up to 40 percent of stock market moves, obfuscate the impact of such metrics (Berkman and Malloch, 2023).

In this chapter, a range of COVID-19 metrics, including positive tests, hospitalisations, ICU cases and deaths, are explored and contrasted. Using a DCC-GARCH approach, the interrelationship between the measures is assessed, to understand the extent to which they capture similar contemporaneous information. Correlations between each metric and changes in the S&P 500 are then examined to quantify links between the measurement of COVID-19 and market performance.

2.2 Previous Literature

To inform challenges surrounding the spread and severity of the disease, healthcare capacity, availability of public services such as education and providing social safety nets, policymakers attempted to interpret public health data. In the US this was beset by difficulties, including differential timing, data gaps, inconsistent definitions and changing scientific interpretations (Galaitsi et al., 2021). Data collection protocols also differed widely internationally, despite the WHO's attempts to establish common conventions. Alternative proxies for COVID-19 spread, such as mobile phone data, have additionally been proposed, also allowing for contact tracing (Grantz et al., 2020).

Cases of unexplained pneumonia began to present in Wuhan, China, in December 2019. The first, subsequently confirmed, case of symptomatic COVID-19 has been established on December 8, 2019 (Singh et al., 2021). By December 30, 2019 human-to-human transmission for patients without exposure to the Wuhan Seafood Market, the initial focus of the epidemiological investigation, is reported (Singh et al., 2021). On January 5, 2020, a notification from the WHO disclosed to member governments an outbreak in Wuhan. The first, latterly confirmed, international case is documented in Thailand on

January 8, 2020 (Singh et al., 2021). The first reported case of COVID-19 in the US, a man returning from China, was documented on January 20, 2020 (Holshue et al., 2020).

By March 15, 2020, 3,499 cases and 60 deaths were attributed to COVID-19 in the US, with the majority in New York, Washington and California (Chowell and Mizumoto, 2020). A national emergency was declared by President Donald Trump on March 13, 2020, leading to a range of social distancing interventions. Such interventions have been associated with a decrease in confirmed COVID-19 cases of up to 9.1 percent (Courtemanche et al., 2020). Without these measures, modelling implies that the spread of COVID-19 would have been up to ten times greater by the end of April 2020 (Courtemanche et al., 2020). Rapid development led to the approval of a Pfizer-BioNTech vaccine for emergency use in the US on December 11, 2020, with first doses administered on December 14. Over the following year, the impact of the vaccine is striking. Suthar et al. (2022) indicates that a 10 % increase in US county vaccination coverage is associated with a 7 % reduction in cases and an 8 % reduction in mortality from COVID-19.

The COVID-19 pandemic had broad-ranging economic consequences for labour, gender, health, discrimination and the environment (Brodeur et al., 2021). While all business sectors were impacted to some extent (Szczygielski et al., 2022), corporate characteristics such as better liquidity, global supply chains and higher corporate social responsibility are associated with strong financial performance during the period (Ding et al., 2021). Furthermore, firms more exposed to Chinese trade underperformed (Ramelli and Wagner, 2020). Critical to the survival of companies during this period were the policies instigated by many governments to support business (Cirera et al., 2021). At the heart of this were liquidity and monetary easing policies, often acting through the banking channel (Demirgüç-Kunt et al., 2021).

The effects of COVID-19 on financial markets, in particular, are striking. The benchmark S&P 500 index rapidly lost up to 34 percent of its value (Gormsen and Koijen, 2023). The associated market volatility rivalled that witnessed during Black Monday 1987 and the Great Crash of 1929 (Baker et al., 2020). The intensity of the stock market decline has been attributed to the extent of the government reaction, particularly social distancing and restrictions on commercial activity (Baker et al., 2020). Declines in the stock market were not confined to the US, with severe dislocations across all developed economies (Zhang et al., 2020). Emerging markets were also impacted, especially those in Asia (Topcu and Gulal, 2020). In spite of the proliferation of information surrounding the spread of the virus, markets reacted significantly to the announcement of the first death from COVID-19 in each country (Heyden and Heyden, 2021).

The financial market impact of the pandemic was not confined to equity markets. In developed economies, the sovereign debt yield decreased, while in emerging economies, there was a positive impact on yields, perhaps indicating a safe haven quality for developed markets' bonds (Nasir et al., 2023). The shock to bonds was not, however, limited to yields, with vast shifts in liquidity also documented (O'Hara and Zhou, 2021), but this was somewhat alleviated by the actions of the Federal Reserve to support the market (Kargar et al., 2021). Similarly, monetary policy announcements led to changes in corporate credit spreads, with the effect found to be heterogeneous across credit rating buckets (Nozawa and Qiu, 2021).

The price of crude oil was particularly impacted, with West Texas Intermediate futures prices turned negative for a period during April 2020 (Fernandez-Perez et al., 2023; Corbet et al., 2020b, 2021b). Safe haven assets such as gold worked to protect bond investors and, to a lesser extent, equity investors during the pandemic (Konstantakis et al., 2023). Cryptocurrencies, long-touted as a hedge for traditional financial markets were indicated to have negative returns correlated with equity and major currency returns during the early stages of the pandemic (Conlon et al., 2024d,g; Conlon and McGee, 2020a). Cryptocurrencies were also found to be substantially impacted by negative COVID-19 sentiment (Corbet et al., 2020c), along with reacting negatively to the subsequent period of heightened inflation resulting from COVID-19 (Conlon et al., 2021, 2024g).

At the heart of the debate about the implications of the COVID-19 pandemic on financial markets is the specific timing and measurement of events. This chapter seeks to contrast the different metrics regularly cited during the pandemic, cases, hospitalisations and deaths, and to assess their links with financial markets.

2.3 Data and Methodology

2.3.1 Data

COVID-19-related data for this study were collected for the US from the COVID Tracking Project at The Atlantic.[1] The data is compiled from the state-level websites of public health authorities. It is selected due to an earlier start date relative to other sources, a vital characteristic in assessing links with financial markets due to their forward-looking nature.

Daily data are aggregated at a weekly level due to strong day-of-the-week effects, resulting from reduced weekend testing and spikes in reporting. Aggregation is carried out on the Friday of each week. Similar to other COVID-19 data sources such as the CDC, our data is subject to different data definitions across regions, time lags and state-level aggregation. Testing figures may also include multiple tests carried out on the same person.

The first recorded US case of COVID-19 in the data is on January 19, 2020 and a total of 18 cases are recorded up to February 29, 2020. The first recorded death occurred on February 26, 2020. Hospitalisation data is somewhat lagging, with the first documented hospitalisations on March 3, 2020. The data is discontinued on March 7, 2021, due to an improvement in the quality of aggregated data reported by government sources. The period considered, however, captured the most market-relevant period of the pandemic, allowing us to gain an understanding of the links between COVID-19 measures and changes in financial returns.

1 www.covidtracking.com

Market data relating to the S&P 500, an index capturing the performance of 500 large, listed Companies listed on the US exchange, is obtained from EIKON, a division of LSEG Data and Analytics. Weekly returns from January 24, 2020, are examined to align with pandemic-related data. All returns are in US dollars (USD).

2.3.2 Methodology

To assess the relationship between the different measures of COVID-19, along with links between these metrics and financial markets, the DCC-GARCH model of Engle (2002) is employed.

Given a time series s_t of length n, an AR(1) process can be written as,

$$s_t = \mu + a s_{t-1} + \varepsilon_t. \tag{2.1}$$

The residuals of the mean equation are modelled as:

$$\varepsilon_t = H_t^{\frac{1}{2}} z_t. \tag{2.2}$$

z_t is an $n \times 1$ vector of i. i. d. errors and H_t is the conditional covariance matrix of s_t.

Univariate GARCH models are first estimated for each time series. A GARCH(1,1) model is employed here, where the elements of H_t can be written as:

$$h_{i,t} = \omega_i + \alpha_i \varepsilon_{i,t-1}^2 + \beta_i h_{i,t-1}. \tag{2.3}$$

In a second step, the condition correlations are estimated using:

$$H_t = D_t R_t D_t. \tag{2.4}$$

H_t is an $n \times n$ conditional covariance matrix and R_t is the conditional correlation matrix. D_t is a time-varying diagonal matrix with standard deviations on the diagonal.

$$D_t = \operatorname{diag}(h_{1,t}^{1/2}, \ldots, h_{n,t}^{1/2}). \tag{2.5}$$

$$R_t = \operatorname{diag}(q_{1,t}^{1/2}, \ldots, q_{n,t}^{1/2}) Q_t (q_{1,t}^{1/2}, \ldots, \operatorname{diag} q_{n,t}^{1/2}). \tag{2.6}$$

Q_t is a symmetric positive definite matrix, given by

$$Q_t = (1 - \theta_1 - \theta_2)\overline{Q} + \theta_1 z_{t-1} z_{t-1}' + \theta_2 Q_{t-1}, \tag{2.7}$$

where $\overline{Q}$ corresponds to the $n \times n$ unconditional correlation matrix of the standardised residuals and θ_1 and θ_2 are non-negative. The correlation between time series i and j is then given by:

$$\rho_{i,j,t} = \frac{q_{i,j,t}}{\sqrt{q_{i,i,t} q_{j,j,t}}}. \tag{2.8}$$

2.4 Results

This section provides an empirical assessment of the different metrics used to represent the prevalence and severity of the COVID-19 virus in the US. Dynamic correlations between the different metrics are assessed, and then their relationship with changes in the S&P 500 are presented.

2.5 COVID 19 Data

Four primary metrics were widely communicated during the height of the COVID-19 pandemic, namely the number of positive cases, the tally of people hospitalised and in ICU care, and the total number of deaths attributed to the disease at any point in time. Each of these represents a very different perspective on the prevalence of COVID-19.

The weekly change in each of these metrics is presented in Figure 2.1. Starting with positive cases in the top left-hand figure, we observe a gradual increase in the number of weekly cases up to early 2021. While this may provide some reflection of the presence of the virus in society at this point, the accuracy of these estimates may be questionable. The roll-out of testing was slow, with problems in the production of an accurate testing protocol. The ramp-up of sufficient test equipment production also took substantial time. On top of this, the hurdle to qualify for testing was high, limited to people exposed to the virus, especially healthcare workers, and to those displaying specific symptoms. Finally, there were delays between testing and results, which means that the extent of case positivity may, in these early stages, lag the actual extent to which the virus was spreading in society. These issues make case positivity a poor measure of the transmission of COVID-19, at least until the issues discussed were addressed.

Two interrelated alternatives were regularly discussed, representing, as they did, the pressures on the health system and the potential for restrictions to curtail the spread of the virus to prevent hospitals from being overwhelmed. The weekly changes in the number of patients hospitalised with COVID-19 and those in intensive care with COVID-19 are also shown in Figure 2.1. The data indicate a much sharper and striking increase in cases from April 2020. Three distinct waves are evident in the hospitalisation numbers. The first began as the disease spread widely in society, peaking towards the end of May 2020. The second wave followed shortly thereafter, peaking in August 2021, when 21,925 patients were hospitalised in a single week. The third wave occurred during the winter of 2020–2021, where over 25,000 patients were hospitalised each week for nine consecutive weeks. The lack of strong corresponding waves in positive cases acts as a further indicator that the latter did not adequately reflect the spread of the virus during this period.

The trend in ICU patients is concordant with that of hospitalisations. Three waves are observed over the first year of COVID-19, with the first wave peaking in early May 2020. Subsequent waves were less severe, partly due to better early treatments, restrictions preventing the spread of the disease in locations such as nursing homes, improved

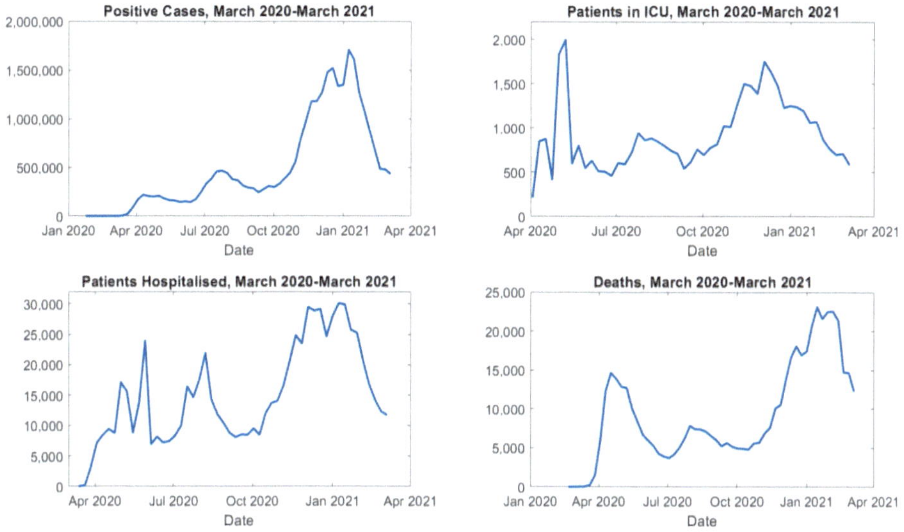

Figure 2.1: Weekly changes in COVID-19 metrics, March 2020–March 2021.
Note: The metrics shown are for positive cases, ICU cases, hospitalisations and deaths. Data reflects changes in the aggregate levels of each measure on a weekly basis, providing an indicator of the new cases, hospitalisations and deaths. Data are calculated on a Friday-to-Friday basis to avoid reporting delays associated with weekends.

public health measures and, potentially, later variants caused less severe illness. The third wave, evident in winter 2020, began to taper from early December, coinciding with the approval of and first vaccinations against COVID-19. One important side effect of vaccination was a substantial decrease in the likelihood of serious illness.

Finally, the number of weekly reported US deaths, incorporating confirmed and probable COVID-19 case diagnoses, is provided. Once again, there are three waves, with the second wave less severe than the others. The final wave peaked in mid-January 2021, with a loss of 23,083 lives in a single week. Notably, this peak arrived one week after the peak in hospitalisations but up to seven weeks after the peak in cases requiring ICU.

This summary highlights many of the issues surrounding the variety of ways in which the effects of COVID-19 were measured. These limitations also partially restrict the use of the metrics in prediction and characterisation, especially in the context of financial markets. Data on hospitalisation and deaths seem like the most plausible metrics, but even these suffer from the challenge of being lagging indicators.

2.5.1 Relationship Between Different Measures

Next, the DCC-GARCH model described in Section 2.3.2 is applied to dynamically estimate the level of contemporaneous correlation between the various COVID-19 measures. This analysis allows us to get a high-level understanding of the extent to which these mea-

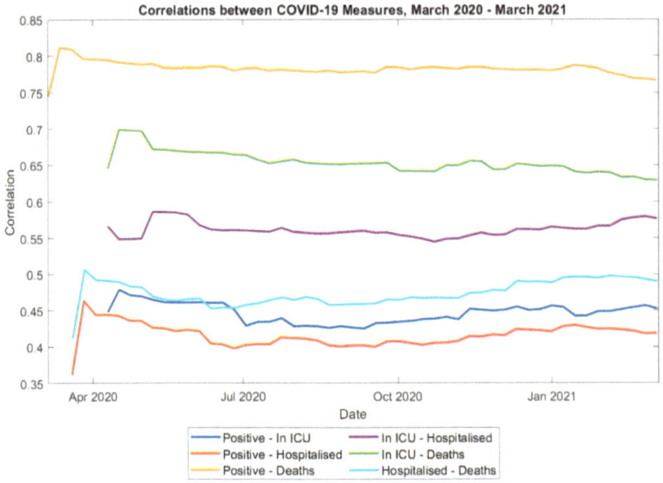

Figure 2.2: Intra-correlations between COVID-19 metrics, 2020–2021.
Note: This figure details the extent of the correlations over time between changes in i) positive cases, ii) Deaths, iii) hospitalisations, and iv) ICU cases. A DCC-GARCH model is used to estimate dynamic correlations over the period from March 2020 through March 2021.

sures reflect similar information and, perhaps, to identify any outliers. Results are detailed in Figure 2.2 and the different correlation start dates reflect the variety in the collection of the data.

Starting from top to bottom, the highest correlations are observed between positive cases and deaths. Although decreasing slightly over time, these correlations are, on the face of it, likely to be causal but with a lag. The correlations may be a cause of underreporting in both measures in the early stages of the pandemic, but also delays in rolling out the vaccine, resulting in a greater alignment of the third wave, with the vulnerable vaccinated first, bringing the decrease in deaths down in line with the leading positive case indicator.

This is followed by the correlations between the numbers of patients in the ICU and hospitalisations and deaths, with averages of 0.56 and 0.65, respectively. A high correlation is to be expected here, given that extremely ill hospitalised patients may be moved to the ICU and that these same patients are the most likely to subsequently pass away due to the virus. Given that they are often separated by an intermediate stage, correlations between changes in hospitalised patients and deaths are lower, with an average value of 0.47. The correlation level peaked at 0.51 towards the beginning of the pandemic and returned close to these levels by January 2021.

Finally, correlations between positive cases and those hospitalised or in the ICU are found to be lowest. There are a variety of explanations for this. First, there is a delay between the first diagnosis and being hospitalised with the virus. Low testing capacity in the early stages of the pandemic would also have contributed to the low correlation, alongside reporting delays. As testing became more commonplace, this may have then

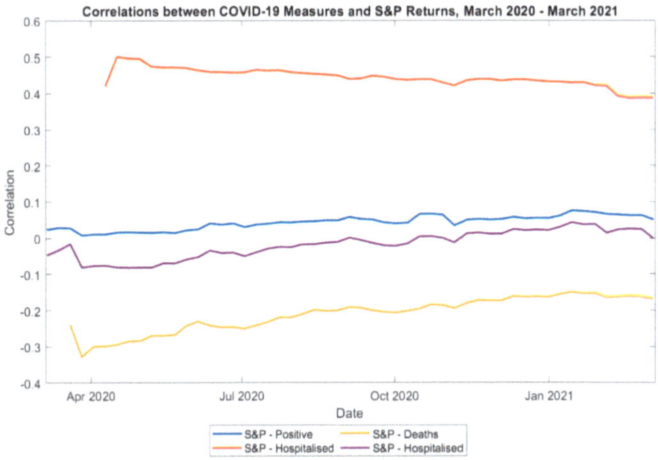

Figure 2.3: Correlations between COVID-19 and S&P 500 returns.

Note: This figure details the extent of the correlations over time between weekly returns of the S&P 500 and changes in i) positive cases, ii) deaths, iii) hospitalisations, and iv) ICU cases. A DCC-GARCH model is used to estimate dynamic correlations over the period from March 2020 through March 2021.

altered the relationship. Changes in the severity of the virus, along with the phased introduction of the COVID-19 vaccine, would also have resulted in a reduction in the number of cases requiring hospitalisation and especially the volume of patients in the ICU.

These correlations highlight considerable variety in the relationship between the set of measures commonly used to assess the spread and severity of the pandemic. While this analysis does not assess the causal effect or any lead-lag inter-dependencies, it does indicate distinct differences in the metrics. The implication for an analyst deciding which of these to select as an indicator of the virus is that care must be taken, especially in the early stages of the virus, where reporting was substandard, subjective and without agreed protocols.

2.5.2 COVID-19 and Financial Markets

Dynamic links between changes in each of the COVID-19 measures and financial market returns are examined next. Specifically, the DCC-GARCH correlation between the weekly change in COVID-19 and the returns of the S&P 500 is quantified. Should increases in the spread and severity of the virus be construed as bad news, one would expect a negative relationship between increases in COVID-19 and stock returns. Results are displayed in Figure 2.3.

The correlation between the number of patients hospitalised and S&P 500 returns is found to be strongly positive, taking values between 0.39 and 0.50. While these findings might appear to be counterintuitive, increased hospitalisations may have acted as a credible signal to policymakers on the severity of the pandemic, leading them to provide greater fiscal and monetary stimulus. This would, in turn, be regarded as positive news by financial markets. The decrease in correlation towards the end of the sample may also indicate that the introduction of the vaccine helped to break the link between hospitalisation data and financial market performance. Finally, companies in the S&P 500 may have exposure to markets other than the US, meaning that they are impacted by the spread of the disease in other countries, along with government restrictions and social distancing rules.

Correlations between S&P returns and the change in positive cases hover just above zero, having an average value 0.044. In other words, the reaction of financial markets to changes in the number of positive cases is negligible. While one driver of this may be the exposures that US companies have to overseas economies, reporting inaccuracies may have led participants to focus on other measures which better reflect the true impact on the economy. Furthermore, the forward-looking nature of financial markets would imply that forecasts of the future trajectory of cases may be of more value relevance to investors.

A weak correlation is found to exist between changes in the number of hospitalised patients and S&P returns. This correlation is negative in the early stages of the pandemic, taking the value −0.08 in late March 2020, but steadily increasing to 0.0432 in January 2021. This may indicate that the market responded, to some extent, to increases in hospitalisations. As information on the pandemic emerged, there were widespread concerns about the impact on the economy, with financial markets reflecting this. As the pandemic progressed, news on government economic supports and the introduction of various vaccination alternatives tempered this relationship.

The final, and most interesting, analysis is the relationship between changes in deaths from COVID-19 and S&P 500 returns. This is the only metric demonstrating the consistent negative expected relationship with market returns. Over the one-year period examined, the average correlation varied from −0.32 to −0.15, showing a relative weakening over time. Why is this relationship the most persistent among those examined? Deaths may be the strongest determinant of market sentiment resulting from COVID-19. Increases in deaths are, among the measures examined, the most likely to result in stricter lockdowns and an associated reduction in economic activity. Increases in deaths may also have the greatest immediate influence on consumer sentiment, reducing spending. Finally, deaths are a more reliable indicator of the severity of the pandemic, as they are not influenced by testing rates or reporting inconsistencies associated with comorbidities.

While not providing a causal relationship between the various measures of COVID-19 and S&P returns, this analysis demonstrates strong differences in the response of market returns to the metrics. This highlights the difficulties faced by an analyst in attempting to evaluate the relevance of the pandemic on financial markets. In retrospect, only data on deaths helps explain stock market returns in the expected direction, but this may even act as a proxy for other underlying factors, such as government restrictions or state support.

2.6 Concluding Comments

The emergence of the COVID-19 virus in December 2019 profoundly affected all aspects of society. The immediate impacts were felt through illness, deaths and a range of ongoing health problems collectively referred to as Long COVID. The emergency measures put in place to stop the spread of the virus had a range of societal impacts on health and well-being, education, social interactions and supply chains. The economic impacts of COVID-19 were substantial, including increased unemployment, a global recession, economic inequality and increases in government debt. A longer-term implication was an increase in inflationary pressures due to disrupted supply chains. Financial markets responded rapidly and adversely to the spread of the virus, with many countries entering a bear market by March 2020. The recovery was, however, swift, with markets regaining most or all of their losses by the end of 2020.

Society was broadly unprepared for the pandemic. Healthcare systems were overwhelmed, there was limited global cooperation, economies were fragile, and many sectors were disproportionately prepared. Many countries also lacked systems to allow the detection and tracking of emerging infectious diseases. The latter issue meant that data about the extent and severity of the pandemic was lacking, especially in the early stages. Commonly tracked metrics included positive cases, hospitalisations, ICU cases and deaths from COVID-19. As discussed in this chapter, each of these presented its own challenges, ranging from limited testing capacity, varying protocols on diagnosis, an evolving virus, and data quality issues.

This chapter provides some support for data quality issues, especially surrounding the proliferation of positive cases, where the extent of the week-on-week changes is moderate in the early stages of the virus, compared to hospitalisations and deaths. Assessing the correlations between changes in the different metrics, the relationship between positive cases and deaths is found to be strongest. Correlations between changes in hospitalisations and ICU cases with deaths and positive cases tend to be much more subdued. Assessing the relationship between financial market performance and COVID-19, very disparate findings are evident. Hospitalisations tend to be strongly positively correlated with returns of the S&P 500, counter to expectations and perhaps a consequence of lagged information relative to the market. The relationship between COVID-19 deaths and the S&P is firmly negative, in keeping with the prior that the severity of the virus is construed as bad news for firms. The relationship between stock returns and COVID-19 measures act as a prism for the wider societal implications of deficient pandemic data quality. As markets tend to be able to efficiently incorporate new value-relevant information (Rösch et al., 2017), one would expect them to respond swiftly and decisively to COVID-19 data. The somewhat limited, and in the case of hospitalisation data, unexpected relationship found with heavily-monitored COVID-19 measures highlights the dilemma in using such metrics in setting policy in response to the virus. Possible workarounds to the poor data quality would be the use of combination forecasts, shown to provide more accurate predictions in economic data (Conlon et al., 2024h).

A number of policy implications arise from the preceding analysis. Madhav et al. (2023) estimates that the COVID-19 pandemic is not a once-in-a-century risk, but an event of this magnitude has a 2–3 per cent chance of occurring year-on-year. From a data collection perspective alone, measures can now be put in place to ensure limited delays in understanding the extent and severity of any future pandemic. A predefined data collection approach, with learnings from the COVID-19 pandemic, but designed to allow flexibility to adapt to future events, is a basic requirement. Metrics arising from this should be standardised and made available promptly in response to an outbreak. Similarly, an adaptive rapid testing capacity should be put in place to respond to any emerging viral threat. Finally, pre-agreed local, national and global aggregation mechanisms will allow for coordinated policy responses. In the context of expected losses of up to $700 per annum from pandemics each year (Glennerster et al., 2022), these data exigencies are nominal. Even the costs of preparedness for rapid vaccination production and supply-chain to respond to new viruses are limited compared to the estimated social costs (Glennerster et al., 2022). Measurement is key to informing the response to the challenge of future pandemics and should be part of any pandemic-response framework which emerges from the COVID-19 outbreak.

3 Early Financial Market Detection of COVID-19

In this chapter, we focus on the early response of financial markets to the eventual realisation of the severity of the problem faced, focusing on points of detection and the impact of the crisis on financial markets. We begin by discussing how underestimations concerning the severity of the virus and a delay in the release of clear information surrounding its subsequent spread contributed sharply to the eventual extreme market stresses that persisted. The chapter notes that this information lag was largely responsible for the sharp fall in asset prices experienced, presenting several additional points that authorities might have to consider in future scenarios, including the role of liquidity management and cross-country collaboration and coordination of response.

3.1 Introduction

Upon the realisation of the true severity of the COVID-19 pandemic, international financial markets experienced sharp episodes of exceptional stress, not just isolated to equity markets but across many distinct asset classes. It is important to note that not all asset prices fell, as some, such as pharmaceuticals and medical-related corporations, increased in value. However, in some sectors such as transportation and hospitality, the sudden realisation of forthcoming stresses and pressures led to widespread decline. More broadly, it was largely two major issues that garnered the most significant concern: first, the increasing potential for lockdowns and border closures, presenting exceptional challenges for international trade and the supply of goods and services; and second, significant flights-to-safety which could potentially propagate substantial bubbles in some asset markets, while excessively depressing the prices of others, both of which could directly influence national balance sheets depending on reliance. For investors, one of their primary concerns stemmed from such sudden shifts in investor sentiment, leading to sudden and severe liquidity deterioration, evidence of which is presented in Figure 3.1. As markets became increasingly volatile, the availability of liquid assets, defined as those that can be easily converted to cash without significant loss of value, became more important to investors, therefore elevating their respective value. In particular, investors sought to convert holdings into cash or cash-equivalent assets, driving up demand for U. S. Treasuries and other safe-haven securities (Acharya and Steffen, 2020), where substantial doubt and uncertainty surrounding the depth and duration of the pandemic drove such fear.

In response to these challenges, international central banks attempted to take decisive action to stabilise and reassure financial markets, particularly due to deteriorating sentiment conditions. The Federal Reserve Bank in the United States and the European Central Bank, for instance, implemented a series of emergency measures, including rapid decisions to implement a series of interest rate cuts to levels close to a zero rate, while simultaneously launching extensive quantitative easing programs in an at-

https://doi.org/10.1515/9783111707990-003

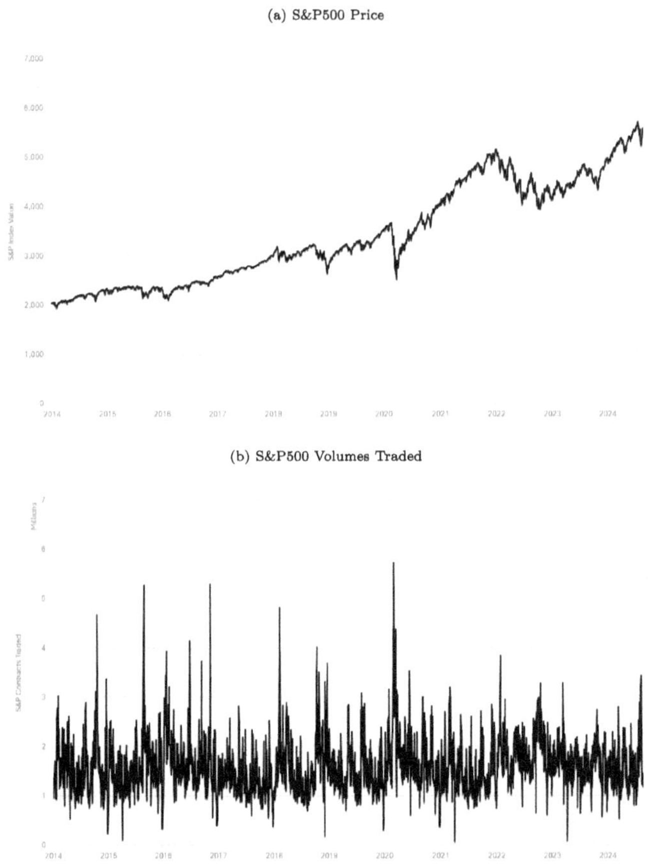

Figure 3.1: S&P 500 price and volumes traded. *Note*: Data obtained from LSEG Eikon.

tempt to alleviate additional pressures. While some functionality issues persisted due to the severity of the shock, the signal presented to the markets of leaders willing to go outside of traditional channels appeased investors during periods of rest-bite. Central banks further established several credit facilities to support the functioning of financial markets, examples of which are presented in Tables 3.1 and 3.2, respectively.

External interventions we targeted in an attempt to ensure that businesses and financial institutions were able to access the necessary funds to continue regular operations and meet forthcoming short- and medium-term obligations, to prevent deeper, secondary economic effects through potential layoffs and downsizing that might follow. Those working in vulnerable sectors such as hospitality, leisure, and transportation sought support due to imposed layoffs, many of which were a direct result of social distancing and work-from-home regulations imposed in an attempt to protect against the spread of the pandemic. Corporations with strong balance sheets, particularly those with better access to liquidity found themselves in a stronger position to mitigate the

Table 3.1: European Central Bank (ECB) monetary policy responses due to the COVID-19 pandemic.

Date	Type	Description
Mar 18, 2020	Pandemic Emergency Purchase Programme (PEPP)	In response to the COVID-19 pandemic, the ECB launched the Pandemic Emergency Purchase Programme (PEPP), a €750 billion temporary asset purchase program aimed at stabilising financial markets and supporting the Eurozone economy. This program provided additional flexibility compared to previous QE programs, allowing the ECB to respond more dynamically to market conditions
Jun 4, 2020	PEPP Expansion	The ECB expanded the PEPP by an additional €600 billion, bringing the total to €1.35 trillion, and extended the program until at least June 2021. This expansion reflected the ECB's commitment to supporting the Eurozone economy through the prolonged economic impact of the COVID-19 pandemic
Dec 10, 2020	Further PEPP Expansion	The ECB increased the PEPP by another €500 billion, bringing the total to €1.85 trillion, and extended the duration of purchases to at least March 2022. The ECB also re-calibrated its TLTROs to ensure favourable borrowing conditions remained available to banks, further supporting credit flows to the economy
Jul 22, 2021	New Monetary Policy Strategy	The ECB adopted a new monetary policy strategy, setting a symmetric 2 % inflation target over the medium term. This change represented a shift from the previous target of "below, but close to, 2 %," and allowed for temporary overshoots of inflation to maintain economic stability
Dec 16, 2021	PEPP Tapering and End Date Announcement	The ECB announced that net purchases under the PEPP would be reduced starting in March 2022 and would end by March 2023. However, the ECB indicated that it would continue to reinvest maturing securities and maintain favourable financing conditions as long as necessary to support the recovery from the pandemic
Jul 21, 2022	Interest Rate Hike	The ECB raised its key interest rates by 50 basis points, marking its first rate hike in 11 years. The main refinancing rate was increased to 0.50 %, as the ECB shifted its focus to tackling inflation, which had risen sharply due to supply chain disruptions, energy price shocks, and the impact of the war in Ukraine
Sep 8, 2022	Interest Rate Hike	The ECB raised interest rates by another 75 basis points, bringing the main refinancing rate to 1.25 %. This aggressive hike was part of the ECB's efforts to combat the highest inflation rates seen in decades, driven by rising energy costs and ongoing supply chain disruptions
Oct 27, 2022	Interest Rate Hike	The ECB increased its key interest rates by another 75 basis points, bringing the main refinancing rate to 2.00 %. This hike reflected the ECB's commitment to addressing persistent inflationary pressures despite concerns about slowing economic growth in the Eurozone
Dec 15, 2022	Interest Rate Hike	The ECB raised rates by 50 basis points, bringing the main refinancing rate to 2.50 %. This decision continued the ECB's effort to rein in inflation, which remained significantly above target, while also considering the risks of an economic slowdown in the Eurozone

Table 3.1 (continued)

Date	Type	Description
Feb 2, 2023	Interest Rate Hike	The ECB raised rates by another 50 basis points, bringing the main refinancing rate to 3.00 %. This move was part of the ongoing series of rate hikes to return inflation to the ECB's 2 % target, as inflationary pressures remained elevated across the Eurozone
Mar 16, 2023	Interest Rate Hike	The ECB raised rates by 50 basis points, bringing the main refinancing rate to 3.50 %. This hike was a continuation of the ECB's aggressive stance on inflation, which persisted despite concerns about the impact of higher rates on economic growth and financial stability
May 4, 2023	Interest Rate Hike	The ECB increased rates by 25 basis points, bringing the main refinancing rate to 3.75 %. This smaller hike indicated a slight moderation in the ECB's tightening pace, as it balanced the need to control inflation with concerns about the economic outlook
Jun 15, 2023	Interest Rate Hike	The ECB raised rates by another 25 basis points, bringing the main refinancing rate to 4.00 %. This hike reflected the ECB's ongoing efforts to combat inflation, which remained above target, while also considering the cumulative impact of previous rate hikes on the Eurozone economy

Note: Data obtained from ECB News Releases available here.

Table 3.2: US Federal Reserve monetary policy responses due to the COVID-19 pandemic.

Date	Type	Description
Mar 3, 2020	Emergency Rate Cut	The Federal Reserve made an emergency rate cut of 50 basis points to 1.00 %–1.25 % in response to the rapidly spreading COVID-19 pandemic. This was the first emergency cut since the financial crisis, aimed at supporting the economy as the pandemic began to cause significant disruptions
Mar 15, 2020	Emergency Rate Cut	In a second emergency move, the Fed cut the federal funds rate to 0.00 %–0.25 % and announced large-scale asset purchases. This aggressive action was in response to the escalating COVID-19 crisis, aiming to cushion the economic impact and ensure the smooth functioning of financial markets
Mar 23, 2020	Quantitative Easing (QE)	The Fed announced unlimited QE, committing to purchase Treasury securities and MBS "in the amounts needed" to support market functioning. This unprecedented move reflected the Fed's determination to stabilise financial markets and support the economy through the pandemic's uncertainty
Jun 16, 2021	Begin Tapering Discussions	The Federal Reserve began discussing the eventual tapering of asset purchases as economic conditions improved with the recovery from the COVID-19 pandemic. The Fed acknowledged rising inflation but maintained that it was largely transitory, indicating no immediate policy shift
Nov 3, 2021	Tapering QE	The Fed announced it would begin reducing the pace of its asset purchases by $15 billion per month, starting in November 2021. This decision was driven by substantial progress in the labour market and inflation running well above the Fed's long-term target
Mar 16, 2022	Federal Funds Rate Hike	The Fed increased the federal funds rate by 25 basis points to 0.25 %–0.50 %, beginning a tightening cycle to combat rising inflation, which had surged due to supply chain disruptions, strong demand, and the ongoing impact of the pandemic. This was the first hike since December 2018
Jun 15, 2022	Federal Funds Rate Hike	The Fed raised the rate by 75 basis points to 1.50 %–1.75 %, the largest hike since 1994, in response to persistently high inflation. This marked a more aggressive stance by the Fed to rein in inflation, with further rate increases expected
Feb 1, 2023	Federal Funds Rate Hike	The Fed increased the rate by 25 basis points to 4.50 %–4.75 %, continuing its efforts to combat inflation, which remained well above the Fed's 2 % target despite signs of slowing economic growth. The Fed signalled a commitment to further tightening if necessary
May 3, 2023	Federal Funds Rate Hike	The Fed raised the rate by another 25 basis points to 5.00 %–5.25 %, reflecting ongoing concerns about inflationary pressures. The Fed reiterated its focus on achieving price stability, even as it monitored potential risks to economic growth

Note: Data obtained from US Federal Reserve News Releases available here.

initial shock and to better manage operational headwinds. Evidence of strategic management of cash reserves held in banks is evident in Figure 3.2 from data focusing on the United States, presenting evidence of the importance of liquidity management during periods of significant systemic risks (DeAngelo and Stulz, 2015; Acharya and Thakor, 2016; Dell'Ariccia and Ratnovski, 2019).

The threat posed by the pandemic highlighted the elevated interconnectedness of global financial markets and the speed at which liquidity can disappear during periods of sharp financial crises, as evidenced by Figure 3.3 when considering global COVOL. It

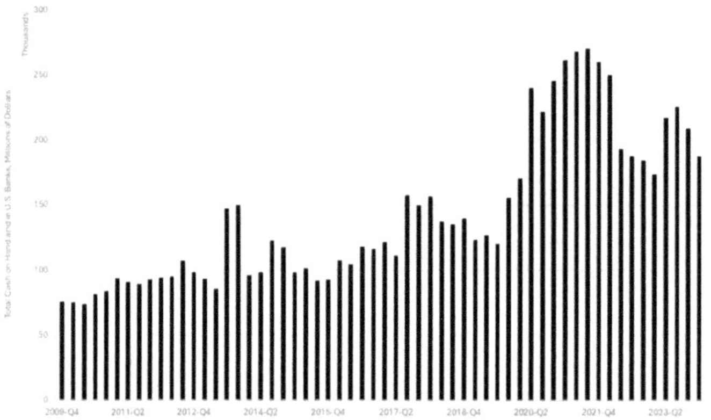

Figure 3.2: U. S. corporations total cash on hand and in U. S. banks, millions of dollars.
Note: Further information related to the Quarterly Financial Report survey can be found here, while methodology details can be found here. U.S. Census Bureau, Quarterly Financial Report: U.S. Corporations: All Information: Total Cash on Hand and in U. S. Banks [QFRTCASHINFUSNO], retrieved from FRED, Federal Reserve Bank of St. Louis; https://fred.stlouisfed.org/series/QFRTCASHINFUSNO.

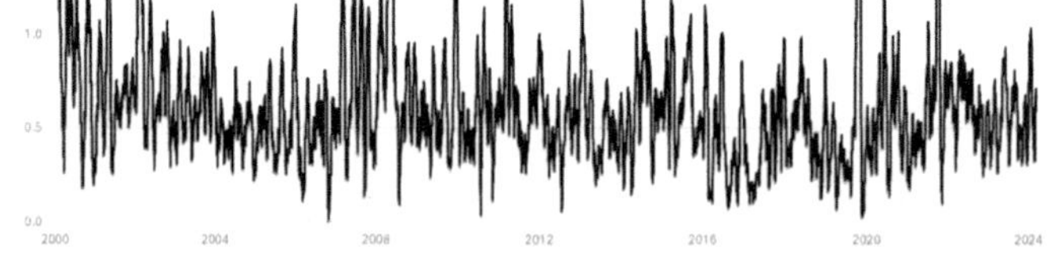

Figure 3.3: Global COVOL.
Note: Data obtained from here, and based on the work of Engle and Campos-Martins (2023). The COVOL time series is a time series of shocks that are common across all assets in the dataset, while to smooth the series, a 22-day moving average is used. Higher values indicate a larger common shock across all countries.

is quickly apparent that such asset comovement elevated sharply during the escalation of the COVID-19 pandemic, resulting in limited places where diversification opportunities could be obtained. As investors sought shelter, market values sharply deviated from long-term averages as premia and large discounts became available due to inherent threats that persisted from holding certain assets, where, in some cases, liquidity dissipated entirely due to sharp demand shifts. In such cases, central banks had to operate as a lender of last resort to ensure market functionality and to provide reassurance.

3.2 Timeline of Early COVID-19 Detection

In mid-October 2019, it was thought that COVID-19 likely began circulating undetected in Hubei Province, China, preceding the first documented case on November 17, 2019 (Pekar et al., 2021). Cases relating to the common cold, or broad seasonal illness, masked the presence of the virus, and without any detection systems in place, it began to spread rapidly before initial identification. It was not until 31 December 2019 that the World Health Organisation (WHO) formally outlined the existence of COVID-19, focusing on the precise threats and precautions that should be considered. The period surrounding year-end is traditionally associated with decreased financial market trading activity, with many taking holidays. Such an announcement during a traditionally quiet trading period, this might explain some of the relatively minute response, however, financial markets remained broadly unresponsive to the emerging risk during this period, as the virus's impact had yet to manifest internationally through a formally announced cross-border spread. The delay in clear, transparent reporting of the severity of the pandemic in some countries, coupled with the absence of local early warning systems, then contributed to a significant lag in response from investors, leading to such a sharply negative response at the time of eventual realisation (Lau et al., 2021; Albani et al., 2021). Such negativity was amplified when it became apparent that COVID-19 had reached other parts of the world, leading to more immediate disruption to supply chains and sharp shifts of consumer demand (Shahed et al., 2021; Moosavi et al., 2022). A sharp shift of corporate focus was evident as preparedness and corporate resilience became central themes, with governments significantly ramping up rhetoric of support as information became more available surrounding the threats posed.

The global contagion effects of COVID-19 became broadly evident quite rapidly after the initial identification, where Table 3.3 presents evidence of the first dates of the formal release of statistics surrounding deaths by the WHO and governments of several major countries, while Figure 3.4 presents evidence of the sharp elevation of cases and deaths during the entire pandemic. Retrospective analyses add further evidence that not only in China had cases relating to COVID-19 circulating undetected, but also in Europe and the United States before official documentation (Deslandes et al., 2020). Retrospective analyses of blood samples and sewage detected the presence of antibodies and viral

Table 3.3: Date of First Confirmed Case as reported by national governments and the WHO.

Country	Date of First Confirmed Case
China	December 8, 2019
Brazil	February 26, 2020
Nigeria	February 27, 2020
Mexico	February 28, 2020
Thailand	January 13, 2020
Japan	January 15, 2020
South Korea	January 20, 2020
United States	January 20, 2020
France	January 24, 2020
Australia	January 25, 2020
Canada	January 25, 2020
Germany	January 27, 2020
India	January 30, 2020
Italy	January 31, 2020
United Kingdom	January 31, 2020
Russia	January 31, 2020
Spain	January 31, 2020
Saudi Arabia	March 2, 2020
South Africa	March 5, 2020

Note: Data obtained from respective national governments and the WHO Newsroom page, available here.

(a) Daily Globally-Announced Cases and Deaths relating to COVID-19

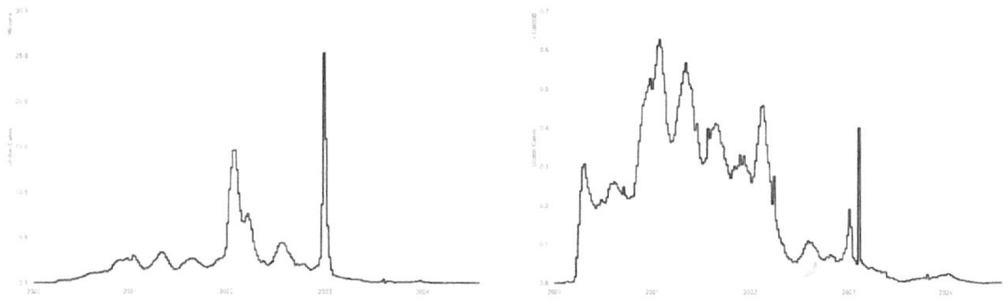

(b) Cumulative Globally-Announced Cases and Deaths relating to COVID-19

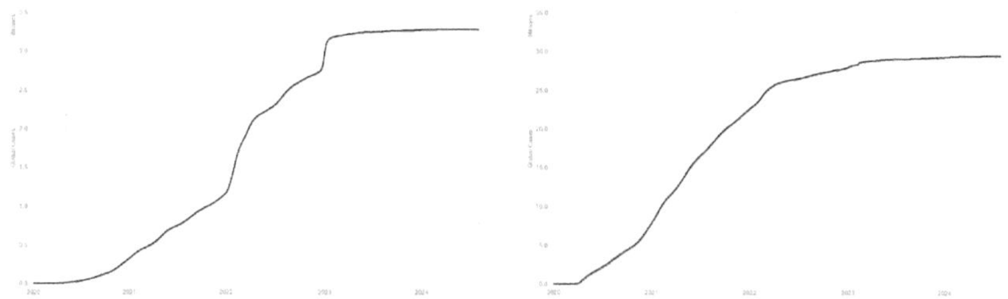

Figure 3.4: Globally-announced COVID-19 cases and deaths statistics.
Note: Data obtained from the WHO and Johns Hopkins University Covid Databases.

traces relating to COVID-19 in advance of formal identification (La Rosa et al., 2020), leading to the view of a more immediate global spread, rather than that traced by official release statistics.

The WHO issued the first of several reports relating to COVID-19 in early January 2020, and by 30 January 2020, it formally declared COVID-19 to be a Public Health Emergency of International Concern (PHEIC), emphasising the vital need for an international coordinated response, with several key events relating to the pandemic outlined in detail in Table 3.4, including the formal identification of a global pandemic by the WHO on 11 March 2020, which acted as a catalyst for a sharp shift in focus by international governments, which realised that this announcement predicated the transfer of responsibility, as retrospective analyses of protection measures would consider this date to be that on which governments could not claim innocence due a lack of warning and understanding. At this point, several governments began to introduce a range of packages and

Table 3.4: List of all formal WHO announcements relating to the COVID-19 pandemic.

Date	Event
December 31, 2019	WHO was informed of cases of pneumonia of unknown cause in Wuhan, China, and began monitoring the situation
January 9, 2020	WHO announced that Chinese authorities had identified a novel coronavirus as the cause of the pneumonia cases in Wuhan
January 30, 2020	WHO declared the outbreak a Public Health Emergency of International Concern (PHEIC)
February 11, 2020	WHO officially named the disease caused by the novel coronavirus as 'COVID-19'
March 11, 2020	WHO declared COVID-19 a global pandemic as the virus spread rapidly across multiple countries
March 18, 2020	WHO launched the COVID-19 Solidarity Response Fund to raise funds for pandemic response efforts
April 24, 2020	WHO and its partners launched the Access to COVID-19 Tools (ACT) Accelerator to ensure equitable access to COVID-19 diagnostics, treatments, and vaccines
July 9, 2020	WHO acknowledged emerging evidence of airborne transmission of COVID-19 in crowded and poorly ventilated settings
December 31, 2020	WHO issued an Emergency Use Listing for the Pfizer-BioNTech COVID-19 vaccine, making it the first vaccine to receive WHO validation for emergency use
March 29, 2021	WHO updated its recommendations on the use of masks, advising their use in areas where the virus is spreading
May 5, 2021	WHO approved the first COVID-19 vaccine under the COVAX initiative for global distribution
July 6, 2021	WHO declared that COVID-19 vaccines were effective against severe disease and variants of concern
October 6, 2021	WHO recommended the widespread use of the RTS,S/AS01 malaria vaccine, which was developed with considerations related to COVID-19
May 5, 2023	WHO declared that COVID-19 no longer constituted a Public Health Emergency of International Concern (PHEIC)

Note: Data obtained from WHO Newsroom page, available here.

regulations to mitigate the effects of the pandemic, but unfortunately, the early stages exposed many areas of deficiency that existed in the health services of many countries, particularly surrounding disease isolation, critical care and national surveillance and traceability. Some countries were further hampered by legislation surrounding personal data protection, to which solutions had to be identified and debated at political levels. Broadly, the delay in recognising the virus as a serious global threat allowed it to spread largely unhindered, thereby magnifying its global reach and impact.

In some countries, political focus shifted to identifying and attributing responsibility to the source of the pandemic, with an early focus surrounding the Huanan Seafood Wholesale Market. Political "points-scoring" and deflection were quickly apparent, widely considered as attempts to mask sovereign deficiency and response, and rallying right-wing sentiment against China as "the source". In effect, such rhetoric and behaviour did little to alleviate the immediate associated pressures. As the pandemic continued to evolve, financial markets began to react quite negatively. Substantial uncertainty and the realisation of the severity of the forthcoming disruption sharply increased volatility, with announcements surrounding corporate cost-cutting measures, the suspension of dividends and the renegotiation of credit facilities quickly followed.

3.3 Initial Market Reactions

While initially, financial markets showed little concern about the potential global economic impact of the pandemic was not yet fully understood. Investors largely assumed that the outbreak might remain localised, similar to previous health emergencies such as SARS (Pagnottoni et al., 2021; Spelta et al., 2023), which had quite limited global repercussions. Consequently, the initial market reaction was muted, with most investors adopting a holding, or "wait-and-see" approach (Conlon and McGee, 2020a; Fernandez-Perez et al., 2021; Corbet et al., 2020d, 2022a,c,d; Lang et al., 2024; Conlon et al., 2020, 2024c). However, as the situation in China deteriorated in January 2020. The official PHEIC acknowledgement by the WHO generated a notable change in investor sentiment, preceding sharp declines in major asset markets as investors moved to reduce exposure and risk in their portfolios (Corbet et al., 2021b). Major stock indices, including the S&P 500, as presented in Figure 3.1, experienced significant and rapid devaluation as it became more abundantly clear that the pandemic would not be contained within China, and that its impact on the global economy would be severe. The market's response was characterised by broad-based selling as investors sought to reduce risk in their portfolios amid this mounting uncertainty.

The effects of this stock market response varied dramatically across sectors, where those most negatively affected by the imposition of travel restrictions and social distancing regulations were most affected. Airlines, hotels, and companies in the oil industry, for example, faced immediate negative responses as fears of a global slowdown persisted, with the potential for a broad, deep recession. In contrast, both the technology and the healthcare sectors demonstrated incredible levels of resilience. The technology sector is benefiting directly from increased demand for technological services, particularly those providing strong communication and video conference services as a result of the broad shift towards remote working. Further, the healthcare sector generated sustained interest as the demand for medical supplies and pharmaceuticals grew exponentially, thereby increasing revenues and associated valuations.

Traditional financial market volatility was directly influenced and strongly exacerbated by the tremendous uncertainty that persisted as a result of pandemic contagion. Announcements relating to travel restrictions, lockdowns and imposed quarantines exacerbated already elevated tensions and stoked further fear and uncertainty while diminishing market sentiment (Ashraf, 2020a; Alaoui Mdaghri et al., 2021; Tuna and Tuna, 2022). Some of the largest single-day losses were experienced during the pandemic, driven largely by the black-swan[2] nature of the pandemic, and continued uncertainty with perceptions of a lack of firm control, created an environment where market sentiment wavered dramatically at extreme speeds (Buckman et al., 2020; Huynh et al., 2021; John and Li, 2021; Conlon et al., 2022, 2024d). Investors began to purchase safe-haven assets to preserve value, particularly gold, which has significant historical evidence of providing such storage in the presence of volatility (Tanin et al., 2022; Bentes et al., 2022; Esparcia et al., 2022; Conlon et al., 2024b). Similarly, government bonds experienced a sharp decline in yields due to elevated demand (Vissing-Jorgensen, 2021; He et al., 2022; Zhou and Meng, 2023), driven by their perceived safety and the assurance that they would retain value even as riskier assets faced steep declines. For investors, access to liquid assets such as bonds and cash became a central point of focus, which meant holding smaller portions of their portfolios in volatile equities and other riskier assets (Suardi et al., 2022; Al Farooque et al., 2023). Such heightened demand for liquidity simultaneously led to strains in short-term funding markets, prompting central banks to implement non-standard monetary policy tools to ensure the smooth functioning of markets.

3.4 Impact of Public Health Announcements

The PHEIC declaration by the WHO acted as a catalyst for wider markets to truly appreciate the gravity of the situation which confronted investors and the wider public (O'Hara and Zhou, 2021; Elsayed et al., 2022; Fatica and Panzica, 2024). The sell-off that followed in equity markets signalled widespread expectations of widespread economic disruption and inherent risks of an immediate slowdown or recession. Central banks attempted to step outside traditional comfort zones to reassure investors so as to stabilise

2 The term "*Black Swan*" (Taleb, 2007) refers to an extremely rare event possessing severe consequences, and is often viewed as predictable in hindsight. COVID-19 can be considered a Black Swan due to its sudden emergence, global impact, and significant economic and social disruption.

markets (Haas et al., 2020; Fischer, 2021; Berger et al., 2021; Grasselli, 2022; Aizenman et al., 2022) and relieve strain on financial systems as fears of frozen credit markets, similar to those experienced during the global financial banking crises of 2012 began to manifest, directly affecting households and businesses alike (Çolak and Öztekin, 2021; Mayer and Schnabl, 2021; Long et al., 2022; Georgarakos and Kenny, 2022; Dunz et al., 2023). Government response through lockdowns and travel restrictions had immediate, profound impacts on global markets (Baker et al., 2020; Caporale et al., 2022), albeit such measures were largely necessary to reduce the spread of the virus. The closure and restriction of key sectors such as hospitality, travel, and retail, simultaneously occurring with manufacturing delays, created significant bottlenecks and backlogs in global supply chains (Belhadi et al., 2021; Ozdemir et al., 2022), coinciding with a sharp decline in consumer spending due to mobility restrictions, leading to further deterioration of asset values and an elevated financial market volatility (Bachas et al., 2020; Hodbod et al., 2021; Georgarakos and Kenny, 2022).

The pandemic also uncovered substantial vulnerabilities in financial market efficiency, particularly about the non-absorption of readily available information, or more specifically, substantial mispricing of risk, such as that quite evident in financial markets during the propagation of the pandemic. Quite simply, investors struggled to accurately assess the severity of the pandemic, leading to a broad hesitation when pricing in the potential associated downside, resulting in an acute market correction once the threat became evident to the broader investment community. However, the novelty of the developing situation was a key factor contributing to this delayed reaction. Quite simply, in recent times, while contagious diseases had commonly occurred, nothing similar to the scale of the COVID-19 pandemic had been identified, with many, refusing to believe that it could be capable of completely stifling the global economy for many years to follow. Without such previous grounds to assess risk accurately, the situation was further exacerbated by continued revisions of policy and regulation concerning the tools being used to fight against the spread of the pandemic, which had negative effects on market sentiment and trust in the capability of the government to generate an effective mitigation strategy.

3.5 Concluding Comments

The delicate nature of the relationship between sentiment, effective news releases, public health information and financial markets was all displayed during the onset of the COVID-19 pandemic. Broad miscalculation regarding the severity of the pandemic led to a more acute negative investor response upon sudden realisation, where this lag correlated with substantial information asymmetry and the availability of unclear data regarding the true scale and contagion experienced. The market response was characterised by a rush to liquid asset reserves and those assets traditionally associated with flight-to-safety, such as bonds and gold. Fear of information suppression was also a concern once the true severity of the pandemic was identified. Some feared that government authorities were withholding information to avoid causing excessive panic among citizens, which could lead to overly negative perceptions and estimations of value.

Although an extremely expensive lesson, financial markets will now perceive the threat of future pandemics with added weight. The use of reactive responses rather than proactive ones in terms of corporate risk management left many corporations in quite desperate situations at the beginning of the pandemic, with many facing liquidity crunches, margin calls and a widespread scramble for infrastructural supplies to maintain safe customer interaction. However, government support and innovative technological support went some way to moderating such negative effects. Furthermore, the disparity identified across national responses to the pandemic and the resulting impacts on financial markets highlights the need for a more cohesive and coordinated international approach in managing not only global health crises but perhaps many other types of international crises. The differential cross-country implementation of public health measures created a patchwork of responses that further complicated the global economic economy, where regions were found to be only as strong as the weakest link found within, leading to even more disjointed market reactions and increased uncertainty.

4 COVID-19 and the Effects of Social Distancing

The COVID-19 pandemic initially led to the adoption of social distancing measures as a key tool to counteract the significant contagion effects. While essential for the protection of the broader public and to alleviate pressure from public health services, their implementation had profound and far-reaching economic repercussions. This chapter investigates some of these economic impacts, focusing specifically on key structural changes induced by the pandemic, while identifying how the implementation of social distancing contributed to significant contractions in many industries, particularly those heavily reliant on physical interactions, such as retail, hospitality, and manufacturing. Social distancing also heavily increased many inequalities faced by small businesses and marginalised communities, which this chapter investigates.

4.1 Introduction

The onset of the COVID-19 pandemic in late 2019 and early 2020 marked an unprecedented global health crisis, compelling global governments to implement many public health measures designed primarily to protect national healthcare systems but also possessing deep, inherent secondary effects that had the potential to generate crises in other sectors. As the WHO announced the existence of a global pandemic in early 2020, as the virus propagated, governments faced the dual challenge of containing its spread while mitigating its economic fallout; unfortunately, a substantial period after the pandemic had crossed many borders (Corbet et al., 2020e; Conlon and McGee, 2020a; Conlon et al., 2020, 2024d; Lang et al., 2024; Kyriazis and Corbet, 2024). Immediate responses included implementing widespread social distancing measures, lockdowns, and restrictions on non-essential activities to reduce further transmission of the virus. These measures, though critical in saving lives, initiated a variety of significant economic disruptions that reverberated through virtually every sector of the global economy (Sukharev, 2020; Kuznyetsova et al., 2021).

Social distancing, a strategy involving the maintenance of physical space between individuals to prevent virus transmission, became the cornerstone of public health directives. Several examples relating to the global implementation of several strategies are presented in Table 4.1, with many key similarities in stringency and monitoring identifiable, further presented in Table 4.2, with countries self-selecting a range of criteria from complete lockdowns to partial restrictions on movement and gatherings. These measures often included closing schools, workplaces, and public spaces, alongside restrictions on travel and social interactions. The primary goal surrounding the implementation of such divisive regulations, or in some cases, advisories, was to reduce the secondary contagion, referred to as "flattening the curve" of infections. Such a design was an attempt to reduce pressures on an already stressed healthcare system, to stop it from becoming further overwhelmed (Thu et al., 2020; Siedner et al., 2020; McGrail et al., 2020), noting that many of the cases had transferred to the medics and front-line

https://doi.org/10.1515/9783111707990-004

Table 4.1: Select international social distancing restrictions due to COVID-19.

Country	Date	Key social distancing measures	Authority/agency responsible	Penalties for non-compliance
US	Mar-20	Nationwide recommendation to maintain 6 feet distance in public spaces; local governments set specific regulations	Centers for Disease Control and Prevention (CDC); State and local governments	Fines, closure of non-compliant businesses, arrests in some states
UK	Mar-20	Mandatory 2-meter distancing in public spaces; "Rule of Six" limiting gatherings; lockdowns with varying restrictions by tier	Department of Health and Social Care (DHSC); Public Health England (PHE)	Fines ranging from £100 to £10,000 for severe breaches
Australia	Mar-20	1.5-meter social distancing, limits on gatherings, closure of non-essential businesses, state-specific lockdowns	Australian Department of Health; State governments	Fines up to A$11,000, potential jail time for repeated non-compliance
Germany	Mar-20	1.5-meter distancing in public spaces, limits on private gatherings, mask mandates in enclosed public spaces	Federal Ministry of Health; State governments (Länder)	Fines ranging from €50 to €500, closure of businesses
Japan	Apr-20	1–2 meter distancing recommended, voluntary limits on gatherings, encouraged telework, closure of entertainment venues	Ministry of Health, Labour and Welfare (MHLW)	No legal penalties, strong reliance on public compliance
Canada	Mar-20	2-meter distancing in public spaces, limits on gatherings, closure of non-essential services, provincial-specific rules	Public Health Agency of Canada (PHAC); Provincial governments	Fines up to CA$750,000, imprisonment for severe violations
N. Zealand	Mar-20	2-meter distancing in public spaces, strict lockdown measures, limits on gatherings, alert level system to manage response	Ministry of Health; Managed Isolation and Quarantine (MIQ)	Fines up to NZ$4,000, potential imprisonment
France	Mar-20	1-meter distancing in public spaces, bans on large gatherings, nationwide lockdowns with restrictions on movement	Ministry of Health; Prefects in local departments	Fines up to €135 for first offence, escalating fines for repeat offences
Italy	Feb-20	1-meter distancing in public spaces, nationwide lockdowns, bans on gatherings, closure of non-essential businesses	Ministry of Health; Regional governments	Fines up to €3,000, potential imprisonment for serious breaches
S. Korea	Feb-20	1-meter distancing, restrictions on gatherings, extensive contact tracing, closure of high-risk facilities	Korea Disease Control and Prevention Agency (KDCA)	Fines up to ₩3 million, potential jail time for quarantine breaches

Table 4.1 (continued)

Country	Date	Key social distancing measures	Authority/agency responsible	Penalties for non-compliance
China	Jan-20	Strict lockdowns, social distancing in public spaces, restrictions on travel and gatherings, closure of non-essential businesses	National Health Commission (NHC); Local governments	Severe penalties including fines, imprisonment, forced quarantine
Brazil	Mar-20	Social distancing recommendations varied by state, limits on gatherings, mask mandates in some regions	Ministry of Health; State and municipal governments	Penalties varied by state, including fines and business closures
Sweden	Mar-20	1-meter distancing recommended, limits on public gatherings initially set at 500, then reduced to 50	Public Health Agency of Sweden (Folkhälsomyndigheten)	No significant legal penalties, reliance on public adherence
Singapore	Apr-20	1-meter distancing in public, strict enforcement of mask mandates, limits on social gatherings, closure of high-risk venues	Ministry of Health; Ministry of Home Affairs	Fines up to S$10,000, imprisonment for serious violations
S. Africa	Mar-20	1.5-meter distancing in public spaces, nationwide lockdown, limits on gatherings, closure of non-essential services	National Department of Health; Provincial governments	Fines up to ZAR 5,000, imprisonment for serious breaches
Spain	Mar-20	1.5-meter distancing in public, national lockdown, limits on movement and gatherings, mask mandates in indoor and outdoor spaces	Ministry of Health; Regional governments	Fines ranging from €100 to €600,000 depending on the severity of the breach
Argentina	Mar-20	1.5-meter distancing in public, nationwide lockdown, limits on movement and gatherings, closure of non-essential businesses	Ministry of Health; Provincial governments	Fines up to ARS 100,000, potential imprisonment

Note: Data obtained from the Centres for Disease Control and Prevention (CDC) and state/local governments in the United States; the Department of Health and Social Care (DHSC) and Public Health England (PHE) in the United Kingdom; the Australian Department of Health and various state governments in Australia; the Federal Ministry of Health and state governments (Länder) in Germany; the Ministry of Health, Labour and Welfare (MHLW) in Japan, the Public Health Agency of Canada (PHAC) and provincial governments in Canada, the Ministry of Health and Managed Isolation and Quarantine (MIQ) in New Zealand; the Ministry of Health and local prefects in France; the Ministry of Health and regional governments in Italy; the Korea Disease Control and Prevention Agency (KDCA) in South Korea; the National Health Commission (NHC) and local governments in China; the Ministry of Health and state/municipal governments in Brazil; the Public Health Agency of Sweden (Folkhälsomyndigheten) in Sweden; the Ministry of Health and Family Welfare and state governments in India; the Ministry of Health and Ministry of Home Affairs in Singapore; the National Department of Health and provincial governments in South Africa; the Ministry of Health and regional governments in Spain; and the Ministry of Health and provincial governments in Argentina. These agencies were instrumental in formulating, enforcing, and communicating the social distancing measures in response to the pandemic.

Table 4.2: Select international lockdown restrictions due to COVID-19.

Country	Date	Key lockdown measures	Authority/agency responsible	Penalties for non-compliance
US	Mar-2020	Stay-at-home orders in many states, closure of non-essential businesses, restrictions on interstate travel in some regions	State and local governments; Centres for Disease Control and Prevention (CDC)	Varies by state: fines, business closures, potential imprisonment
UK	Mar-2020	Nationwide lockdown with restrictions on movement, stay-at-home orders, closure of non-essential shops, regional tiered system later introduced	Department of Health and Social Care (DHSC); Public Health England (PHE)	Fines ranging from £100 to £10,000 for severe breaches
Australia	Mar-2020	State-specific lockdowns with stay-at-home orders, interstate travel bans, mandatory quarantine for international arrivals, closure of non-essential businesses	Australian Department of Health; State governments	Fines up to A$11,000, potential jail time for repeated non-compliance
Germany	Mar-2020	Nationwide lockdown, stay-at-home orders, closure of non-essential shops, limits on domestic and international travel	Federal Ministry of Health; State governments (Länder)	Fines ranging from €50 to €500, escalating fines for repeated offences
Japan	Apr-2020	Nationwide state of emergency declared, voluntary restrictions on movement, closure of non-essential businesses, no legal enforcement of lockdowns	Ministry of Health, Labour and Welfare (MHLW)	No legal penalties, reliance on public cooperation
Canada	Mar-2020	Provincial lockdowns with stay-at-home orders, closure of non-essential services, restrictions on interprovincial travel, mandatory quarantine for international arrivals	Public Health Agency of Canada (PHAC); Provincial governments	Fines up to CA$750,000, imprisonment for severe violations
N. Zealand	Mar-2020	Nationwide lockdown with stay-at-home orders, strict movement restrictions, closure of non-essential services, alert level system used to manage restrictions	Ministry of Health; Managed Isolation and Quarantine (MIQ)	Fines up to NZ$4,000, potential imprisonment
France	Mar-2020	Nationwide lockdown with stay-at-home orders, restrictions on movement beyond 1 km from home without a valid reason, curfews in certain areas, closure of non-essential businesses	Ministry of Health; Prefects in local departments	Fines up to €135 for first offence, escalating fines for repeat offences

Table 4.2 (continued)

Country	Date	Key lockdown measures	Authority/agency responsible	Penalties for non-compliance
Italy	Feb-2020	Nationwide lockdown, strict stay-at-home orders, closure of non-essential businesses, restrictions on travel between regions, curfews introduced later	Ministry of Health; Regional governments	Fines up to €3,000, potential imprisonment for serious breaches
S. Korea	Feb-2020	No nationwide lockdown, but strict restrictions on movement in affected regions, extensive contact tracing, mandatory quarantine for international arrivals	Korea Disease Control and Prevention Agency (KDCA)	Fines up to ₩3 million, potential jail time for quarantine breaches
China	Jan-2020	Strict lockdowns in Wuhan and other cities, stay-at-home orders, restrictions on movement, nationwide travel bans, quarantine for all international arrivals	National Health Commission (NHC); Local governments	Severe penalties including fines, imprisonment, forced quarantine
Brazil	Mar-2020	State-specific lockdowns with stay-at-home orders, varying restrictions on movement, closure of non-essential businesses, quarantine for international arrivals in some regions	Ministry of Health; State and municipal governments	Penalties varied by state, including fines and business closures
Sweden	Mar-2020	No formal lockdown, but recommendations for self-isolation and limited movement, restrictions on large gatherings, closure of high-risk venues	Public Health Agency of Sweden (Folkhälsomyndigheten)	No legal penalties, strong reliance on public adherence
Singapore	Apr-2020	Circuit Breaker lockdown, stay-at-home orders, closure of non-essential services, restrictions on movement and gatherings, mandatory quarantine for arrivals	Ministry of Health; Ministry of Home Affairs	Fines up to S$10,000, imprisonment for serious violations
S. Africa	Mar-2020	Nationwide lockdown, stay-at-home orders, closure of non-essential businesses, restrictions on movement, phased reopening with continued restrictions	National Department of Health; Provincial governments	Fines up to ZAR 5,000, imprisonment for serious breaches

Table 4.2 (continued)

Country	Date	Key lockdown measures	Authority/agency responsible	Penalties for non-compliance
Spain	Mar-2020	Nationwide lockdown, stay-at-home orders, closure of non-essential services, restrictions on movement between regions, curfews in some areas	Ministry of Health; Regional governments	Fines ranging from €100 to €600,000 depending on severity
Argentina	Mar-2020	Nationwide lockdown, strict stay-at-home orders, closure of non-essential businesses, restrictions on movement, quarantine for international arrivals	Ministry of Health; Provincial governments	Fines up to ARS 100,000, potential imprisonment

Note: Data obtained from the Centres for Disease Control and Prevention (CDC) and state/local governments in the United States; the Department of Health and Social Care (DHSC) and Public Health England (PHE) in the United Kingdom; the Australian Department of Health and various state governments in Australia; the Federal Ministry of Health and state governments (Länder) in Germany; the Ministry of Health, Labour and Welfare (MHLW) in Japan, the Public Health Agency of Canada (PHAC) and provincial governments in Canada, the Ministry of Health and Managed Isolation and Quarantine (MIQ) in New Zealand; the Ministry of Health and local prefects in France; the Ministry of Health and regional governments in Italy; the Korea Disease Control and Prevention Agency (KDCA) in South Korea; the National Health Commission (NHC) and local governments in China; the Ministry of Health and state/municipal governments in Brazil; the Public Health Agency of Sweden (Folkhälsomyndigheten) in Sweden; the Ministry of Health and Family Welfare and state governments in India; the Ministry of Health and Ministry of Home Affairs in Singapore; the National Department of Health and provincial governments in South Africa; the Ministry of Health and regional governments in Spain; and the Ministry of Health and provincial governments in Argentina. These agencies were instrumental in formulating, enforcing, and communicating the social distancing measures in response to the pandemic.

defenders who were becoming ill simply from proximity to those who needed medical assistance. These issues were particularly pronounced in the early stages of contagion as governments attempted to increase their understanding of transmission dynamics. The immediate impact of social distancing measures on mobility and daily life was profound. Major urban areas were simply transforming into relative ghost towns as people stayed away. While these policies were effective in reducing the spread of COVID-19, they also led to significant disruptions in economic activities, particularly in sectors reliant on physical presence and consumer mobility.

The economic ramifications of social distancing were visible when businesses closed, leading to immediate job losses and a broad collapse in economic sentiment. Supply chains were severely disrupted, with significant problems identified in trading partners possessing non-comparable health and safety standards, such as those found in food processing, while the retail, hospitality, and entertainment industries were amongst the hardest hit, facing prolonged closures and a sudden collapse in consumer demand. While some attempts were made to gradually reopen under certain conditions, and social distancing limitations were imposed, it was quickly apparent that fear was widespread amongst certain cohorts of the population, particularly the most vulnerable. The impact was not limited to these sectors alone; the manufacturing and services sectors experienced severe contractions due to interrupted supply chains and decreased consumer spending, as presented in Figures 4.1 and 4.2. The global economy witnessed an unprecedented contraction, with many countries entering deep recessions. At the same time, unemployment rates increased dramatically as businesses could not sustain their operations and laid off millions of workers. However, implementing several international rescue packages mitigated some of this economic decline.

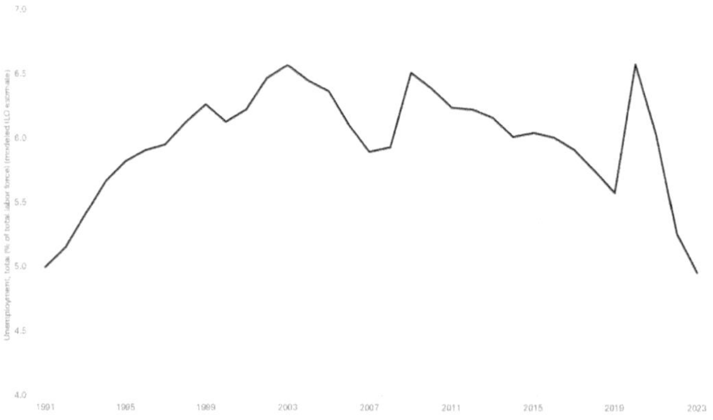

Figure 4.1: Unemployment, total (% of total labour force) (World Bank modelled ILO estimate).
Note: Data from World Bank Group, obtained from here. Unemployment, total (% of the total labour force) (modelled ILO estimate). International Labour Organisation. "ILO Modelled Estimates and Projections database (ILOEST)" ILOSTAT. Accessed June 18, 2024.

Figure 4.2: GDP per capita growth (annual %).
Note: World Bank national accounts data, and OECD National Accounts data files.

This chapter discussed the economic consequences of social distancing measures by examining the immediate and long-term impacts on various economic sectors and population cohorts. It aims to understand how these measures reshaped international economies while considering the differential impacts on small businesses, large corporations, and vulnerable populations, highlighting the uneven burden that was experienced. Additionally, the chapter will investigate the spillover effects on global supply chains and input-output linkages, which exacerbated the economic downturn. Understanding the economic ramifications of social distancing is crucial for formulating policies that balance public health objectives with economic stability. We also consider the long-term structural changes induced by the pandemic, such as the acceleration of digital transformation and shifts in consumer behaviour. As businesses adapted to the 'new normal', many embraced remote working, e-commerce, and digital services, which have lasting implications for future economic activities (Kim, 2020; Kurniasih and Akbar, 2021), presenting the potential to reshape labour markets, productivity, and economic growth.

4.2 The Impact of Social Distancing on Economic Activity

The outbreak of COVID-19 and subsequent implementation of social distancing measures disrupted normal global economic dynamics and functionality, generating a sharp, immediate decline in economic activities across most countries (Apostolakis et al., 2021; Hunjra et al., 2021; Izzeldin et al., 2021; Kusumahadi and Permana, 2021). The cessation of non-essential businesses and restricted mobility led to a steep reduction in consumer spending, confidence and business investments (Coibion et al., 2020; Gupta et al., 2021a). This contraction was unprecedented in scale, generating economic downturns as severe in both speed and severity as that of the global financial crisis instigated by the collapse of the subprime mortgage system. The initial shock to economic activity was experienced across all sectors, but some were more severely impacted due to their reliance on physical presence and intermediate goods. For instance, the mining, oil, and gas sectors experienced a sharp decline as global demand for energy products plummeted with an associated expectation of a global economic slowdown (Jiang et al., 2021). This was compounded by a significant fall in the value of commodities, further straining the financial conditions of companies and, in some cases, directly threatening their continued viability within these industries. The entertainment and hospitality sectors were damaged severely, as social distancing measures forced the closure of cinemas, theatres, hotels, and restaurants (Jiang and Wen, 2020; Gursoy et al., 2021; Dube et al., 2021; Gursoy et al., 2021). Data presented in Table 4.3 presents evidence of the sharp collapse in global box office revenues due to the pandemic, with year-on-year gross sales falling by 81.4 %. These industries, heavily dependent on limited consumer social distancing and significant interaction, faced an existential crisis, with revenues collapsing; however, in many cases, costs remained. In the manufacturing sector, disruptions were particularly pronounced due to the collapse of several supply chains, initiating incredible competition for limited resources globally at competitive prices. Many manufacturing plants were forced to shut down or, in some cases, operate at reduced capacity. Such decisions led to substantial delays and shortages in the production of goods, which had an unfortunate cascading effect on other industries that relied on manufactured inputs, exacerbating the overall economic downturn. Additionally, the automotive industry saw a significant reduction in demand as consumers deferred purchases of expensive items amidst economic uncertainty. Repairs also took extended periods of time to carry out, as many companies, even with social distancing measures imposed and safe working environments created, could simply not identify materials and parts to continue operations during such hostile economic conditions.

Retail, especially non-essential retail, experienced substantial setbacks as physical stores closed, and consumers shifted to online shopping (Koch et al., 2020; Shaw et al., 2022). However, while this change in consumer preference did not fully compensate for the loss of in-store sales, it led to widespread bankruptcies and short-term layoffs. Further, as presented in Figure 4.3 the transportation sector, including airlines, railways, and public transit faced severe disruptions (Amankwah-Amoah, 2020; Sharma and Nicolau, 2020; Yang et al., 2021; Liu et al., 2021b; Sun et al., 2021, 2022; Corbet et al., 2022a, 2023; Hu et al., 2024). Travel bans and reduced passenger numbers led to exceptional revenue losses and elevated operational challenges, many of which occurred with limited expectations or were generated as by-products of unforeseen situations that had manifested elsewhere. Airlines, for example, had to ground large portions of their fleets and lay off thousands of employees, while public transit systems observed a sharp drop in ridership, affecting their financial sustainability. Many countries observed an immediate transition towards the use of cars, as many selected not to use public transport for safety reasons, and selected to travel in bubbles rather than exposing themselves to additional risks.

Table 4.3: Measures implemented by various countries to reduce housing evictions during the COVID-19 pandemic.

Year	Total gross	%± LY	Releases	Average	#1 release
1977	$443,497,461	290.60 %	9	$49,277,495	Star Wars: Episode IV – A New Hope
1978	$826,413,013	86.30 %	13	$63,570,231	Grease
1979	$1,229,428,453	48.80 %	40	$30,735,711	Superman
1980	$1,642,400,771	33.60 %	68	$24,152,952	Star Wars: Episode V – The Empire Strikes Back
1981	$898,686,960	−45.30 %	56	$16,047,981	Superman II
1982	$3,001,761,432	234 %	132	$22,740,616	E. T. The Extra-Terrestrial
1983	$2,738,195,414	−8.80 %	149	$18,377,150	Star Wars: Episode VI – Return of the Jedi
1984	$3,066,288,000	12 %	169	$18,143,715	Ghostbusters
1985	$3,017,379,323	−1.60 %	191	$15,797,797	Back to the Future
1986	$3,065,297,715	1.60 %	201	$15,250,237	Top Gun
1987	$3,343,230,996	9.10 %	226	$14,793,057	Beverly Hills Cop II
1988	$3,542,179,944	6 %	239	$14,820,836	Who Framed Roger Rabbit
1989	$4,084,060,815	15.30 %	235	$17,378,982	Batman
1990	$4,326,824,577	5.90 %	236	$18,334,002	Ghost
1991	$4,336,073,530	0.20 %	253	$17,138,630	Terminator 2: Judgement Day
1992	$4,519,644,026	4.20 %	247	$18,298,153	Batman Returns
1993	$4,823,116,106	6.70 %	267	$18,064,105	Jurassic Park
1994	$5,061,909,583	5 %	259	$19,544,052	The Lion King
1995	$5,106,129,264	0.90 %	291	$17,546,835	Batman Forever
1996	$5,600,750,973	9.70 %	306	$18,303,107	Independence Day
1997	$6,077,250,085	8.50 %	310	$19,604,032	Men in Black
1998	$6,696,278,852	10.20 %	334	$20,048,739	Titanic
1999	$7,340,708,198	9.60 %	448	$16,385,509	Star Wars: Episode I – The Phantom Menace
2000	$7,476,224,972	1.80 %	439	$17,030,125	How the Grinch Stole Christmas
2001	$7,959,296,828	6.50 %	412	$19,318,681	Harry Potter and the Sorcerer's Stone
2002	$9,164,913,438	15.20 %	570	$16,078,795	Spider-Man
2003	$9,232,953,228	0.70 %	667	$13,842,508	Finding Nemo
2004	$9,354,636,012	1.30 %	700	$13,363,765	Shrek 2
2005	$8,833,618,311	−5.60 %	676	$13,067,482	Star Wars: Episode III – Revenge of the Sith
2006	$9,203,041,941	4.20 %	746	$12,336,517	Pirates of the Caribbean: Dead Man's Chest
2007	$9,679,019,852	5.20 %	775	$12,489,057	Spider-Man 3
2008	$9,652,648,585	−0.30 %	725	$13,313,998	The Dark Knight
2009	$10,615,886,283	10 %	646	$16,433,260	Transformers: Revenge of the Fallen
2010	$10,585,388,159	−0.30 %	651	$16,260,196	Avatar
2011	$10,155,695,359	−4.10 %	731	$13,892,880	Harry Potter and the Deathly Hallows: Part 2
2012	$10,843,641,372	6.80 %	807	$13,436,978	The Avengers
2013	$10,955,524,800	1 %	826	$13,263,347	Iron Man 3
2014	$10,368,861,849	−5.40 %	849	$12,213,029	Guardians of the Galaxy

Table 4.3 (continued)

Year	Total gross	%± LY	Releases	Average	#1 release
2015	$11,148,780,747	7.50 %	845	$13,193,823	Jurassic World
2016	$11,375,225,455	2 %	855	$13,304,357	Finding Dory
2017	$11,075,387,520	−2.60 %	854	$12,968,837	Star Wars: Episode VIII – The Last Jedi
2018	$11,892,160,011	7.40 %	993	$11,975,991	Black Panther
2019	$11,363,361,617	−4.40 %	910	$12,487,210	Avengers: Endgame
2020	$2,113,386,800	−81.40 %	455	$4,644,806	Bad Boys for Life
2021	$4,483,010,556	112.10 %	441	$10,165,556	Spider-Man: No Way Home
2022	$7,369,521,886	64.40 %	499	$14,768,580	Top Gun: Maverick
2023	$8,908,297,471	20.90 %	590	$15,098,809	Barbie
2024	$5,423,126,617	-	421	$12,881,535	Inside Out 2

Note: Data obtained from Box Office Mojo, IMDbpro, available here.

Figure 4.3: Thompson Reuters Global Passenger Transportation Services Index.
Note: Data obtained from Thompson Reuters Global Passenger Transportation Services Index,. TRXFLDGLPUI46 (TRDPRC_1).

The construction industry suffered sharp, immediate losses as a result of the pandemic, as projects were delayed or cancelled due to health concerns and supply chain disruptions (Ogunnusi et al., 2020, 2021; Dobrucali et al., 2022). As presented in Figure 4.4, the price of shipping goods soared due to a reduction in staffing and global shortages of availability due to the transition of many shipping lanes to emergency deliveries. The slowdown in construction activities not only affected employment in the sector but also had ripple effects on industries related to construction materials and real estate. Furthermore, the agriculture sector experienced disruptions in both production and distribution. Labour shortages due to health concerns, travel restrictions, and transportation difficulties led to supply chain issues. This affected food supply and agricultural exports, contributing to economic instability in regions heavily dependent on agriculture (Henry, 2020; Laborde et al., 2020; Barrett, 2020; Torero, 2020; Alabi and Ngwenyama, 2023).

(a) .XSICFESE Far East to South America East Coast

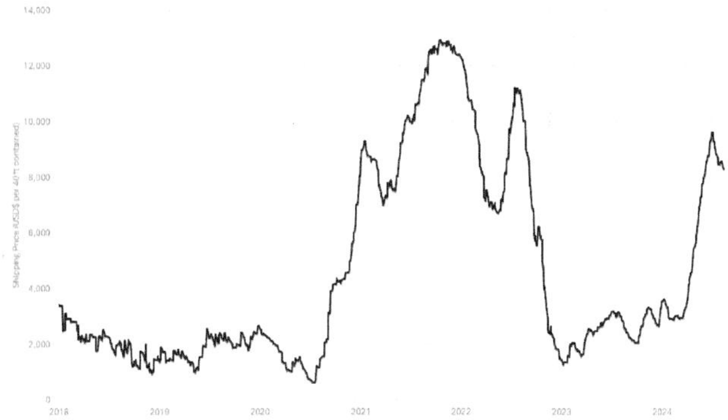

(b) .XSICNEUE North Europe to US East Coast

(c) .XSICFENE Far East to North Europe

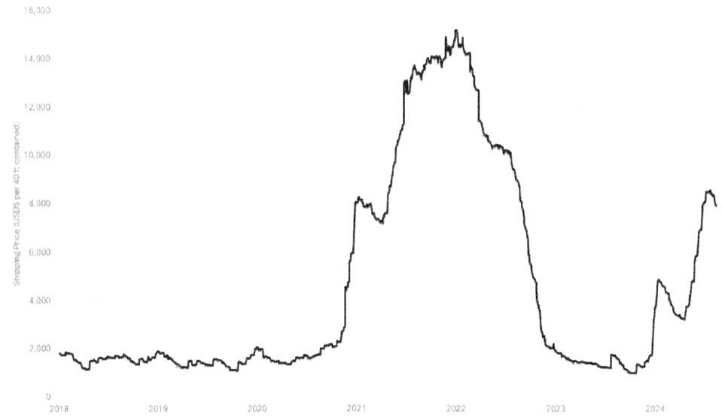

Figure 4.4: Select global shipping indices.
Note: Data from LSEG Eikon. Xeneta Shipping Index by Compass (XSIC, the Indices or the Index) represent BMR-compliant indices for rolling short-term Freight All Kind (FAK) rates valid for less than 32 days for a 40' container. They are calculated daily and published at 4pm London time.

Broadly, the combined effect of the COVID-19 pandemic and social distancing measures led to an unprecedented global economic downturn. The shock was felt across all sectors, with industries reliant on physical presence and intermediate goods being the hardest hit. This economic contraction highlighted the vulnerabilities in global supply chains and the need for resilience in economic planning and policy-making. The lessons learned from this crisis will be crucial in shaping future responses to global economic disruptions.

4.3 The Effects of Social Distancing on Small Businesses and Entrepreneurship

The COVID-19 pandemic has profoundly impacted small-to-medium businesses, leading to an unprecedented decline in their number and the probability of success without adequate support. Small businesses, which often operate with limited financial reserves and dependent on daily operations and in-person interactions were especially vulnerable to the rapid stoppage of economic activity. The persistence of low activity levels among small businesses can be attributed to several ongoing challenges. First, the uncertainty surrounding the pandemic's duration and the potential for future lockdowns made it difficult for businesses to plan and invest in recovery efforts (Gupta et al., 2020; Corbet et al., 2020d, 2021b, 2022b; Corbet and Oxley, 2023; Meehan and Corbet, 2023; Goodell et al., 2024). Secondly, consumer behaviour changes, such as reduced spending and a shift towards online shopping, altered demand for many small businesses' products, particularly those reliant on foot traffic and in-person services, as evidenced by Figure 4.5. Third, the varying levels of state and local restrictions meant that businesses in different regions faced different operational constraints, complicating efforts to return to normal-

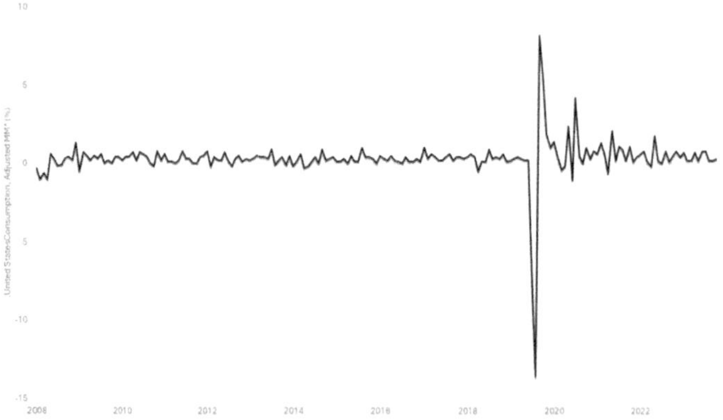

Figure 4.5: United States consumption, adjusted MM*(Jul 2024).
Note: Personal Outlays, Personal Consumption Expenditure, Overall, Total, AR, SA, Chg P/P. Available from here. Seasonally adjusted. Source: BEA - Bureau of Economic Analysis, U.S. Department of Commerce.

ity and creating unequal opportunities for resurgence based on the quality and level of support provided. More specifically, a small business operating in a country with exceptional support would theoretically possess an elevated probability of survival compared to those small companies that received such support. However, in a competitive market, strong support could potentially provide competitive advantages. Moreover, the financial relief measures introduced by many governments, while helpful, were not equally accessible to all small business owners. In the United States, for example, the Paycheck Protection Program (PPP) and other aid initiatives faced criticism for their complex application processes and inequitable distribution of funds (Hubbard and Strain, 2020; Autor et al., 2022; Bailey et al., 2022).

Another factor contributing to the prolonged struggle of small businesses is the disruption of supply chains. Social distancing measures and lockdowns affected the availability and cost of supplies, leading to delays and increased operational costs. However, small businesses, possessing limited bargaining power and potentially less financial reserves, could not absorb these additional costs compared to larger competitive firms. This supply chain disruption directly impacted the ability of small businesses to meet customer demands and maintain future profitability. Further, the pressure to adapt quickly to new business models, such as online sales and delivery services, required financial investment and a rapid acquisition of new skills and technologies, which many small business owners found challenging or, in some cases, impossible to afford.

4.4 Inequality Within Vulnerable Populations as a Result of Social Distancing

The economic fallout of social distancing measures has been identified to have disproportionately affected the poorest and most vulnerable cohorts of society, amplifying pre-existing socioeconomic inequalities. The economic impacts of these measures are both immediate and far-reaching, exacerbating issues such as unemployment (Petrosky-Nadeau et al., 2020; Bianchi et al., 2023), domestic violence (Kofman and Garfin, 2020; Evans et al., 2020; Boserup et al., 2020), and mental health crises (Hossain et al., 2020; Rajkumar, 2020; Xiong et al., 2020). Income reduction and unemployment were most pronounced amongst already denoted low-wage workers, particularly those in precarious job situations, who often lacked the financial support and savings to mitigate prolonged periods of economic inactivity. Unemployment sharply increased during the pandemic, with the most significant impacts observed among marginalised groups (Daly et al., 2020; Lee et al., 2021b), and those in sectors predominantly associated with low salaries, such as those in the service industry, including retail, hospitality, and personal care. These sectors are the most heavily dependent on physical interactions; they were among the first to close and the last to reopen, resulting in workers with limited alternatives for income generation. In some cases, such low-income workers were amongst those regularly taking the highest risks of illness as a result of the pandemic, with negotiated hazard payments largely inadequate to fairly compensate for the true risk being absorbed.

Elevated unemployment also led to a sharp rise in mental health issues, with many individuals experiencing heightened levels of stress, anxiety, and depression as a result of significant changes in their employment situation. Uncertainty surrounding employment stability and future prospects generated particularly damaging environments, which often were the most difficult for those categorised as the most vulnerable in society. Mental health services, many of which were already under incredible strain before the pandemic, struggled to cope with the increased demand, leaving many without adequate support during a critical time. The resulting mental health crises possessed significant long-term implications, potentially affecting individuals' ability to regain economic stability and similar working conditions to those experienced prior to the pandemic. Domestic violence incidents sharply elevated as a result of the lockdowns and social distancing measures (Boserup et al., 2020), while the stress of economic hardship, combined with the forced confinement of families in their homes, created a volatile environment for many. Victims of domestic abuse found it even more challenging to seek help or escape abusive situations due to the restrictions on movement and the reduced availability of support services.

Social safety nets, while crucial during this period, revealed significant gaps in coverage and effectiveness. Unemployment benefits, food assistance programs, and emergency financial aid were essential in providing temporary relief to those affected by the pandemic. However, the sudden surge in demand overwhelmed many of these systems, leading to delays and complications in accessing support, a range of which are presented in Table 4.4. Many low-income individuals, particularly those in informal employment or "gig economy" jobs, fell through and did not receive adequate support due to eligibility requirements that did not account for their work situations. Despite the expansion of unemployment benefits and direct financial aid, these measures often proved insufficient to meet the needs of the most vulnerable (Blustein et al., 2020; Couch et al., 2020; Petrosky-Nadeau et al., 2020). For many low-income families, the financial assistance provided did not cover basic living expenses, leading to increased food insecurity and housing instability. The expiration of certain benefits, coupled with ongoing economic uncertainty, left many without a safety net as the pandemic dragged on. The inadequacies of these support systems underscored the need for more robust and inclusive social safety policies.

Access to online resources and remote work opportunities were also significantly lower among low-income families, who often lacked reliable internet access and digital devices (Ruiz-Martínez and Esparcia, 2020; Early and Hernandez, 2021; Korkmaz et al., 2022). This divide affected children's education as remote learning became a significant tool to provide education, but due to technological inadequacies and affordability, many students from disadvantaged backgrounds struggled to keep up with their studies. The long-term educational impacts of this divide are likely to perpetuate cycles of poverty

Table 4.4: Selected pandemic unemployment assistance programmes.

Country	Benefit program	Details	Eligibility	Duration
United States	Pandemic Unemployment Assistance (PUA)	Provided benefits to those not traditionally eligible, such as freelancers and gig workers	Workers affected by COVID-19	Up to 39 weeks
Canada	Canada Emergency Response Benefit (CERB)	Provided $2,000 per month to those who lost income due to COVID-19	Workers who lost income due to COVID-19	Up to 28 weeks
United Kingdom	Universal Credit & Job Retention Scheme	Enhanced Universal Credit and wage subsidies up to 80 % of salary for furloughed workers	Employees and self-employed workers	Varied by program
Germany	Kurzarbeit (Short-Time Work Scheme)	Government paid up to 60 % (70 % for those with children) of lost wages for reduced working hours	Employees with reduced working hours	Up to 12 months
France	Chômage Partiel (Partial Unemployment Scheme)	Government subsidized 70 % of gross salary for reduced working hours	Employees affected by reduced working hours	Up to 12 months
Australia	JobSeeker Payment & JobKeeper Payment	JobSeeker provided financial assistance to unemployed; JobKeeper subsidized wages of employees	Employees and self-employed affected by COVID-19	Varied by program (6–12 months)
Spain	ERTE (Temporary Employment Regulation Files)	Temporary suspension of contracts with government support of up to 70 % of salary	Employees under suspended contracts	Duration of the state of emergency
Italy	Cassa Integrazione Guadagni (CIG)	Wage supplementation for employees affected by reduced hours or temporary layoffs	Employees with reduced hours or layoffs	Up to 12 months
Japan	Employment Adjustment Subsidy	Subsidies provided to companies to maintain employment by covering a portion of employee wages	Companies maintaining employment	Up to 12 months
Brazil	Emergency Employment and Income Maintenance Program	Temporary suspension of contracts with government support of up to 70 % of salary	Employees with suspended contracts	Up to 6 months
New Zealand	COVID-19 Wage Subsidy Scheme	Wage subsidies to support employers and employees affected by COVID-19	Employers and self-employed	Up to 8 weeks (extended as needed)
South Korea	Employment Retention Subsidy	Financial support to employers to retain workers by covering up to 90 % of wages during work suspension	Employers experiencing significant business losses	Up to 180 days

Table 4.4 (continued)

Country	Benefit program	Details	Eligibility	Duration
South Africa	Temporary Employer/Employee Relief Scheme (TERS)	Wage subsidies provided to workers who could not work due to the pandemic	Employees unable to work due to COVID-19	Up to 3 months (extended)
India	Atmanirbhar Bharat Rozgar Yojana	Incentive scheme to boost employment by covering EPF contributions for new hires	Employers hiring new employees during COVID-19	2 years
Mexico	Support Program for Workers in the Informal Sector	Financial assistance to informal sector workers who lost income due to the pandemic	Informal sector workers	One-time payment
Argentina	Emergency Family Income (IFE)	Monthly cash payments to unemployed and informal workers impacted by the pandemic	Unemployed and informal workers	Up to 3 months
Russia	Increased Unemployment Benefits	Enhanced unemployment benefits, including additional payments for families with children	Unemployed individuals and families	Duration of unemployment
Sweden	Increased Unemployment Insurance	Temporarily raised unemployment benefits and eased eligibility requirements	Unemployed individuals	Up to 300 days

Note: The information for this table was compiled from a variety of reliable sources, including official government publications, international organization reports, and news articles. Specific sources include the International Labour Organization (ILO), OECD reports, and government websites such as the U. S. Department of Labor, Service Canada, UK Government, Bundesagentur für Arbeit (Germany), Ministère du Travail (France), Australia's Services Australia, New Zealand's Ministry of Social Development, South Korea's Ministry of Employment and Labor, South Africa's Department of Employment and Labour, India's Ministry of Labour and Employment, Mexico's Ministry of Labor, Argentina's National Social Security Administration (ANSES), Russia's Ministry of Labor, and Sweden's Arbetsförmedlingen.

and inequality. Further, housing insecurity emerged as a critical issue, with many low-income families facing eviction and homelessness. The economic strain of the pandemic made it difficult for many to keep up with rent payments (Gupta et al., 2021b), and while eviction moratoriums provided temporary relief, as presented in Table 4.5, they did not address the underlying issue of unaffordable housing. The threat of losing one's home added another layer of stress and instability for already vulnerable populations, with long-term implications for both physical and mental health. The pandemic also highlighted the importance of community support networks and grassroots organisations in filling the gaps left by formal social safety nets. Many local organisations and mutual aid groups mobilised to provide essential services such as food distribution, financial assistance, and mental health support. These community-driven efforts were crucial in mitigating some of the worst impacts of the pandemic, demonstrating the resilience and resourcefulness of local communities in times of crisis.

4.5 Mobility and Case Trajectories

Social distancing policies during the COVID-19 pandemic significantly influenced mobility patterns (Dingil and Esztergár-Kiss, 2021; Wellenius et al., 2021; Abouk and Heydari, 2021; Zhang et al., 2023). By utilising anonymised and aggregated mobility data from opted-in users, researchers could assess the efficacy of these policies in curbing movement and thereby slowing the spread of the virus. Such data provided crucial insights into how human behaviour changed in response to governmental directives and the resultant epidemiological outcomes. Using mobility data offered a novel approach to understanding public adherence to social distancing guidelines. These data sets, derived from the location histories of millions of users, presented a detailed picture of mobility trends before, during, and after the implementation of various restrictions. By comparing mobility patterns across different states with varying levels of restrictions, researchers were able to gauge the effectiveness of these measures in reducing public movement as presented in Table 4.1.

Analysing the mobility data revealed significant reductions in visits to places such as retail stores, workplaces, and parks, which corresponded with the timing of stricter social distancing policies (Table 4.1). The data showed a marked decline in non-essential travel, indicating that people largely adhered to the guidelines, which was crucial in the initial efforts to control the virus's spread. These reductions were most pronounced in states that implemented early and stringent lockdown measures. Moreover, the correlation between reduced mobility and slower COVID-19 case growth was apparent (DeLuca et al., 2020). States that experienced greater declines in mobility typically saw a subsequent decrease in the rate of new infections (Badr et al., 2020). This relationship underscored the importance of early and decisive action in pandemic response strategies. The data provided empirical support for the argument that limiting movement could effectively slow down transmission rates, giving healthcare systems time to prepare and re-

Table 4.5: Measures implemented by various countries to reduce housing evictions during the COVID-19 pandemic.

Country	Measures implemented	Details	Date
United States	Eviction Moratorium	Federal moratorium preventing evictions for non-payment of rent. Extended multiple times	March 27, 2020
Canada	Eviction Ban & Rent Deferrals	Provinces like Ontario and British Columbia implemented temporary bans on evictions and allowed rent deferrals	March–April 2020 (varies by province)
United Kingdom	Eviction Ban	Suspension of evictions and extension of notice periods. Financial support provided to tenants	March 26, 2020
Australia	Eviction Moratorium & Rent Relief	Temporary bans on evictions for tenants facing hardship, with some regions offering rent relief or deferral options	March–April 2020 (varies by state)
Germany	Postponement of Evictions & Rent Deferrals	Postponement of evictions and deferred rent payments without penalties	April 1, 2020
France	Eviction Ban & Rent Deferrals	Banned evictions and allowed rent payment deferrals, extending the winter truce on evictions	March 27, 2020
Spain	Eviction Moratorium & Financial Support	Imposed an eviction moratorium and provided financial assistance to vulnerable tenants	March 31, 2020
Italy	Suspension of Evictions	Suspension of all eviction proceedings and financial assistance provided to tenants and landlords	March 25, 2020
New Zealand	Temporary Freeze on Rent Increases & Evictions	A freeze on rent increases and a ban on evictions for rent arrears	March 26, 2020
Ireland	Eviction Ban & Rent Freeze	Ban on evictions and freezing of rent increases	March 27, 2020
Brazil	Suspension of Evictions & Rent Deferrals	Measures in certain cities and states to suspend evictions and allow for rent deferrals	April 2020 (varies by region)
South Africa	Eviction Moratorium & Rent Relief	Suspension of evictions and provision of rent relief in some provinces	March 26, 2020
India	Suspension of Evictions & Rent Relief in Some States	Temporary bans on evictions and offered rent relief or deferments in some states	April 2020 (varies by state)
Japan	Financial Assistance for Rent	Financial assistance provided to help tenants pay rent, though no eviction moratorium was implemented	Apr-20

Table 4.5 (continued)

Country	Measures implemented	Details	Date
Mexico	Suspension of Evictions in Some Regions	Suspension of evictions and limited financial assistance in certain states and municipalities	April 2020 (varies by region)
Argentina	Eviction Moratorium & Rent Freeze	Eviction moratorium and freezing of rent increases	March 29, 202

Note: The data for the measures implemented to reduce housing evictions during COVID-19 was sourced from various government publications, legal documents, and reports from international organisations such as the United Nations, World Bank, and OECD. Additionally, information was gathered from news articles and official statements from national and regional governments, including the U. S. Centers for Disease Control and Prevention (CDC), Canada's provincial announcements, the UK government's official COVID-19 response updates, and similar sources from Australia, Germany, France, Spain, Italy, New Zealand, Ireland, Brazil, South Africa, India, Japan, Mexico, and Argentina.

spond. Quantifying the impact of these policies involved examining the extent to which mobility changes affected COVID-19 case trajectories. Experts developed models to predict case growth based on mobility trends, finding that areas with more substantial mobility reductions saw lower case numbers (Nouvellet et al., 2021). These models took into account various factors such as population density, existing healthcare infrastructure, and the baseline level of virus transmission, ensuring a thorough analysis. The findings from these studies also highlighted disparities in the impact of social distancing across different regions and communities. Urban areas, with higher population densities and greater reliance on public transportation, exhibited more significant reductions in mobility compared to rural areas (Park et al., 2021; Chang et al., 2021). This discrepancy pointed to the need for tailored public health interventions that consider the unique characteristics of different locales. Additionally, the mobility data helped identify potential hot spots of virus transmission. By mapping movement patterns, researchers could pinpoint areas where social distancing was less effective, allowing for targeted interventions. This approach was particularly useful in managing outbreaks in high-risk environments such as nursing homes, correctional facilities, and densely populated urban neighbourhoods.

Integrating mobility data into public health policy provided a real-time feedback mechanism for officials. It enabled a dynamic response to the pandemic, where policies could be adjusted based on observed behaviour and its impact on virus spread. For instance, countries could ease restrictions in areas where mobility data indicated strong adherence to guidelines and low transmission rates while reinforcing measures in areas with higher mobility and rising case numbers (Beck and Hensher, 2020). One of the critical insights from this analysis was the varying lag times between mobility changes and their impact on case numbers. The data showed that significant reductions in movement typically led to noticeable declines in new cases after a delay of one to two weeks (DeLuca et al., 2020; Wellenius et al., 2021). This lag underscored the importance of maintaining restrictions even when immediate effects were not visible, as premature relaxation could lead to a resurgence of cases.

4.6 Spillover Effects and Input–Output Linkages

The onset of COVID-19 generated economic barriers for companies in sectors creating intermediate goods and severe disruption to production chains, thereby exacerbating even greater economic disruptions. This shock uncovered incredible system-wide vulnerabilities exacerbated by the interconnectedness of globally-focused economies. Firms heavily reliant on selling intermediate goods to sectors severely affected by social distancing, such as hospitality, retail, and transportation, faced particularly unprecedented challenges. Though not the direct targets of restrictions, these intermediate goods producers experienced significant downturns as their primary consumers curtailed their short-to-medium-term operations and simply shut down entirely. This interdependence underscores the complex nature of economic networks, where disturbances in one sector can precipitate widespread financial instability in other seemingly disconnected sectors. Production bottlenecks and halts deeply disrupted the flow of operations. Industries such as automotive manufacturing, which depend on the steady supply of parts and raw materials from various sectors, encountered severe disruptions, which further cascaded through the supply chain, affecting production schedules, increasing costs, and ultimately reducing output. The contraction in demand from affected sectors further compounded these issues, as suppliers faced diminished orders and heightened uncertainty.

Moreover, it was identified that the scale of a firm and its financial health played crucial roles in determining its resilience to these shocks (Laeven, 2022; Akyildirim et al., 2020, 2022, 2023, 2024b). Larger firms with diversified supply chains and substantial cash reserves were better positioned to weather the disruptions (Akyildirim et al., 2024a; Scrimgeour et al., 2024). These firms could absorb short-term losses and maintain liquidity, allowing them to continue operations or pivot strategies to mitigate the impact. In contrast, smaller firms with limited financial buffers and less diversified supply chains faced greater insolvency risks. The disparity in resilience between large and small firms highlighted the uneven economic burden of the pandemic and the importance of financial preparedness. The indirect effects of social distancing also manifested in decreased investments and delayed capital expenditures across sectors. Firms facing uncertain demand and disrupted supply chains were hesitant to commit to new investments, further stalling economic recovery (Hoang et al., 2022a; Tawiah and O'Connor Keefe, 2022). This hesitation was particularly evident in capital-intensive industries, such as construction and heavy manufacturing, as presented in Figure 4.6, where long-term investments are critical for growth. The delay in investments not only affected immediate economic activity but also had long-term implications for productivity and innovation. Additionally, the interconnectedness of global supply chains meant that the economic disruptions were not confined to national borders (Moosavi et al., 2022; Cordeiro et al., 2022). International trade faced significant hurdles as countries implemented varying degrees of lockdowns and social distancing measures. Export-oriented industries suffered from reduced demand abroad, while import-dependent sectors had to contend with supply shortages and elevated competition for resources. The global nature of supply chains amplified the economic impact of social distancing, as disruptions in one region could reverberate worldwide, affecting production and trade flows on a large scale.

4.7 Concluding Comments

The outbreak of COVID-19 necessitated unprecedented public health measures, including extensive social distancing protocols, which profoundly impacted worldwide economic conditions. While essential for controlling the spread of the virus, these measures induced significant disruptions, particularly in sectors dependent on physical presence

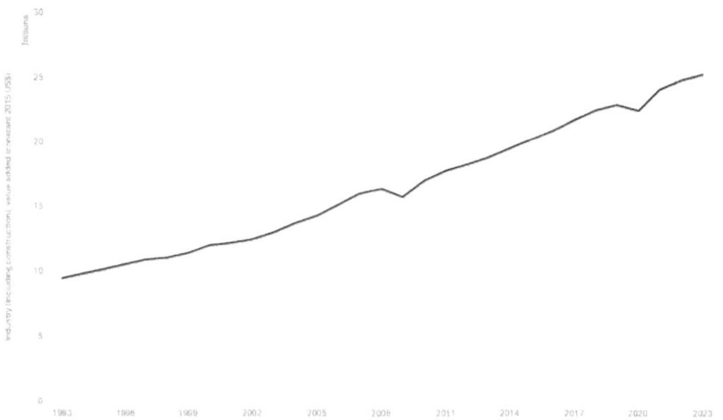

Figure 4.6: Industry (including construction), value added (constant 2015 US$).
Note: From the World Bank national accounts data and OECD National Accounts data files. Notes that "Industry (including construction) corresponds to ISIC divisions 05–43 and includes manufacturing (ISIC divisions 10–33). It comprises value added in mining, manufacturing (also reported as a separate subgroup), construction, electricity, water, and gas. Value added is the net output of a sector after adding up all outputs and subtracting intermediate inputs. It is calculated without making deductions for depreciation of fabricated assets or depletion and degradation of natural resources. The origin of value added is determined by the International Standard Industrial Classification (ISIC), revision 4. Data are in constant 2015 prices, expressed in U. S. dollars" and "The reporting period for national accounts data is designated as either a calendar year basis (CY) or a fiscal year basis (FY). For this country, it is fiscal year-based (fiscal year-end: March 20). Also, an estimate (PA.NUS.ATLS) of the exchange rate covers the same period and thus differs from the official exchange rate (CY). In addition, the World Bank systematically assesses the appropriateness of official exchange rates as conversion factors. In this country, multiple or dual exchange rate activity exists and must be accounted for appropriately in underlying statistics. An alternative estimate ("alternative conversion factor" – PA.NUS.ATLS) is thus calculated as a weighted average of the different exchange rates in use in the country. Doing so better reflects economic reality and leads to more accurate cross-country comparisons and country classifications by income level. For this country, this applies to the period 1960–2006. Alternative conversion factors are used in the Atlas methodology and elsewhere in World Development Indicators as single-year conversion factors."

and intermediate goods. The initial lockdowns resulted in unprecedented economic decline, with sectors such as entertainment, hospitality, and manufacturing experiencing the most severe contractions. This initial shock propagated through various economic linkages, affecting even those sectors not directly targeted by social distancing measures.

Small businesses were particularly vulnerable, with many nations experiencing a sharp reduction in active companies during the early months of the pandemic, where many simply had to shut down as a temporary measure in an attempt to survive before a range of economic support was eventually provided in some countries. The economic effects as a result of social distancing measures disproportionately affected the most vulnerable populations across many societies, exacerbating pre-existing inequalities. Low-income workers, often employed in sectors with high physical contact, faced severe job losses and income reduction. The compounded effects of unemployment, food insecurity, and a lack of access to healthcare intensified the problems experienced along with the severity of the situation for these groups. Data suggests that the implementation of many lockdown procedures also led to increased instances of domestic violence and mental health crises as stressed social support systems struggled to cope with rising demands. Broadly, the pandemic highlighted the complex interdependencies within economies, where the impact on one sector could reverberate through others via input-output linkages. The direct and indirect effects of social distancing on stock market performance further illustrated the economic vulnerabilities exposed by the pandemic.

5 Comparing the Financial Impact of COVID-19 with other Global Disasters

How did financial assets perform during the COVID-19 crisis, and are there similarities with previous crises? This chapter quantifies the performance of the S&P 500 during the COVID-19 bear market and contrasts this with previous bear markets. Large pandemic-related losses occurred rapidly and were recovered quickly than in previous bear markets. Gold and Treasury bonds provided relative respite for equity investors during the COVID-19 bear market. Other equity bear markets are noteworthy for the lack of consistent diversification opportunities available to investors.

5.1 Introduction

A bear market in equities, taken to mean a decline in market prices of 20 per cent or greater, acts as an indicator of investors' worries about the economy more generally. During the COVID-19 pandemic, the US stock market dropped by over 34 percent, presenting one of the steepest and swiftest falls in history. This notwithstanding, equity bear markets are not all that remarkable, with 65 reported between 1800 and 2000 (Gonzalez et al., 2005). Given their frequency, what can investors do to protect themselves from significant bear market losses?

In addition to their aversion to large equity losses, diversified investors are also concerned about the performance of other assets during periods when equity prices are depressed. Alongside reducing specific risk, diversifying across a range of assets helps in minimising portfolio losses during downturns. Treasury bonds, traditionally thought of as having a low correlation with equities due to the flight-to-quality effect, are one mechanism to hedge risk, but may be subject to time-varying correlations and term-premia (Kozak, 2022). Commodities, including gold and crude oil, may also have diversification properties due to limited correlation with equities (Bessler and Wolff, 2015).

This chapter compares the duration and severity of the COVID-19 equity bear market with previous crises to provide context for investors. This is followed by a performance assessment of a set of diverse assets during bear markets. This provides two contributions. First, it highlights the potential diversification benefits available to equity investors during the COVID-19 crisis. Second, it allows for a comparison of diversification, hedging, and safe haven attributes during multiple periods of extreme downside risk, which are of critical importance to investors.

The research findings emphasise the severity of the COVID-19 bear market. Compared to previous bear markets, the S&P 500 dropped more rapidly and recovered far more quickly than in previous market downturns. Furthermore, the magnitude of the drop in prices was greater than in three of the other six bear markets examined over a 50-year period. Commodities and crude oil provided no respite for investors, and their

https://doi.org/10.1515/9783111707990-005

value dropped during the crisis. Gold and treasury bonds, although volatile in the early stages of the crisis, provided a store of value for investors. Evidence of heterogeneity emerges during previous bear markets. Commodities and crude oil provide outperformance, relative to equities, during a number of the bear markets examined, but losses in others. Gold underperforms during the inflation-related bear market, which started in 1980, but provides relative stability during other crises. Finally, Treasury bonds outperformed equities during the pandemic, along with the dot-com and global financial crisis bear markets, but fell in price during the most recent inflation-driven bear market.

The implications for investors are complex. No single asset provides respite for investors across all of the bear markets examined. Macroeconomic fundamentals, such as inflation and interest rates, appear to have a substantial influence on diversification performance during bear markets. Furthermore, some of the supposed diversifiers, such as crude oil, actually produce increased losses for investors, counter to their intended purpose. Given this uncertainty in terms of which assets investors should hold to mitigate bear market losses, a portfolio approach may be best placed to determine the optimal weights. Furthermore, other asset classes such as hedge funds may provide further protection during bear markets (Conlon et al., 2007). These suggestions are left for future research.

5.2 Previous Literature

Bear markets, defined as periods when an equity market drops in value by more than 20 percent, have received much focus in the literature (Chen, 2009; Meric et al., 2008; Butler and Joaquin, 2002). Various ways to identify bear markets have been proposed (Kole and Van Dijk, 2017; Maheu and McCurdy, 2000), while the ability to forecast bear markets is still an open research question (Haase and Neuenkirch, 2023; Nyberg, 2013). The importance of understanding bear markets is grounded in their influence upon asset allocation, with increasing correlation during regimes influencing optimal portfolio weights (Conlon et al., 2023c; Carroll et al., 2017; Ang and Bekaert, 2004; Campbell et al., 2002).

The benefits of holding uncorrelated assets during periods of crisis have been well documented. Gold has been shown to act as a diversifier, hedge and safe haven for commodity markets (Ryan et al., 2024; Bredin et al., 2015; Baur and Lucey, 2010). Government bonds demonstrate flight to quality properties during bear markets (Beber et al., 2009), but only long-dated bonds, not one-year Treasuries, have strong safe-haven properties. More recently, assets such as green bonds (Naeem et al., 2022) and cryptocurrencies (Conlon et al., 2024g; Conlon and McGee, 2020a; Corbet et al., 2020c) have been examined as possible hedges against downside risk in equities. While the focus in this chapter is on US equity markets, which act as a barometer of markets internationally, other markets were also severely impacted by the crisis (Corbet et al., 2021b).

The COVID-19 crisis has proven to be a formidable test of the diversification, hedging and safe haven capacity of assets. Gold has been shown by some to have failed the test (Cheema et al., 2022) and by others to have provided safe haven benefits (Salisu et al., 2021). In keeping with some of the findings documented below, Akhtaruzzaman et al. (2021) demonstrate that the pandemic safe haven properties of gold were sharply time dependent. A further factor impacting the benefits of diversification throughout the COVID-19 pandemic is the timing of vaccine deployment (Pham et al., 2023). When a wide set of markets is considered, Attig and Sy (2023) demonstrate that international diversification is the optimal risk-reduction tool through a series of crises, including the COVID-19 pandemic.

5.3 Data and Methodology

The data used in this chapter were obtained from Eikon, a division of LSEG Data and Analytics. Daily price data from December 31, 1972 through December 31, 2023 are extracted and returns calculated. Bear markets, defined as periods during which equities drop in value by more than 20 percent, are represented using the S&P 500 index. A list of the bear markets alongside an indication of the driver, the start and end dates (the date by which the market recovered all losses from the bear market) and the length of the period from when the market started its decline to when it recovered all losses are described in Table 5.1.

Table 5.1: S&P 500 bear market timing.

Event	Start date	Finish date	Number of days
USD Devaluation/Oil Crisis/Inflation	11/01/1973	17/07/1980	1,961
Inflation	28/11/1980	03/11/1982	504
Black Monday	25/08/1987	26/07/1989	502
Dot-Com Crash	24/03/2000	30/05/2007	1,968
Global Financial Crisis	09/10/2007	28/03/2013	1428
COVID-19	19/02/2020	18/08/2020	130
Post-COVID Inflation	03/01/2022	N/A	N/A

Note: This table shows the timing of bear markets, downward price movements of more than 20 percent in the S&P 500. The start date corresponds to the date of the market peak before the bear started, the finish date refers to the date at which the market regained all losses, while the number of days is the length of the bear market and subsequent recovery in terms of trading days.

The performance of a series of other assets, often described as diversifiers, is also examined. The Goldman Sachs Commodity Index (GSCI) is preferred as representative of the broad commodity market, and selected due to the evidence that important constituents such as precious metals and soft commodities have some safe haven properties (Rubbaniy et al., 2022; Bredin et al., 2015). Gold, long known for its diversification, hedging and safe haven properties, alongside inflation hedging characteristics, is also examined (Baur and Lucey, 2010; Bredin et al., 2017; Conlon et al., 2018b). Crude oil, often considered as a diversifier for equity investors, is further examined (Bessler and Wolff, 2015). Finally, Treasury bonds are regularly included in diversified portfolios as a means to improve the risk-return tradeoff (Bessler et al., 2017). The start dates for the data are different with, for example, data on crude oil only available from 1983, preventing an analysis of all bear markets across every asset.

5.4 Results

The extent and duration of all S&P 500 bear markets since the 1970s are compared with the COVID-19 bear market in this section. This is then followed by assessing the impact this has on other asset classes and whether they follow a similar trend or offer diversification and hedging opportunities. While the analysis does not explicitly speak to portfolio opportunities, it provides investors with some broad guidance as to the impact of bear markets on other asset classes.

Figure 5.1 shows the performance of the S&P throughout the seven different bear markets that have occurred since the 1970s, in a manner similar to that presented by Gormsen and Koijen (2023). The COVID-19 bear market can be clearly differentiated from the others. First, the speed at which the market decreased is almost unprecedented, with only the Black Monday crash of 1987 dropping more rapidly in value (albeit after a subdued initial fall). Among the other crises, the stock market took a much longer time

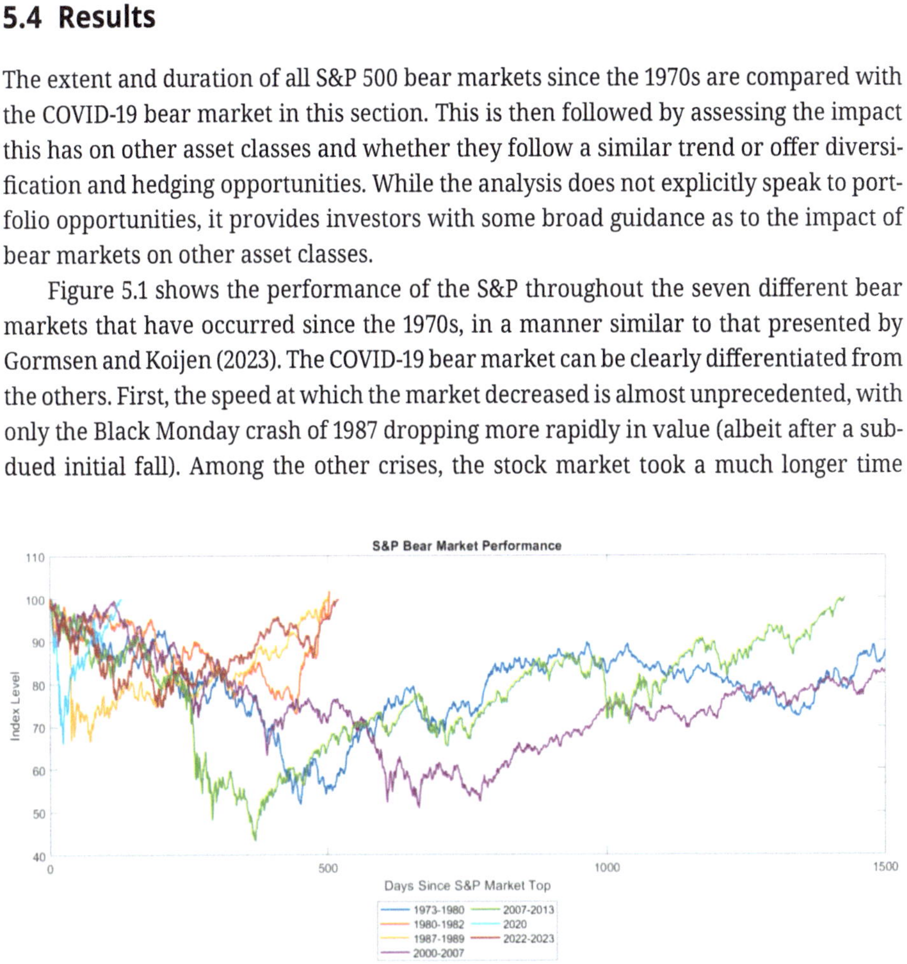

Figure 5.1: S&P 500 performance during and after Bear Markets.
Note: This figure shows the performance of the S&P 500 index from the point at which the market peaked until it returned to this level, or 1,500 days have passed. The S&P bear markets detailed are from 1973–1980, 1980–1982, 1987–1989, 2000–2007, 2007–2013, 2020 and 2022–2023. All data are rebased to a value of 100 at the beginning.

to reach its lowest value. Taking the global financial crisis as an example, the market topped out in October 2007, having only recently fully recovered fully from the dot-com turmoil, beginning a slow decline which accelerated towards summer 2008 but only reached its low in March 2009.

Second, the market recovered all losses within a much shorter window than in any previous crisis, regaining all losses in just 130 trading days. Again, comparing with the global financial crisis, the latter took over 1,000 trading days to recover all losses from the crisis, experiencing some further large drawdowns along the way. Finally, the extent of the peak losses, while sizable, is modest compared to those experienced by investors during the global financial crisis, the bursting of the dot-com bubble and the bear market instigated by the US dollar devaluation, alongside the oil crisis and inflation in the 1970s. Total losses in the S&P 500, as of March 19, 2020 came to 34 percent, much lower than the extremes of other crises, such as the global financial crisis, where markets lost 57 percent of their value. In this context, the COVID-19 crisis was substantially less harrowing for investors.

These data also illustrate the effectiveness of the coordinated monetary and fiscal response to the COVID-19 crisis. The timing of the market turnaround coincides with announcements regarding the extent of non-traditional monetary policy interventions to stem the economic impacts of the crisis. This response far exceeded that of previous crises, resulting in a turnaround in expectations that led to a swift recovery. Of note, much of the promised quantitative easing was not required, with the announcement sufficient to generate a swift turnaround in market sentiment.

The following sections examine the performance of other assets during the S&P 500 bear markets documented here.

5.4.1 Commodities

Using the GSCI as a barometer of the commodity complex, we determine the performance of commodities during the bear market periods depicted in Figure 5.1. Specifically, using indices rebased to 100 at the start of each bear market in equities, we examine how commodity prices changed in response to bear market conditions. From a diversified, risk averse, investors' perspective, this provides some guidance as to the potential to hedge losses in equities using commodity markets during periods of maximal market turmoil.

The rebased GSCI index is shown in Figure 5.2. During the COVID-19 crisis, commodities dropped sharply, losing up to 48 percent of their value in just 45 trading days, a slightly longer window of decline than observed for the S&P 500. Much of this drop in value can be attributed to the dramatic decline in oil prices, with spot prices turning negative for a short period (Corbet et al., 2021b, 2020b). By the time the S&P 500 regained all losses from the crisis, and commodities had regained almost half their losses, with the index at 75, compared to the starting level of 100.

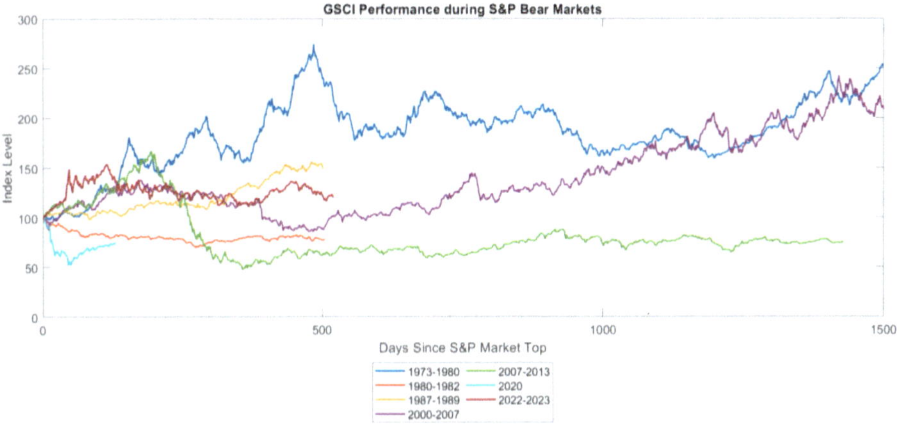

Figure 5.2: Goldman Sachs Commodity Index Performance during and after S&P 500 Bear Markets.
Note: This figure shows the performance of the GSCI during the period where the S&P 500 index peaked until it returned to this level or 1,500 days have passed. The S&P bear markets detailed are from 1973–1980, 1980–1982, 1987–1989, 2000–2007, 2007–2013, 2020 and 2022–2023. All data are rebased to a value of 100 at the beginning.

Comparing the performance of commodities during other S&P bear markets points to some potential for diversification opportunities. During the 1973–1980 crisis, associated with high inflation and increases in oil prices, commodities provided considerable outperformance. While such outperformance may be linked to commodities acting as an inflation hedge, evidence suggests that this is only the case for industrial and precious metals (Liu et al., 2023). This outperformance, while significant, is also found to be volatile over the period to 1980.

Similarly, commodities provided relative respite to equity investors during the Black Monday crash of 1987 and the inflation crisis of 2022. After the Black Monday crash, commodities were unaffected, growing in price steadily over the following years. This points to the crisis being financially led, rather than macroeconomically led, where the latter might have resulted in a decrease in commodity demand. Over the 2022 bear market, commodities initially outperformed, growing in price by over 50 percent before falling back. While initially thought of as a hedge, rising interest rates, intended to dampen demand, may have resulted in this return in value.

The 1980–1982 bear market was strongly linked to runaway inflation alongside drastic monetary policy, with interest rates hitting over 20 percent. This had the effect of driving down commodity prices alongside equities, with the former not recovering anything close to their original levels. The global financial crisis stands out, with very significant growth in commodity prices over the first year or so and a substantial subsequent decline. One determinant of this increase is the growth in price of energy commodities over the period, attributed to increases in demand (Hamilton, 2009). Commodity prices began a steep decline in July 2007, losing over 70 percent of their value from top to bottom. By the time the S&P 500 recovered all losses, commodities were still only trading at 75 percent of their original value.

These findings highlight some hedging potential for equity investors in commodities, but also indicate risks. Inflationary pressures and associated interest rate hikes can have significant effects on commodities, although an initial spike in prices, despite equity markets declining, is noted in two cases. The COVID-19 decline in commodities has the greatest resonance with the decrease in prices from July 2007, during the global financial crisis. In both cases, suppressed demand led to a rapid and dramatic decrease in commodity prices.

5.4.2 Gold

The performance of gold during bear markets is illustrated in Figure 5.3. During the COVID-19 bear market in equities, gold was somewhat volatile, increasing in price initially, decreasing by about 12 percent subsequently and then recovering steadily over the following 100 days to a level of 124. While the initial decrease in value was considerable, gold still acted as a store of value relative to equities during the initial part of the crisis. The subsequent increase in value may have been a result of the vast quantitative easing unleashed by central banks globally, with investors concerned about inflationary risks. While there is some debate about whether gold acted as a hedge during the COVID-19 crisis (Cheema et al., 2022; Salisu et al., 2021), the very short time span and limited decline in gold prices must be taken into account.

Figure 5.3: Gold Performance during and after S&P 500 Bear Markets.
Note: This figure shows the performance of gold prices during a period where the S&P 500 index peaked until it returned to this level, or 1,500 days have passed. The S&P bear markets detailed are from 1973–1980, 1980–1982, 1987–1989, 2000–2007, 2007–2013, 2020 and 2022–2023. All data are rebased to a value of 100 at the beginning.

Gold's performance during previous bear markets is more mixed than the literature might imply. During the seven equity bear markets assessed, gold was found to be a store of value in six, experiencing limited or no drops in price while equity markets were concurrently decreasing. The 1980–1982 crisis is an exception, however, with gold dropping for most of the bear market and finishing the period priced lower than at the start. Similarly, during the 1987 Black Monday bear market, although gold initially acted as a hedge, it dropped in price during the equity market recovery.

During the 1973–1980 bear market, gold, although volatile, did appreciate in value by over 200 percent. This may be a consequence of the well-documented inflation hedging properties of gold (Conlon et al., 2018b). The global financial crisis presented a firm test of gold as a store of value. This crisis contained a deflationary period, followed by considerable monetary easing, which left investors worried about runaway inflation. Gold appreciated in price considerably throughout the crisis, finishing over 100 percent higher. Although some volatility is evident, there is a strong contrast with the GSCI commodity index, which appreciated considerably and lost a large proportion of its value during this bear market. Finally, during the fall associated with the bursting of the dot-com bubble, gold retained its value, followed by an appreciation in price in tandem with the strengthening of markets.

Compared with the broad commodity market, gold appears to have provided strong diversification and hedging properties throughout the majority of crises faced by the stock market. Moreover, in five of the seven bear markets, gold investors would have increased their wealth by the time that equity markets returned to their base value of 100. While not indicated as a guaranteed hedge against bear market losses, gold may form part of a portfolio approach to reducing downside risk.

5.4.3 Crude Oil

Next, we assess the performance of crude oil during S&P 500 bear markets in Figure 5.4. Although there are similarities with the GSCI, some notable differences also emerge. Crude oil suffered the curious fate of having negative prices early in the pandemic.[3] This exceptional circumstance was instigated by oversupply, a huge drop in demand and negative sentiment. Oil prices recovered quickly, however, and by the culmination of the bear market cycle they had returned to 80 percent of their starting price.

The COVID-19 bear market was, by a considerable stretch, the worst performance of crude oil during S&P 500 bear market recessions. Of the five bear markets for which data are available, crude oil prices finished at a level higher than when the bear market losses began. There were, however, periods of substantial volatility. Following the 1987

3 For ease of calculation, the lowest price is set to 0 here. Negative spot prices were present for only one day in the time series.

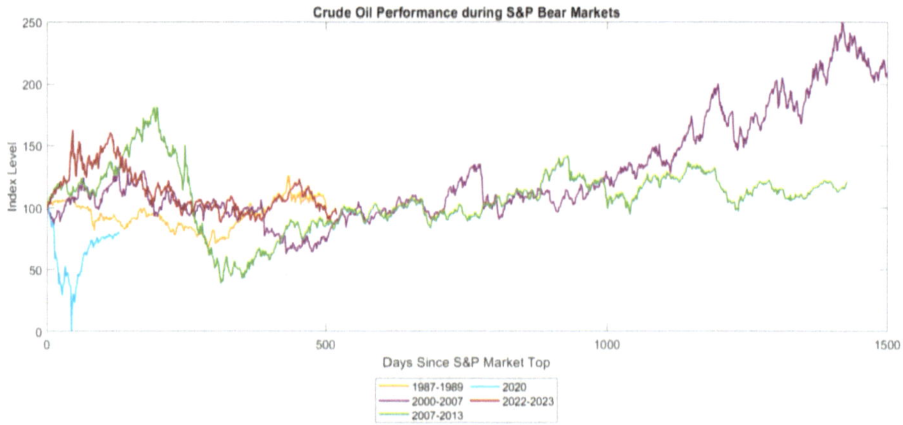

Figure 5.4: Crude Oil Performance during and after S&P 500 Bear Markets.
Note: This figure shows the performance of crude oil prices during period where the S&P 500 index peaked until it returned to this level or 1,500 day have passed. The S&P bear markets detailed are from 1987–1989, 2000–2007, 2007–2013, 2020 and 2022–2023. All data are rebased to a value of 100 at the beginning.

Black Monday crash, crude oil dropped by over 26 percent in the first year and a half of trading. In the subsequent months, in line with the increase in the S&P 500, crude oil also appreciated in price. The dot-com burst coincided with an initial increase in crude oil prices by up to 33 percent, followed by a lengthy decrease down to about 62 percent of the original value. Prices then increased substantially over the following years, during the period when stock markets only returned to their original level.

The price dynamics of crude oil during the period surrounding the global financial crisis-led bear market are similar to those observed for the S&P 500. Prices appreciated considerably, followed by a large and swift decline at the height of the crisis, when demand dried up. Oil recovered in value reasonably quickly and remained within a tight range for the following years. Finally, during the most recent bear market corresponding to the return of inflation and interest rate increases, crude oil initially appreciated by over 50 percent but then returned to close to its starting level. Investors, however, would not have experienced meaningful losses over the period.

5.4.4 US Treasury Bonds

US government bonds are among the main beneficiaries of the flight to safety that occurs during bear markets. Investors selling risky assets such as stocks move their capital into safer assets, particularly government bonds. Furthermore, during crises, central banks often cut interest rates, making higher-paying existing bonds more appealing to investors. The aggregate performance of US Treasury bonds during four bear markets is shown in Figure 5.5.

Figure 5.5: US Treasury Bonds Performance during and after S&P 500 Bear Markets.
Note: This figure shows the performance of US Treasury Bonds during a period where the S&P 500 index peaked until it returned to this level, or 1,500 days have passed. The S&P bear markets detailed are from 2000–2007, 2007–2013, 2020 and 2022–2023. All data are rebased to a value of 100 at the beginning.

For the first three bear markets, Treasury bonds performed as expected, appreciating considerably. In each case, the bear market was associated with decreasing interest rates. Over the COVID-19-linked bear market, Treasury bonds initially appreciated and, similar to gold, depreciated in price again, followed by a subsequent increase and retention of value. In this sense, although there was some price volatility, Treasury bonds were a store of value during the crisis. For each of the dot-com and global financial crisis-initiated bear markets, Treasury bonds performed strongly, returning between 25 and 40 per cent to investors.

The more recent bear market, however, was difficult for Treasury bond investors. To fight inflation, the Federal Reserve had to raise interest rates, making older issued bonds with lower yields less valuable. In sharp contrast with previous bear markets, investors would have lost up to 13 percent, adding to their losses from a portfolio perspective. While Treasury bonds are often proposed as critical to diversification, these results indicate an element of conditionality. Treasuries have acted as a hedge and a diversifier during decreasing interest rate environments, but when the bear market is a consequence of rising interest rates, investors may suffer a double impact from both stocks and bonds simultaneously decreasing in value. While the present data does not permit further analysis of the performance of Treasury bonds during bear markets coinciding with rising interest rate environments, further work needs to be done to validate these findings.

5.5 Concluding Comments

Bear markets are part of the lore of investing, indicating at least a decrease of 20 percent in equity markets. Risk-averse investors seek to soften the blow during bear markets by holding a diversified portfolio of assets, some of which hold their value during stock market decreases. This has given rise to an interest in hedges and safe havens to protect capital. In this chapter, the performance of the S&P 500 during the COVID-19 bear market is compared with previous crises, assessing both the initial decrease in value and the recovery. The performance of a series of other assets, including commodities, Treasury bonds, gold and crude oil during bear markets is then quantified.

The COVID-19 bear markets in equities are shown to be exceptional, in terms of the speed at which the market decreased, the depth of the decrease and the time for full recovery. After falling by over 30 percent in a matter of weeks, the market recovered fully within 130 days. Compared to previous bear markets, the bear markets of the 1980s were the quickest to recover, taking a little over 500 trading days. This recovery is also notable by the level of monetary and fiscal support provided by the government, allowing the market to brush off losses rapidly. Furthermore, unlike previous crises, some noteworthy sectors outperformed considerably during the crisis, especially prominent ones such as technology, which were critical to business and education during the crisis.

The performance of the other asset classes during bear markets is then assessed to get an indication of their capacity to protect investors against losses. Commodities lost considerable value during the bear market and were still substantially undervalued when the bear market ended. During previous crises, the performance of commodities was mixed. With the exception of the bear market associated with the 1987 Black Monday decline, commodity performance was volatile, even when outperformance was found.

Gold, a traditional hedge and safe haven for equity markets, provided some protection for investors during the COVID-19 bear market, but the performance was volatile during the initial stages of the crisis. During previous bear markets, gold provided a refuge during four of the crises. During the crises of the 1980s, however, its performance was more mixed. The price of crude oil declined precipitously in the early stages of the pandemic, attributable to both supply and demand drivers. While a strong recovery was evident by the end of the bear market, this was insufficient to return crude oil to its initial starting price. While crude oil declined in value during previous crises, the slumps were less dramatic than during the COVID-19 pandemic or those found for equity markets.

Finally, Treasury bonds, referring to US government-issued debt securities, provided relative immunity to the COVID-19 bear market, although they did experience a temporary, albeit sharp, drop in value in the early stages of the crisis. During the bear markets associated with the global financial crisis and the dot-com bubble, Treasury bonds consistently performed and provided a valuable hedge for equity investors. The benefits of Treasury bonds for diversification were tested; however, during the most recent bear market, brought on by the surge in inflation and associated interest rate increases from 2022. Treasury bonds dropped substantially in value, resulting in simultaneous losses for investors diversified into equities and government bonds.

Further research is required to formalise the optimal strategy for investors to limit losses during bear markets. The findings above do not indicate a single asset that provides consistent diversification strategies throughout all bear markets. Understanding the specific drivers of hedging and safe haven assets, such as their performance during periods of high inflation and rising interest rates, will help in selecting an appropriate portfolio of well-diversified assets. Furthermore, an examination of other assets known for their diversification benefits, such as hedge funds, during bear markets is warranted. Finally, while daily data is examined in this study, risk characterisation has been shown to alter at different return intervals, perhaps influencing the diversification and risk reduction outcomes (Conlon et al., 2018a, 2024d). Further research in this vein is also required.

6 The Impact of COVID-19 on Global Sports Finance

This chapter examines the significant financial and operational impact of the COVID-19 pandemic on the global sports industry. The pandemic brought about unprecedented disruptions, halting live events, diminishing revenues from ticket sales, broadcasting rights, and sponsorships, and triggering widespread financial distress across all levels of sports. We explore the immediate effects on major leagues, grassroots clubs, and the broader sports ecosystem, highlighting the role of liquidity management and the shift towards digital and virtual engagement as critical responses. The chapter also addresses the long-term financial implications, including the uneven recovery across regions, exacerbating existing inequalities, and the necessary evolution of financial strategies within the industry. Additionally, we discuss the social and cultural shifts catalysed by the pandemic, particularly regarding gender equity, racial justice, and mental health in sports.

6.1 The Immediate Shock to Global Sports

The COVID-19 pandemic affected all sectors in some manner, including sports. The industry broadly slowed down due to global lockdowns and social distancing measures for infection prevention. Events from local matches to international championships were abruptly cancelled, causing significant financial losses. Disruptions hit teams, athletes, leagues, media, advertising, and local economies. Tickets, TV, sponsorship, and product losses were substantial due to the Tokyo 2020 Olympics[4] and professional league seasons being cancelled or postponed. These sports industry shocks destabilised stable financial organisations.

Historically, the sports industry has demonstrated remarkable resilience in the face of economic downturns. For instance, during the 2008 financial crisis, major sports leagues and organisations managed to mitigate such headwinds, eventually restoring themselves to solid profitability relatively unscathed (Andreff, 2011). The sector's inherent ability to generate substantial revenue through media rights, sponsorships, and live events provided a buffer against economic shocks. However, the impact of the

---

4 The Tokyo 2020 Olympics were postponed to 2021 due to the COVID-19 pandemic, marking the first time in the event's history that the Games were rescheduled rather than cancelled outright. The decision was made in March 2020 after growing concerns about the safety of athletes, officials, and spectators as the pandemic spread globally. In agreement with the Japanese government, the International Olympic Committee (IOC) and the Tokyo Organising Committee concluded that postponing the Games were necessary to protect public health and ensure that the event could be held under safer conditions. The postponement created significant logistical and financial challenges, including the need to renegotiate contracts, adjust schedules, and manage the upkeep of venues. The delay also increased costs for the host city, estimated to be billions of dollars, due to the additional year of preparations required. Despite the challenges, the Tokyo Olympics were eventually held in July 2021, albeit with strict health protocols and without international spectators to minimise the risk of COVID-19 transmission.

https://doi.org/10.1515/9783111707990-006

COVID-19 pandemic was fundamentally different. It was not merely an economic downturn but a global health crisis that directly targeted the operational core of the sports industry—mass gatherings. The ban on in-person attendance at sports events, a primary revenue stream for many organisations, exposed the vulnerability of a business model heavily reliant on physical presence (Deloitte Sports Business Group, 2020). As a result, the pandemic catalysed widespread operational disruptions, forcing a reevaluation of the industry's financial strategies.[5] Furthermore, the pandemic underscored the importance of having robust fan databases and analytics capabilities to personalise experiences and maintain relationships even when live events are disrupted. As the industry recovers, there is an opportunity to reconstruct business models with a greater emphasis on digital offerings, data-driven operations, and flexible revenue streams that can better withstand future crises. Adapting quickly and embracing technological innovation may prove crucial for sports organisations aiming to thrive in the post-pandemic era. The pandemic also underscored the critical importance of liquidity and cash reserves in ensuring organisational survival during periods of crisis. As revenues plummeted due to cancelled events and reduced sponsorships, many sports organisations struggled to cover fixed costs, including player salaries, facility maintenance, and other operational expenses. The lack of liquidity became a significant issue, particularly for smaller clubs and organisations that operated with thin financial margins even in normal times (Nauright et al., 2020; Hammerschmidt et al., 2021; Ratten et al., 2021; González-Serrano et al., 2023). This sudden cash crunch led to a heightened focus on preserving liquidity (Bolton et al., 2011; Williamson, 2012; Adrian et al., 2017), with organisations increasingly prioritising cash reserves over new investments. Sports entities were sometimes compelled to seek emergency funding, restructure debts, or cut costs drastically to stay afloat.[6]

---

5 According to Deloitte Sports Business Group (2020), the crisis accelerated several pre-existing trends in the industry, particularly the shift towards digital fan engagement and the importance of data-driven strategies. As live events were suspended, sports franchises had to quickly pivot to alternative channels to maintain fan connections, leveraging social media, esports, and streaming platforms. This highlighted the value of a multichannel approach to fan engagement, less dependent on in-person attendance and traditional broadcasting.

6 The COVID-19 pandemic created severe financial challenges for sports organisations globally. In response, various bailout and relief efforts were initiated. FIFA announced a $1.5 billion relief fund for its 211 member associations, providing grants and loans to help offset lost revenues. Further, the English Premier League and English Football League agreed on a £250 million bailout package to support lower league clubs facing financial difficulties. There was debate over whether government bailouts were appropriate for professional sports leagues. Some argued wealthy leagues like the Premier League should support lower divisions, while others contended government intervention was necessary to preserve the wider football ecosystem. Proposed solutions included government bailouts, loans, salary caps, and selling equity stakes to private investors. However, there were concerns about taking on debt or giving up future revenues. Broadly, the crisis highlighted existing financial vulnerabilities in sports, with many clubs operating at a loss even before the pandemic.

Explicitly, the pandemic generated financial instability, forcing sports corporations to reassess their financial and operational approaches. Organisations understood they needed more resilient financial systems to withstand unanticipated shifts, including increasing cash flow management, liquidity, and revenue diversification to reduce dependence on single sources. The absence of live events may quickly erode broadcasting rights and sponsorships, which provide financial security. Thus, sports organisations today seek considerable cash reserves as a buffer against future unpredictability, understanding that financial shocks must be rapidly addressed for long-term existence. COVID-19 has shaken sporting organisations' business and financial methods, but after the crisis, the industry must rebuild stronger and faster, utilising data-driven decision-making, diverse income streams, rigorous liquidity management, and digital engagement will characterise the sports corporation. Companies learning from these lessons will be better prepared for health crises, economic downturns, and other catastrophes. The pandemic may compel the sports industry to embrace more sustainable and flexible business models to thrive in an unstable global climate.

6.2 Financial Impact on Major Leagues and Events

The financial impact of COVID-19 on major sports leagues and global events was profound, fundamentally altering the international sports industry. The suspension of games, tournaments, and events across major leagues like the European Champions League, Champions Cup Rugby, NBA, NFL, and MLB led to unprecedented revenue losses. These leagues, heavily reliant on multiple revenue streams such as media rights, ticket sales, and sponsorships, faced an immediate financial downturn as the pandemic forced the cancellation or postponement of entire seasons. The NBA, for instance, saw a drastic reduction in media revenue, constituting roughly half of the league's total income.[7] This shortfall was further exacerbated by the loss of ticket sales, a significant

7 The NBA's decision to move all games to Disney during the COVID-19 pandemic was a groundbreaking response to an unprecedented crisis. On March 11, 2020, the league suspended its 2019–2020 season after Utah Jazz player Rudy Gobert tested positive for COVID-19. As the pandemic continued to unfold, the NBA explored options to safely resume play, ultimately landing on the concept of a "bubble" environment. In early June 2020, the league announced its plan to restart the season at Walt Disney World Resort in Orlando, Florida. The choice of Disney World was strategic and influenced by several factors. The resort's ESPN Wide World of Sports Complex offered multiple courts and ample space for practices, while the expansive hotel capacity could accommodate teams, staff, and league personnel. Disney's experience in managing large-scale events and Florida's year-round outdoor climate were additional advantages. The "NBA Bubble" officially opened on July 7, 2020, encompassing three hotels for lodging, three arenas for games, practice courts, medical facilities, and leisure areas. Twenty-two of the 30 NBA teams were invited to participate in the bubble based on their standings when the season was suspended. This included the 16 teams in playoff position and six teams within six games of a playoff spot. The NBA implemented strict health and safety protocols, including daily COVID-19 testing, mask requirements outside of games and

source of revenue, especially for smaller-market teams that depend more heavily on gate receipts. The ripple effects extended to associated businesses, including broadcasters and advertisers, which were left scrambling to renegotiate contracts and deal with the financial fallout of empty arenas and reduced viewership.

During the COVID-19 pandemic, when fans were barred from attending matches in person, several English football clubs, particularly in the Premier League, introduced a controversial pay-per-view (PPV) model for games not selected for regular television broadcast. In October 2020, the Premier League announced that matches not already scheduled for TV coverage would be available on a PPV basis for £14.95 per game, accessible through BT Sport Box Office and Sky Sports Box Office platforms. This move was ostensibly to provide fans with access to all matches while generating revenue to offset the significant financial losses caused by empty stadiums. However, the initiative was met with widespread criticism and backlash from supporters, who viewed the pricing as excessive, especially given the economic hardships many were facing due to the pandemic. Fan groups organised boycotts, with many choosing to donate the PPV fee to local food banks instead of watching the matches. The negative reception was so strong that by November 2020, just a few weeks after its introduction, the Premier League abandoned the PPV scheme, reverting to making all matches available through existing broadcast partnerships at no additional cost to viewers. This episode highlighted the delicate balance clubs and leagues faced between financial necessities and maintaining goodwill with their fan base during an unprecedented crisis.

The COVID-19 pandemic profoundly impacted global sporting events, forcing unprecedented changes and cancellations across the industry. The Tokyo 2020 Olympics faced the most significant disruption, postponed for the first time in Olympic history to the summer of 2021. This delay disrupted athletes' preparations and inflicted severe

---

practices, restricted movement within the bubble, and a no-visitors policy until later stages of the playoffs. The schedule within the bubble was carefully structured. Teams arrived in early July for training, followed by eight "seeding games" per team from July 30 to August 14. A play-in tournament was held for the 8th seed in the Western Conference, and the playoffs began on August 17, concluding on October 11. Without fans in attendance, the NBA introduced innovative broadcast features, including virtual fan screens, enhanced audio with artificial crowd noise, and new camera angles to provide a more immersive viewing experience. While the bubble cost the NBA an estimated $180 million to operate, it allowed the league to fulfil most of its TV contracts and mitigate potential losses that could have exceeded $1 billion. The bubble was largely considered a success, with zero COVID-19 cases reported among players, coaches, or staff within the bubble. The season was completed, culminating with the Los Angeles Lakers winning the NBA championship, and it provided a model for other sports leagues to follow. However, the bubble experience was not without challenges for players, who faced extended separation from families and friends, potential mental health concerns due to isolation, and limited entertainment options within the confines of the bubble. Despite these difficulties, the NBA bubble represents a unique chapter in sports history, demonstrating the league's ability to adapt to extraordinary circumstances. It has since been studied as a model of COVID-19 containment and large-scale event management during a pandemic, solidifying its place as an innovative solution to an unprecedented global crisis in professional sports.

financial damage on Japan and the International Olympic Committee. The costs of maintaining venues, rescheduling logistics, and lost tourism revenue soared, creating a financial burden likely to persist for years. The uncertainty surrounding the event's execution amid ongoing health concerns added complexity and financial risk for sponsors, broadcasters, and local businesses dependent on global visitors. Similarly, other major tournaments faced significant challenges. UEFA rescheduled Euro 2020, originally planned as a pan-European event across 12 countries, to 2021, with some host cities withdrawing due to health concerns and logistical difficulties. The 2021 Copa America faced last-minute changes when Colombia and Argentina relinquished their co-hosting duties weeks before the tournament, citing rising COVID-19 cases and social unrest. The competition was hastily moved to Brazil despite that country's high infection rates (de Souza et al., 2020; Vale et al., 2021). These high-profile cases underscore the severe disruptions caused by the pandemic, forcing sporting bodies and host nations to make difficult decisions balancing public health concerns, economic implications, and the integrity of major sporting events. The broader economic impact extended beyond host nations, affecting global companies and international markets tied to these events, which faced reduced investment returns due to the diminished scale and altered perception of the competition.

These financial challenges were not isolated but reflected a broader trend across major international sporting events during the pandemic. Cancelling and changing the parameters associated with numerous competitions, from regional tournaments to world championships, resulted in cascading financial losses across the sports ecosystem. Organising committees faced contractual penalties, while sponsors and broadcasters had to contend with unmet contractual obligations and diminished returns on investment. The financial strain on these events also highlighted vulnerabilities in the business models of sports organisations, particularly their over-reliance on live events and in-person attendance for revenue generation. This period underscored the necessity for diversification and exploring alternative revenue streams, such as digital and virtual engagement, to mitigate future risks.

6.3 Employment and Economic Repercussions

The cancellation of sporting events due to the COVID-19 pandemic profoundly impacted low-wage workers essential to the operation of live sports and associated events. Ticket vendors, ushers, concession stand operators, security personnel, and maintenance staff suddenly found themselves unemployed as venues closed. For many, this meant losing their primary or sole source of income, exacerbating financial insecurities and leading to increased requests for unemployment benefits and food assistance. The loss of work also meant the loss of healthcare benefits for those relying on employer-provided insurance. Specifically, the pandemic exposed and intensified the precarious employment conditions prevalent in many sporting organisations, particularly at lower levels and in non-elite sports. These entities have long relied on short-term and zero-hour contracts to maintain flexibility and manage costs. As sports clubs faced severe revenue drops, they often downsized their workforce, leaving casual and part-time employees without income or the safety net of regular employment benefits or severance packages. Many workers in the sports sector, including coaches, support staff, and venue personnel, were not eligible for the same level of government support as full-time employees in other sectors. This disparity highlighted the vulnerability of workers in the sports industry and raised questions about the sustainability and ethics of such employment practices. The crisis led to calls for reform in labour laws and increased scrutiny of employment practices in the sports sector in some countries. It revealed not only the financial fragility of many sports organisations but also shed light on broader issues of worker protection and social security within the industry. This situation may potentially catalyse long-term changes in how sports entities approach workforce management and employee welfare, prompting a reevaluation of the industry's reliance on precarious employment arrangements.

The impact extended beyond just the professional level of sports. Grassroots sports clubs, which are often the lifeblood of community engagement and youth development, were also severely impacted. These clubs typically operate on narrow margins, relying on small-scale local sponsorships, fundraising events, membership dues, and community volunteers to sustain their activities. The pandemic's disruption of normal operations meant that these revenue streams dried up almost overnight. As a result, many grassroots clubs faced the harsh reality of potential closure. The European Parliament raised significant concerns about this issue, noting that the loss of these community institutions could have long-term consequences not only for sports but also for social cohesion and community well-being.[8] The financial strain on grassroots sports clubs was exacerbated by many of these organisations lacking the financial reserves necessary to weather prolonged periods without income. Unlike professional sports organisations that could turn to large-scale sponsorships or government relief programs, these smaller clubs were often left to fend for themselves, with limited access to external support. The closure of these clubs deprived communities of important social hubs and interrupted the development pathways for young athletes, potentially diminishing the future talent pool for professional sports.

---

8 The European Parliament's concerns about the potential loss of community sports institutions during the COVID-19 pandemic reflect a clear understanding of their critical role in society. These institutions serve as pillars of social cohesion, youth development, public health, and local economies. They provide platforms for volunteer engagement, cultural identity preservation, and informal education. Moreover, they contribute significantly to mental health support and community resilience. In recognition of these multifaceted roles, the European Parliament, in its resolution 2020/2646(RSP), emphasised the need for targeted support to the sports sector, acknowledging its "important social function" in promoting "common European values" European Parliament (2021). The Parliament's call for European recovery plans and specific budget instruments underscores the potential long-term consequences of losing these community institutions for sports and overall societal well-being and resilience European Commission (2020).

The economic repercussions of the pandemic on local economies were equally severe. In cities and towns where sports events are a major economic driver, the absence of games had a ripple effect on surrounding businesses (Buheji et al., 2020; Jordà et al., 2022; Corbet et al., 2020d, 2021b, 2022c; Corbet and Larkin, 2024; Conlon et al., 2024c; Kyriazis and Corbet, 2024). Hotels, restaurants, bars, and retail outlets that depend on the influx of fans during sports seasons faced sharp declines in revenue. In some cases, businesses that were already operating on thin margins were forced to close permanently, leading to further job losses and economic downturns in these areas. The multiplier effect of spending associated with sports events was abruptly halted, causing a noticeable contraction in local economic activity. For instance, in cities that host major sports teams, the loss of revenue from home games affected not just the sports franchises but also local vendors, transportation services, and even the tourism sector.[9] The impact was particularly severe in locations that host marquee events, such as championships or international tournaments, which typically bring in substantial visitor spending. With these events cancelled or postponed, entire local economies were left reeling, with some estimates suggesting that the economic impact could last for several years.

The loss of ticket sales, merchandise revenue, and sponsorships further compounded sports organisations' financial challenges. Most sports teams depend on ticket sales; without live events, they lose money. As fans cut spending due to economic uncertainties, merchandise sales also saw a steep decline as fans shifted their spending priorities in the face of economic uncertainty. Sponsorships, which are closely tied to visibility and brand association with live sports, were renegotiated or cancelled altogether, leading to further financial strain on sports organisations. This financial pressure forced many teams and organisations to make difficult decisions, including further layoffs, salary cuts, and reductions in operational budgets. In some cases, teams had to reconsider their long-term investment strategies, postponing or cancelling plans for new facilities, marketing campaigns, and player purchases. The broader sports ecosystem, which includes suppliers of sports equipment, manufacturers, and service providers like transportation and hospitality, also suffered as the demand for their products and services plummeted. The interconnectedness of the sports industry with various sectors of the economy meant that the financial challenges faced by sports teams had a wide-reaching impact, affecting jobs and businesses far beyond the stadiums and arenas.

---

9 The cancellation of sports events due to the COVID-19 pandemic had significant economic consequences for host cities. In Los Angeles, cancelling the 2020 NCAA Men's Basketball Tournament, which was expected to generate around $10 million in economic activity dealt a blow to the local economy. The loss of the NBA and NHL seasons also affected the city, with each home game for the Lakers, Clippers, and Kings generating an estimated to be worth over $1 million in economic activity for the surrounding area for each game. In Melbourne, Australia, the cancellation of the 2020 Australian Grand Prix, which typically attracts over 300,000 spectators and generates around $40 million in economic activity, had a significant impact, with the effects of further race cancellations felt globally. The city also suffered from the loss of spectators at the 2021 Australian Open tennis tournament.

6.4 Shift to Digital and Virtual Engagement

The COVID-19 epidemic drove the sports sector to adapt quickly in response to the unexpected cancellation of in-person events and the necessity to keep fan participation without the conventional live experiences. Sports organisations resorted to digital platforms when stadiums and arenas collapsed, using technological developments to create virtual experiences that might somewhat imitate the excitement and social elements of live sports. One common way for fans to interact with games together yet still be physically distant was through virtual watch parties, allowing supporters to view live games, communicate in real-time, and even interact with experts and analysts, fostering a new degree of involvement that cut across national borders. This creativity not only kept supporters in touch but also created new income sources via digital advertising and sponsorships, especially for these online gatherings.

Remote training and online contests emerged alongside the digital revolution, and they proved vital for sports' operational continuation under lockdowns. Previously, athletes depended on physical training facilities, so they adjusted to virtual coaching and fitness sessions enabled by video conferencing technologies and specialist apps. As sports companies built and pushed these platforms as part of their larger digital strategy, athletes could keep competitive and preserve their fitness levels thanks to these remote training alternatives. Online contests, especially in sports like rowing and cycling, where participants could compete from home using advanced simulation technologies, became rather common. Often broadcast live, these events drew significant sponsorship and viewership, proving the ability of digital-first sporting events to grab audiences' interest. Having expanded slowly before the epidemic, esports saw a notable surge in acceptance and integration into the mainstream sports ecosystem. Many sports organisations have turned to esports as a substitute for traditional sports leagues, which are on hold to keep fans involved. This was especially clear in the simulation of sports, including football, basketball, and motor racing, in which professional sportsmen participated in virtual contests shown live on TV and internet platforms. Apart from giving fans fresh entertainment, the flawless integration of esports into conventional sports structures gave sports teams insightful knowledge of digital fan involvement. As the lines separating conventional sports from esports blur and provide new money sources through digital sponsorships, television rights, and retail sales, these developments will probably shape future plans.

The epidemic also brought attention to how virtual reality (VR) and augmented reality (AR) might revolutionise sports viewing. Although VR is still in its early years, its usage in sports gives supporters an immersive experience that lets them "attend" games in virtual stadiums or even take part in training sessions alongside their preferred sportsmen. Live broadcasts have also been improved by AR, adding interactive components such as real-time statistics and player profiles that spectators may access on tablets or smartphones. These technologies not only improve the viewing experience but also provide sports teams with fresh chances to interact with supporters in creative ways, thereby strengthening fan loyalty and maybe increasing involvement in both virtual and real-world events. The sports sector is probably going to suffer long-term consequences from the fast digital revolution the epidemic brought about. Organisations are likely to create new business models that give digital and virtual interaction top priority alongside conventional in-person interactions as they keep discovering the possibilities of these technologies. Although the possible benefits—in terms of worldwide reach, fan involvement, and income—are great, this change will call for continuous technological investment as well as a readiness to try new kinds of fan connection. Therefore, including digital platforms and virtual experiences in the sports ecosystem marks not only a temporary adaptation to the difficulties of COVID-19 but also a basic change in how sports are presented and watched.

6.5 Long-Term Financial Implications

COVID-19 has significant long-term financial implications for the sports industry, with recovery taking time and occurring inconsistently across regions and sectors (Brada et al., 2021; Chang et al., 2022; Foroni et al., 2022; Corbet et al., 2022a,d; Hsu et al., 2023; Conlon et al., 2024d). The pandemic diminished the global sports business, and many analysts expect it to take years to recover financially. Many sports organisations have struggled financially due to the pandemic's disruption of traditional revenue streams like ticket sales, broadcasting rights, and merchandise, as well as economic pressures such as reduced consumer spending, health concerns, and the uncertainty of large-scale event returns. Lower ticket sales, broadcasting, and sponsorship revenue have driven sports organisations to renegotiate player contracts, typically resulting in lower compensation (Garcia-Garcia et al., 2020; Weston, 2020). The sponsorship industry, crucial for sporting institutions' financial stability, has seen a major decline, with an estimated 40 % revenue decrease. This drop in sponsorship money has affected the entire sports ecosystem, from top-tier professional leagues to grassroots sports, exacerbating financial issues and jeopardising many smaller teams and organisations.

Due to government support and COVID-19's impact on various countries, sports organisations' financial recovery has been disparate. Major government aid measures, including pay subsidies, tax relief, and direct financial support, have assisted sports organisations in surviving the epidemic in certain regions. Table 6.1 briefly describes these supports. Teams in select nations have maintained operational stability and retained talent owing to these support strategies, allowing them to recover more quickly after the pandemic. In contrast, sports organisations in nations with weaker government funding have struggled to manage the financial impact and retain key players. This differential in government responses has created an international imbalance in the competitive environment, with some teams and leagues emerging from the pandemic in a stronger financial position than others, potentially creating long-term competitive advantages that could reshape the global sports industry. Globally, different government responses

Table 6.1: Government support measures implemented to support sports during the COVID-19 pandemic.

Country	Type of support	Description	Beneficiaries	Date
US	Paycheck Protection Program (PPP)	Low-interest loans provided to small businesses to cover payroll, rent, and utilities. Forgiveness was available if the criteria were met. Some larger sports franchises accessed funds through affiliated small businesses	Small sports teams, minor leagues, and some larger franchises	Mar-20
US	CARES Act (Coronavirus Aid, Relief, and Economic Security Act)	Broad economic relief package providing financial assistance, including tax incentives, to support organisations, including those in the sports industry	Larger sports leagues, stadium operators, and associated businesses	Mar-20
UK	Coronavirus Job Retention Scheme	Government funded 80 % of employee wages for furloughed workers, which included employees of sports clubs and leagues	Sports clubs across various levels, including professional football	Mar-20
UK	Winter Survival Package	A £300 million package including grants and loans to support sports significantly impacted by COVID-19, especially grassroots and lower-league sports	Rugby Football Union, English Football League (lower divisions), horse racing, and other sports	Nov-20
UK	Summer Sport Recovery Package	A £600 million package aimed at ensuring the continuation of sports, particularly for the summer season, including grants and loans for clubs and organisations	Cricket, tennis, rugby league, and other summer sports	Mar-21
Australia	JobKeeper Payment	Wage subsidy provided to employers, including sports organisations, to retain employees during the pandemic	Professional and community sports organisations	Mar-20
Australia	Sport and Recreation Recovery Package	A $50 million package to support recovery of community sports and elite sporting organisations through direct funding and infrastructure investments	National sporting organisations, community sports clubs	Jun-20
Germany	Stabilisation Fund for Professional Sports	€200 million fund to compensate professional sports clubs for losses due to events held without spectators, covering operational costs and financial gaps	Football (soccer), handball, basketball, and ice hockey clubs	Jul-20
Germany	Economic Stabilisation Fund (Wirtschaftsstabilisierungs-fonds)	Broader economic package offering financial support and equity injections to industries, including sports, aimed at preventing insolvency and stabilising large clubs	Larger professional sports clubs, sports venues	Mar-20

Table 6.1 (continued)

Country	Type of support	Description	Beneficiaries	Date
Germany	Bridge Aid III (Überbrückungshilfe III)	Extended support providing additional financial aid to businesses, including sports, for ongoing operational costs during the prolonged impact of the pandemic	Sports clubs, smaller sports associations	Nov-20
Japan	Emergency Subsidy for Sports Organisations	Subsidies provided to maintain operations and athlete development, with a focus on minimising the impact on upcoming international competitions	National and regional sports associations, professional leagues	Apr-20
Japan	COVID-19 Relief Grants for National Sporting Events	Financial grants provided to ensure the continuation of national sporting events, particularly those tied to the Tokyo Olympics and Paralympics	Event organisers, national sports federations	Aug-20
Canada	Emergency Support Fund for Cultural, Heritage, and Sport Organisations	CA$72 million allocated to ensure continuity of sporting events, including assistance for national sports organisations and event organisers	National sports organisations, event organisers, sports leagues	May-20
Canada	Sport Relief Fund	Additional CA$14 million to help sport organisations cover operational costs and ensure ongoing programming during the pandemic	Grassroots and community sports organisations	Oct-20
New Zealand	Sport Recovery Package	NZ$265 million fund to sustain the sporting sector, including professional and community sports, with a focus on long-term sustainability	Regional sports organisations, professional leagues, grassroots sports	May-20
New Zealand	COVID-19 Resilience Fund	Additional NZ$25 million aimed at helping local and community sports organisations recover from the immediate impact of the pandemic	Community sports clubs and local sports organisations	Aug-20
France	Compensation for Ticket Revenue Losses	Government allocated €107 million to compensate professional sports clubs for revenue losses from ticket sales due to spectator restrictions	Professional sports clubs, particularly in football (soccer) and rugby	Sep-20
France	Emergency Solidarity Fund for Sports Clubs	A €20 million fund aimed at providing direct financial assistance to amateur and grassroots sports clubs impacted by the pandemic	Amateur and grassroots sports clubs	May-20

Table 6.1 (continued)

Country	Type of support	Description	Beneficiaries	Date
France	Additional Support for Professional Sports	Additional €100 million allocated to professional sports clubs facing severe financial difficulties due to the ongoing pandemic and related restrictions	Football (soccer), rugby, and other professional sports leagues	Dec-20

Note: Specifically, the data was collated from the Small Business Administration (SBA) and Department of the Treasury (United States); HM Treasury and the Department for Digital, Culture, Media, and Sport (DCMS) (United Kingdom); the Australian Taxation Office (ATO) and the Department of Health and Sport Australia; the Federal Ministry for Economic Affairs and Energy (BMWi) and the Federal Ministry of the Interior, Building and Community (BMI) (Germany); the Japan Sports Agency (JSA); the Department of Canadian Heritage and Sport Canada; Sport New Zealand; and the Ministry of Sports and Ministry of Economy and Finance (France).

to the COVID-19 epidemic has led to considerable differences in the sports industry recovery. This mismatch has allowed some teams and leagues to recover from the crisis with greater finances than others. Those who can begin operations early or with stronger government support may get better sponsorship deals, retain top people, and invest in infrastructure. This advantage could change the global sports power balance. Well-supported organisations from certain nations or areas may dominate international tournaments and garner more global fan interest and revenue over time. Global sports sector restructuring may result in long-term effects on funding, organisation, and consumption.

These differences could influence league competition in the long run, in addition to financial issues. Government-supported teams may invest more in talent acquisition and infrastructure, widening the gap between financially secure and unstable teams. There could exist further league polarisation as wealthy teams consolidate their dominance and financially disadvantaged teams struggle to compete. Leagues in regions with stronger financial recovery may attract more foreign talent and sponsorship deals, worsening financial and competitive gaps across regions. As the global sports sector rebuilds post-pandemic, these inequities may last for years. Financial differences have also affected sports infrastructure, with some localities maintaining or improving their facilities during the epidemic, while others have declined due to a lack of finances. In places with better government support, improvements in stadiums and training facilities have persisted, keeping these areas competitive internationally. Sports infrastructure has deteriorated in places with less investment, worsening the competitive imbalance. These variations in infrastructure investment may affect teams' performance and global competitiveness in these locations.

6.6 Social and Cultural Changes in Sports

COVID-19 also changed athletics' social and cultural background, highlighting and increasing gender equity, racial justice, and mental health issues. After leagues and competitions were suspended due to the pandemic, athletes used their platforms to advocate for social change and confront systemic disparities that had long been disregarded. Athletes became social influencers, often beyond their competitive duties, throughout this time. Their advocacy raised awareness of many critical social concerns and spread to grassroots levels, where sports groups and participants reassessed their roles in promoting social justice and inclusivity. Sports social involvement increased during the epidemic in reaction to societal changes. Athletes led global rallies against racial injustice, particularly after the murder of George Floyd in 2020. Their positions condemned systematic racism, promoted policy changes, and inspired activism. From kneeling during national anthems to putting social justice inscriptions on jerseys, solidarity acts in sports increased during this time. In addition to racial justice, the pandemic highlighted sports' gender inequality. The pandemic led to a disproportionate impact on women's sports, which have historically had less financing, media coverage, and institutional support (Bowes et al., 2021, 2022; Symons et al., 2022). The athletes and staff of several women's leagues were struggling economically and faced cancellation or a substantial decline in their respective ability to continue. This showed the huge inequalities in the importance of sports funding.

During the pandemic, athletes had extraordinary difficulty in managing routine and career disruptions, making mental health a major issue. Lockdowns, anxiety about the future of sport, and high-level training requirements caused substantial problems. Many suffered psychologically from the sudden end of tournaments and the inability to exercise or make contact with teammates. Younger and amateur athletes could not continue physical activity at the highest level and lost access to support networks. Since sports are known to improve mental and physical health, lockdowns have increased physical inactivity, thus presenting severe repercussions for both aspects of daily life.

6.7 Concluding Comments

The COVID-19 pandemic has altered global sports finance, introducing unprecedented challenges and new risks that must be diligently monitored; however, it has also provided some significant opportunities and revenue streams through new mechanisms where products, viewership of games and associated rights can be sold. The pandemic forced the sports industry to rapidly introduce online viewership solutions, revealing the potential of digital engagement and remote physical activity as sustainable components of the industry's future. As traditional sports events were cancelled or held with limited, and in some cases, no spectators at all, organisations had to explore new ways to maintain fan engagement and revenue streams to ensure the continued viability of respective organisations. This shift led to the growth of new phenomena such as virtual watch parties and the sharp increase in online streaming of events. Such innovation kept fans connected to their favourite sports and opened new revenue models likely to persist post-pandemic. For those that partake in such sports, remote training and online competitions initially adopted out of necessity, demonstrated their viability and have continued to grow to become permanent fixtures in the sports ecosystem. The increased adoption of home fitness equipment and digital fitness platforms has also created new avenues for growth as consumers continue to seek convenient and accessible ways to stay active, with such areas continuing to maintain their market presence even as traditional gyms and sports facilities reopen.

However, the transition to a digitally-driven sports environment was not without its challenges. The sports industry faced incredible difficulty navigating financial recovery after the substantial losses incurred during the pandemic. Many organisations, particularly those at the grassroots and semi-professional levels, struggled with reduced revenues and the elevated threat of insolvency. The sharp decline in sponsorship and advertising revenue and the ongoing uncertainty surrounding the ability to hold large-scale events forced sports organisations to reconsider their respective business models. Developing resilient and diversified financial strategies is now imperative for survival. This includes further exploring alternative revenue streams such as digital content, virtual fan experiences, and new forms of sponsorship that leverage online platforms and incorporate social media channels. The pandemic has also underscored the importance of addressing social issues within the sports industry. The crisis has exacerbated inequalities, particularly in access to sports and physical activity, which must be monitored with great care in the future.

7 How Did COVID-19 Impact Financial Markets in the Short and Medium Term?

The COVID-19 pandemic had widespread public health, social and economic implications. This chapter examines links between changes in COVID-19 metrics and indices representing diverse financial assets. Equity markets show the strongest relationship with COVID-19 metrics, followed by corporate and Treasury bonds. Medium-horizon links are particularly evident in the early stages of the pandemic, but wane as government support for the economy is increased and vaccine-related news is impounded. The empirical findings highlight many of the challenges associated with measuring COVID-19, and the importance of government support to financial markets and the economy more widely during the pandemic.

7.1 Introduction

The COVID-19 pandemic originated in Wuhan, China, in late 2019. The high transmissibility of the virus alongside strong global interconnectedness led to its rapid spread worldwide. The pandemic overwhelmed healthcare systems in many countries, caused millions of deaths, and led to unprecedented lockdowns and travel restrictions. Economically, it triggered a global recession, massive job losses, and disrupted supply chains. The pandemic also spurred rapid scientific collaboration, resulting in the development of vaccines at an unprecedented pace. In this chapter, the links between COVID-19 and financial markets, the latter acting as a proxy for the economy more widely, are examined.

The pandemic was deeply damaging to the global economy and to businesses. Although the economic and financial reaction was initially muted, from March 2020 it triggered widespread economic contractions, with many countries plunging into recession. A major catalyst for this was the various restrictions introduced by governments to curb the spread of COVID-19. These included lockdowns, travel bans, social distancing measures, and work and study from home policies. Companies faced unprecedented challenges, including forced closures, supply chain disruptions, and staff absence due to illness. Policymakers intervened with fiscal and monetary supports, helping to cushion the economy from the extremes of the pandemic. Market responses to these events were rapid and strong. From mid-February, the stock market, acting as a barometer for the wider economy, decreased swiftly in value, entering a bear market. The turnaround was equally swift, with markets rebounding from mid-March and rapidly recovering their earlier losses.

Quantifying the impact of COVID-19 on financial markets is beset by many challenges. Data on the extent and severity of the virus suffer from limited testing, inconsistent reporting, asymptomatic transmission and incorrect attribution, alongside lead-lag effects between the alternative metrics regularly discussed. In this chapter, we attempt

https://doi.org/10.1515/9783111707990-007

to circumvent these issues by using three different metrics, each of which captures a different facet of the spread of the virus. Positive cases represent the spread of the disease within the community, hospitalisations act as a benchmark for the severity of the disease, while data on deaths capture the potential for further restrictions to curb the mortality rate. Further, we use a methodology, the wavelet transformation, which allows us to simultaneously quantify the relationship between changes in COVID-19 and financial markets at each point in calendar time, for multiple horizons, and to determine any lead-lag relationships.

The time-scale relationship between four different financial markets and changes in COVID-19 is examined. Treasury bonds reveal a positive link with COVID-19 cases but a negative link with deaths, implying that markets placed different emphasis on the alternative ways of measuring COVID-19. Similar, albeit stronger, findings are observed for investment-grade corporate bonds, with an early band of long-horizon coherency, followed by smaller bands of short-horizon coherency. Links between commodities and COVID-19 are found to be more limited than for the other markets assessed, focused predominantly on the second wave from August to October 2020. Finally, links between COVID-19 cases and deaths with the stock market are shown to be strong and pervasive, especially in the early stages of the pandemic.

This study highlights the intricate relationships between policy interventions and financial markets. Early government restrictions had a strong impact on companies, resulting in rapid price changes. The introduction of monetary and fiscal supports helped to stymie these decreases, with the market becoming immune to further negative COVID-19-related news. Equally important is the observed differences in reaction from asset classes to the pandemic. This reinforces the fundamental importance of diversification as a risk management strategy, particularly during periods of extreme market stress.

7.2 Previous Literature

The public health implications of the COVID-19 pandemic have been well documented, with reductions in life expectancy found across many countries (Aburto et al., 2022). The repercussions of the pandemic went well beyond public health, however, with implications for education, the environment, consumer behavior, work culture, digital infrastructure and the economy (Nicola et al., 2020). The widespread economic effects are clearly apparent through the stock market, which suffered a rapid and substantial decline (Gormsen and Koijen, 2023).

The extent of such dramatic stock market effects can be partially attributed to the severity of the pandemic, the ease of viral transmission and mortality rates (Baker et al., 2020). Compared to previous viral pandemics, however, the market effects were stronger, despite having much lower mortality than the Spanish Flu, which affected the labour supply sharply (Velde, 2022). Baker et al. (2020) attribute the vast economic effects of the COVID-19 pandemic compared to previous crises on two extant characteristics: international travel and the predominance of the service industries. Moreover, the extent of policy interventions during COVID-19 was greater than during previous pandemics, curtailing economic activity and resulting in vast stock market losses, which were rapidly recovered.

The speed of the drop in equity markets in February and March 2020 is unprecedented, but not equally felt by all companies and markets. In the US, some sectors earned positive returns, including food, healthcare and software companies, while equity markets in real estate, entertainment, energy, and hospitality experienced falls in value (Mazur et al., 2021). Both case numbers and deaths affected emerging market returns and volatility, while the timing of these metrics is found to be influential in developed economies (Harjoto et al., 2021). Evidence from equity derivatives markets points to the late adjustment of market prices to the crisis, with the full impact only evident by March 16, 2020 (Jackwerth, 2020). Similarly, volatility futures prices responded sluggishly to the pandemic up to early March 2020, even though evidence for the vulnerability of society to the pandemic was widespread (Cheng, 2020).

The effects of COVID-19 were not only felt by equity markets. A range of commodity markets, especially crude oil, were impacted by a fall in demand, with the price of West Texas crude oil turning negative for a short period in April 2020 (Corbet et al., 2021a,b, 2020b). As a biproduct of the sharp decrease in price, the ability of commodities, with the exception of aluminium and gold, to act as a hedge or diversifier was limited during the pandemic (Enilov et al., 2023). Announcements surrounding successful vaccine trials and approvals, in addition to boosting equity markets, also had a positive pricing impact on commodity markets (Kucher et al., 2023). Fixed-income markets were also negatively impacted by the pandemic. Treasury bond markets, normally a safe haven for investors during crisis, experienced yield hikes and illiquidity, leading the Federal Reserve to purchase USD 1 trillion of Treasuries (He et al., 2022). Similarly, corporate bond liquidity was adversely impacted in the early stages of the pandemic, with Federal Reserve interventions required to help stabilise the market (O'Hara and Zhou, 2021; Kargar et al., 2021; Nozawa and Qiu, 2021). Notably, these events occurred within a short time frame, highlighting the importance of examining short- and medium-term links between COVID-19 and financial markets.

The application of the wavelet transform to understand relationships within financial markets, and with economic fundamentals more generally, is widespread (Gençay et al., 2001). Wavelets have, inter alia, been used to determine the horizon dependence of systematic risk (Gençay et al., 2003), to discern short- from longer-term high-frequency market volatility (Hasbrouck, 2018), to estimate the optimal scale-dependent financial hedge ratios (Conlon and Cotter, 2012; In and Kim, 2006), to measure horizon dependent asset correlations (Conlon et al., 2008) and to understand the links between financial and economic variables such as inflation (Conlon et al., 2021; Kim and In, 2005). The continuous wavelet transformation has particular benefits, allowing researchers to assess the horizon-dependent links between time series at every point in calendar time. The CWT has been applied to determine links between international equity markets (Rua and Nunes, 2009), to evaluate safe haven properties of financial assets (Bredin et al., 2015), energy commodity comovement (Vacha and Barunik, 2012) and credit interdependency (Choi, 2022). In this work, we apply the wavelet transform to examine short- and medium-term relationships between financial markets and changes in COVID-19 metrics surrounding the pandemic.

7.3 Data and Methodology

7.3.1 Data

This chapter relies on daily US market and COVID-19 data to decompose their short- and medium-term interactions. Daily data are selected to facilitate inference on the reactions of financial markets to the sharp increases in cases, hospitalisations and deaths, especially in the early stages of the pandemic. The wavelet transformation, described in the section to follow, allows us to disentangle the importance of short-run spikes and seasonalities, and common medium-term trends. To ensure data alignment, weekend changes in COVID-19 metrics are calculated from Friday through Monday.

The COVID-19 data used in this chapter are collected for the US from the COVID Tracking Project at The Atlantic.[10] The data is compiled from the state-level websites of public health authorities. It is selected due to an earlier start date relative to other sources, a vital characteristic in assessing links with financial markets due to their forward-looking nature. Specifically, we examine data on changes in COVID-19 positive cases, hospitalisations and deaths.

The first recorded US case of COVID-19 in the data is on January 19, 2020 and a total of 18 cases are recorded up to February 29, 2020. The first recorded death occurred on February 26, 2020. Hospitalisation data is somewhat lagging, with the first documented hospitalisations on March 3, 2020. The data is discontinued on March 7, 2021, due to an improvement in the quality of aggregated data reported by government sources. The period considered, however, captured the most market-relevant period of the pandemic, allowing us to gain an understanding of the links between COVID-19 measures and changes in financial returns.

Market data are collected from EIKON, a division of LSEG Data and Analytics. Daily returns data from March 2, 2020 to March 5, 2021 are obtained for four markets as follows: US Treasury bonds are represented by the S&P US Treasury bond index, corporate bonds are illustrated using the S&P US Investment Grade bond index, commodities are represented by the capitalisation-weighted Goldman Sachs Commodity Index (GSCI) and the stock market are depicted by the S&P 500 index, representing the capitalisation-weighted returns of 500 of the largest stocks listed in the US.

10 www.covidtracking.com

7.3.2 Methodology

This chapter uses the continuous wavelet transformation (CWT) to infer the extend to which the COVID-19 pandemic affected financial markets. The CWT provides a number of characteristics which are critical to our analysis. The localised nature of the CWT allows us to establish the specific points in calendar time where changes in COVID-19 metrics lead to market reactions. Furthermore, the CWT coherency described below allows us to determine whether any relationships are short- or long-term. Finally, the CWT can identify the direction of the relationship, providing insight as to whether financial markets lead or lag COVID information. The CWT framework employed is based on Torrence and Compo (1998), and a detailed description is available in Conlon et al. (2021).[11]

The cross-wavelet power spectrum is a measure that quantifies the shared variance between two time series as a function of both scale and time. This metric is derived from the product of the wavelet coefficients of the respective time series, expressed mathematically as: $W_{\epsilon,\tau}(r,s) = W_{\epsilon,\tau}(r) \cdot W^{*}_{\epsilon,\tau}(s)$ where $W_{\epsilon,\tau}(r)$ and $W_{\epsilon,\tau}(s)$ represent the wavelet coefficients of time series r and s, respectively, at scale ϵ and time τ, and $*$ denotes the complex conjugate operation. It is noteworthy that the cross-wavelet spectrum, analogous to the estimation of covariance between time series, is influenced by the inherent variance of the individual time series under consideration. To address this dependency, the wavelet squared coherency is employed. This measure is obtained by normalizing the smoothed cross-wavelet power spectrum with respect to the smoothed wavelet power spectra of the constituent time series. The wavelet squared coherency is formally defined as:

$$R^2_{\epsilon,\tau}(r,s) = \frac{|S(\epsilon^{-1}W_{\epsilon,\tau}(r,s))|^2}{S(\epsilon^{-1}|W_{\epsilon,\tau}(r)|^2) \cdot S(\epsilon^{-1}|W_{\epsilon,\tau}(s)|^2)}, \tag{7.1}$$

where S denotes a smoothing operator in both time and scale. This formulation of wavelet squared coherency provides a normalised measure of the correlation between two time series in the time-frequency domain, facilitating the identification and analysis of shared periodicities and their temporal evolution.

Squared coherency, $0 \leq \rho^2_{\epsilon,\tau} \leq 1$, implies no comovement when $\rho^2_{\epsilon,\tau} = 0$ and perfect comovement when $\rho^2_{\epsilon,\tau} = 1$. Regions of statistically significant squared coherency are determined using Monte-Carlo methods (Aguiar-Conraria and Soares, 2014). The continuous wavelet transformation can also be used to isolate the direction of the relationship between time series and to uncover any lead-lag effects. The wavelet multi-scale phase between two time series $f(t)$ and $g(t)$ is given by:

---

11 Two forms of wavelet transformation are discussed in the literature, the continuous wavelet transformation, described here, and the discrete wavelet transformation, where the number of retained coefficients reduces going from short to longer horizons (Conlon et al., 2009a,b). Conlon et al. (2018a) provide a theoretical basis and simulation analysis to understand why long-horizon correlations differ from their short-horizon counterparts.

$$\theta_{\epsilon,\tau}(f,g) = \tan^{-1}\left(\frac{\mathfrak{I}\{Q(\epsilon^{-1}W_{\epsilon,\tau}(f,g))\}}{\mathfrak{R}\{Q(\epsilon^{-1}W_{\epsilon,\tau}(f,g))\}}\right), \tag{7.2}$$

where Q is the smoothing parameter. At the same time, $\mathfrak{R}$ and $\mathfrak{I}$ correspond to the real and imaginary components of the wavelet coefficients. Wavelet coherency plots utilise phase arrows to visualise both the direction and timing of relationships between time series. Arrows pointing east (west) indicate in-phase (out-of-phase) movements, while north (south) arrows signify that the second time series leads (lags) the first. A northeast (southeast) oriented arrow implies an in-phase relationship where the second time series leads (lags) the first. Conversely, northwest (southwest) arrows represent out-of-phase relationships with the second time series leading (lagging) the first. For a detailed interpretation, refer to Conlon et al. (2018b).

7.4 Results

The empirical findings, detailing the short- and medium-term relationships between COVID-19 and financial markets, are now provided. Short-term refers to horizons of between 1 and 8 days, while medium term refers to horizons of between 8 and 64 days, the latter corresponding to a 3-month duration. The coherency plots provided below have a simple interpretation. Regions bounded by a thick black line are significant at a 5 % level. Warmer colours (red) signify high coherence (a stronger relationship) while cold colours (blue) indicate no interdependence. As described in Section 7.3.2, the phase arrows can be used to understand the direction and any lead-lead effects.

7.4.1 Treasury Bonds

Wavelet coherency between the returns of US Treasury bonds and changes in positive cases, hospitalisations and deaths, respectively, are shown in Figure 7.1.

Assessing first the links between positive cases and Treasury bonds, we observe a number of bands of high coherence, corresponding to a strong relationship, interspersed with extensive cycles of limited coherence. The findings also provide evidence for a distinct change in behaviour over time. In the early stages of the pandemic, up to August 2020 there is a positive link between cases and returns, pointing to safe haven properties of treasury bonds. This is particularly evident at periods between 16 and 32 days up to May 2020, corresponding to the band of positive coherency. After August 2020, the relationship reverses with left-facing arrows indicating bands of strong negative coherency between Treasury bonds and cases. Substantial quantitative easing, involving purchases of Treasury bonds, may be responsible for this phase change.

Wavelet coherency between COVID-related hospitalisations and US Treasury bond returns are shown in the middle plot. The extended periods of low coherence are indicated by blue colours. Brief bands of high coherence are evident, with only one hav-

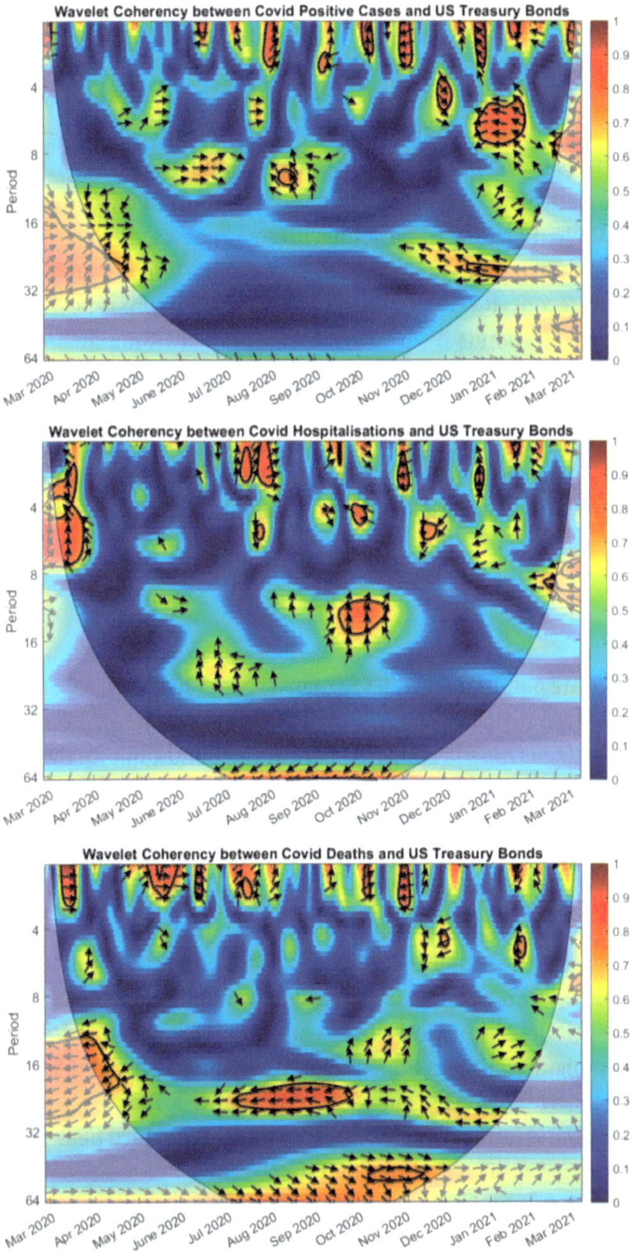

Figure 7.1: Wavelet coherency between COVID-19 and US Treasury Bonds, March 2020–March 2021.
Note: Wavelet coherency between the returns of US Treasury bonds and COVID-19 cases (top), hospitalisations (middle) and deaths (bottom) are shown. The horizontal axis shows calendar time, while the vertical axis shows the coherency at different periods (horizons). Warmer colours (red) depict high coherency, while cooler colours (blue) indicate low coherency. Phase arrows indicate the direction of the relationship and any lead-lag effects and their interpretation is described in Section 7.3.2.

ing period greater than 8 days. The majority of these bands of high coherency have north-facing arrows, indicating that the returns of US Treasury bonds led hospitalisations from COVID-19. In other words, markets were preempting these hospitalisations, based upon information on cases. Hospitalisations are a lagging indicator of the severity of the COVID-19 virus and this is borne out by these empirical findings.

Finally, the relationship between COVID-related deaths and US Treasury bonds are shown in the bottom plot. While there are some similarities with cases, not least in the extended band between 12 and 32 days up to April 2020, some important distinguishing characteristics emerge. The referenced extended band has a negative coherency, corresponding to decreases in Treasury bonds from rising death numbers. Similar findings are evident from July to October 2020, with a period from 20 to 26 days. This may indicate a fear from markets that increased mortality from COVID-19 might result in additional social distancing restrictions, further weakening the economy. Other significant bands of coherence are up to 3 days in period and take both positive and negative sign, highlighting the short-term uncertainty associated with the pandemic.

7.4.2 Corporate Bonds

Relationships between corporate bonds and COVID-19 metrics are considered separately to Treasury bonds, as the severe dislocation associated with the pandemic impacted company default profiles. The focus here is on investment grade bonds, but further disruption was felt among high-yielding bonds during the pandemic.

The top plot in Figure 7.2 highlights the relationship between returns of investment grade corporate bonds and changes in positive COVID-19 cases. The dependency between these is nuanced, with many bands of significant high coherency interspersed with regions of limited interrelationship. A strong medium-term relationship is evident up to August 2020 at horizons greater than 16 days, alongside a band starting in July 2020 and ending in October, between periods of 8 and 16 days. While the coherency is strong, the direction of the relationship is less clear, with both west, east and north-facing phase arrows. This ambiguity mirrors the uncertainty in the market at this time, with a swift short-term response followed by a long-term bull market. Further bands of high coherency are evident around January 2021, corresponding to the third peak in the spread of the virus alongside the initial introduction of the vaccine.

Bands of high coherency between hospitalisations and the returns of investment grade bonds are limited and mostly short-term. The one exception begins in September 2020 at medium-term horizons, corresponding to the conclusion of the second hospitalisation wave. Finally, in the bottom plot, the coherency between COVID-19-related deaths and investment-grade bonds is similar to that found for positive cases. A dominant band at horizons from 10 to 64 days continue up to July 2020, with west and southwest-facing phase arrows. This indicates a negative relationship between the asset class returns and COVID-related deaths, with the market lagging the COVID metric in the longer-term.

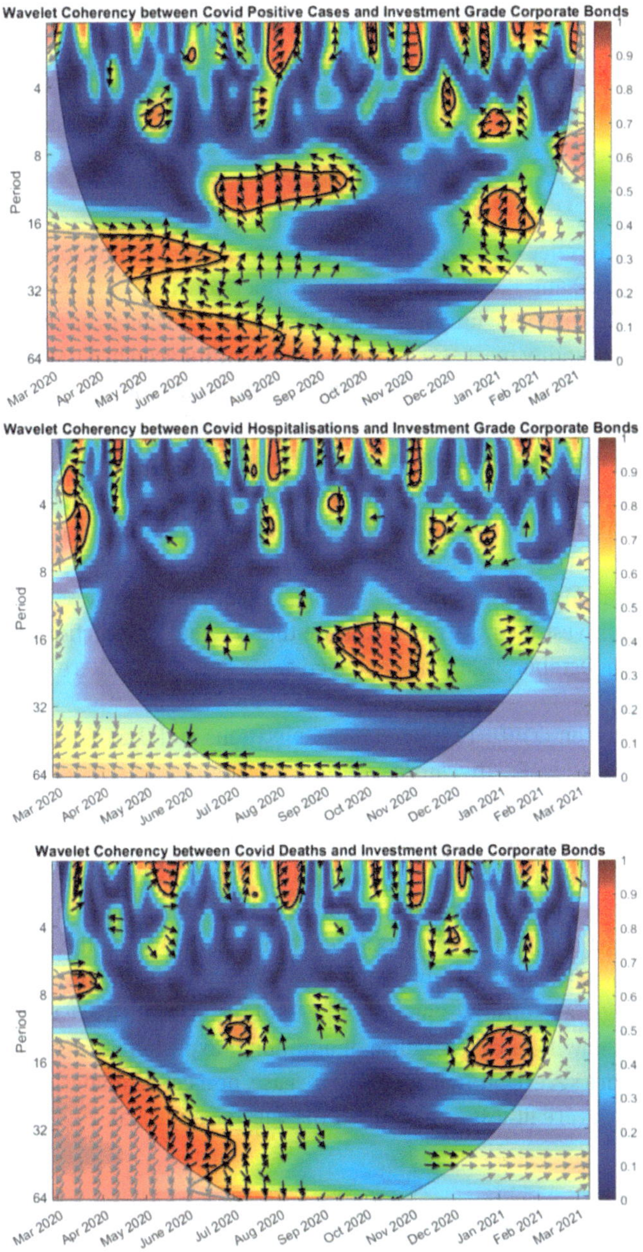

Figure 7.2: Wavelet coherency between COVID-19 and US IG Corporate Bonds, March 2020–March 2021.
Note: Wavelet coherency between the returns of US investment grade corporate bonds and COVID-19 cases (top), hospitalisations (middle) and deaths (bottom) are shown. The horizontal axis shows calendar time, while the vertical axis shows the coherency at different periods (horizons). Warmer colours (red) depict high coherency, while cooler colours (blue) indicate low coherency. Phase arrows indicate the direction of the relationship and any lead-lag effects and their interpretation is described in Section 7.3.2.

A number of smaller bands with positive coherency are also evident, highlighting positive returns in response to increased deaths. This may indicate an expectation of quantitative easing and further corporate supports from government.

7.4.3 Commodities

In Figure 7.3, the wavelet coherency between commodities, represented by the Goldman Sachs Commodity Index (GSCI) and the COVID-19 metrics under consideration are presented. The GSCI is a capitalisation weighted index, dominated by crude oil products. In this context, findings for commodity markets should be heavily influenced by COVID-19, with crude oil futures prices briefly turning negative during the pandemic.

Starting with the top plot, showing the coherency between positive cases and GSCI, the relationship is less striking than observed for bonds. During the early stages of the pandemic, only limited, short-horizon, bands of coherency are evident. This indicates that the negative pricing of crude oil, which occurred in April 2020, was not related to changes in COVID-19 cases. Only from August 2020, during the second wave of the pandemic, do we observe bands of high coherence, ranging from up to 3 days, 4 to 7 days and 10 to 16 days. Southwest-facing arrows indicate that the market reaction lags the changes in deaths. After October 2020, links between cases and the GSCI are again intermittent and brief.

Wavelet coherency between COVID-19-related hospitalisations and the GSCI is limited to brief, short-horizon bands. Furthermore, phase arrows tend to alternate from east- to west-facing, indicating that the market reaction changes dramatically over time. Finally, the bottom plot shows the relationship between COVID-19-related deaths and the GSCI. The timing of coherency is strongly linked to that found for positive cases. One exception is the long-horizon band with south-facing phase arrows evident up to April 2020, indicating that the GSCI market reaction lags changes in deaths. While the direction of the relationship alternates up to October 2020, after this point east-facing phase arrows dominate, indicating that a positive change in the GSCI results from increases in COVID-related deaths. This may be a consequence of additional expected government support in response to a more severe outlook from the disease, or a consequence of the prospects for reductions in severe illness as a result of the vaccine approval.

7.4.4 The Stock Market

Finally, we assess links between changes in COVID-19 and stock market returns. As highlighted in Figure 7.4, the relationship at long horizons, especially with cases and deaths, is pervasive and strong. In contrast to debt markets, the stock market not only reflects the potential for future growth but, as a residual claim holder, the possibility of outright loss. In this context, equity markets are expected to reflect the extent of the COVID-19 pandemic on the economy.

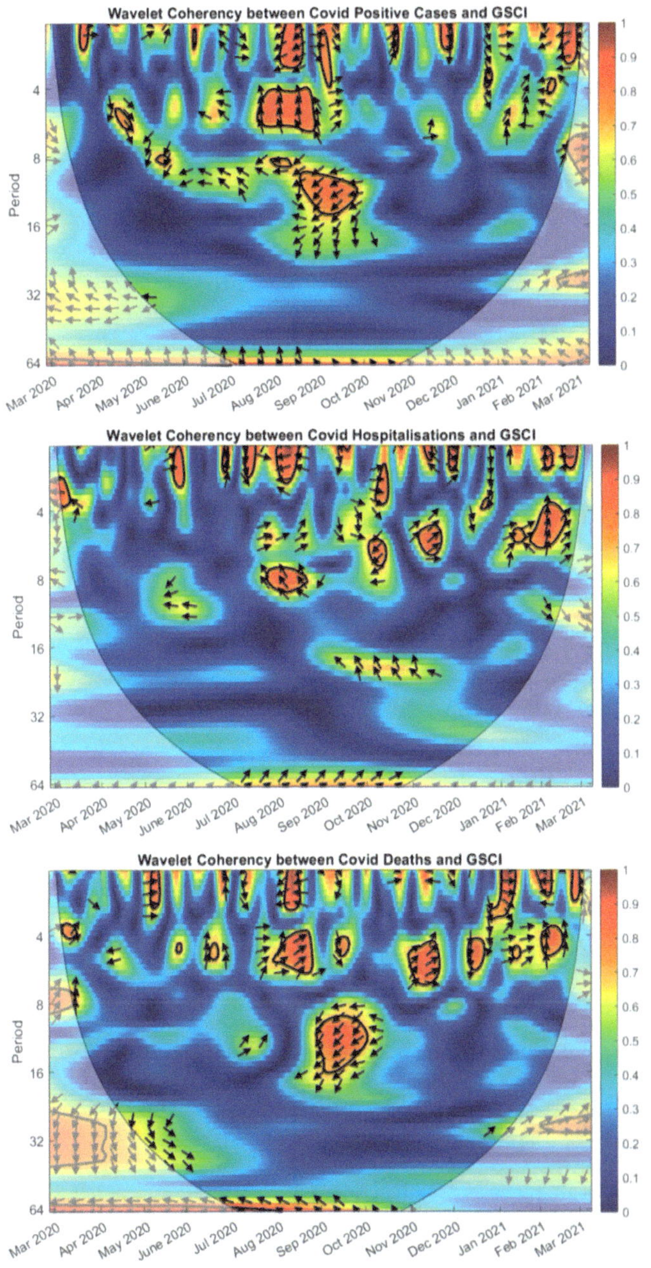

Figure 7.3: Wavelet coherency between COVID-19 and commodities, March 2020–March 2021.
Note: Wavelet coherency between the returns of the Goldman Sachs Commodity Index (GSCI) and COVID-19 cases (top), hospitalisations (middle) and deaths (bottom) are shown. The horizontal axis shows calendar time, while the vertical axis shows the coherency at different periods (horizons). Warmer colours (red) depict high coherency, while cooler colours (blue) indicate low coherency. Phase arrows indicate the direction of the relationship and any lead-lag effects and their interpretation is described in Section 7.3.2.

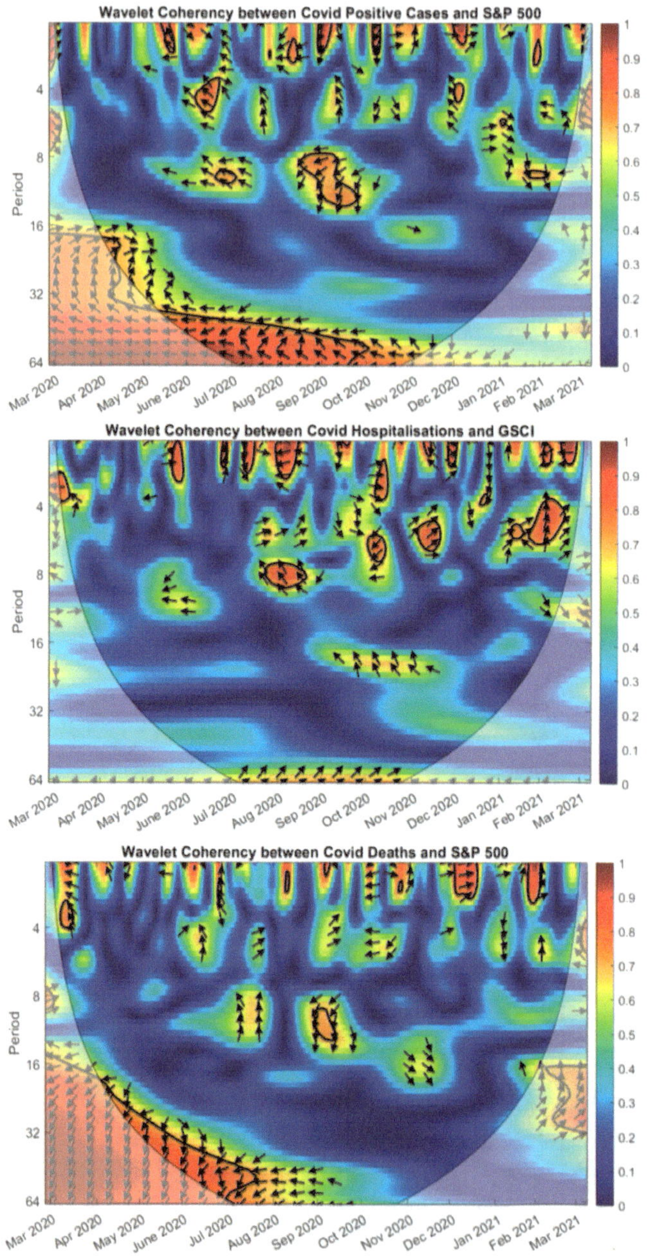

Figure 7.4: Wavelet coherency between COVID-19 and US Stocks, March 2020–March 2021.
Note: Wavelet coherency between the returns of the S&P 500 stock index and COVID-19 cases (top), hospitalisations (middle) and deaths (bottom) are shown. The horizontal axis shows calendar time, while the vertical axis shows the coherency at different periods (horizons). Warmer colours (red) depict high coherency, while cooler colours (blue) indicate low coherency. Phase arrows indicate the direction of the relationship and any lead-lag effects and their interpretation is described in Section 7.3.2.

In the top plot, there is an elongated band of high coherency ranging from 16 up to 64 days, ending in Oct 2020. The predominantly west-facing arrows indicate that a greater number of cases is associated with lower returns, in keeping with expectations. Similarly, there are a number of brief short- and medium-term bands of high coherency up to October 2020, demonstrating a negative relationship between cases and the stock market. After this point, the relationship becomes more variable, with bands of positive and negative coherency visible, pointing to market expectations around vaccine progress.

In keeping with earlier findings for bonds and commodities, the links between COVID-19 related hospitalisations are limited and shifting. This affirms the limited importance of hospitalisation data to financial markets. Wavelet coherency between COVID-19 deaths and S&P 500 returns is shown in the lower plot. The band of longer-run coherency evident for COVID-19 cases is also visible here, but with one notable exception. While the phase bands with cases were west-facing, the dominant alignment for changes in deaths is south-west facing. This indicates that market returns lag changes in deaths, suggesting that it is information on the severity of the disease that has the greatest influence on markets. The market is responding to the potential for further social distancing and economic restrictions to be introduced to prevent further mortality.

7.5 Concluding Comments

Economic information such as GDP, unemployment and inflation can take some months to collate and are prone to revisions, making them of limited use in assessing the state of the economy in real-time. Financial markets, however, are forward-looking, anticipating what the economic outlook will be, how this will affect companies, consumers and governments, and adjusting prices to reflect this. As such, they provide a valuable lens to assess the links between the pandemic and the economy.

This chapter uses the continuous wavelet transform to assess dynamic links between COVID-19 metrics and four financial markets: US Treasury bonds, US investment grade bonds, commodities and Stocks. The strongest links with financial markets are found for changes in COVID-19 cases and deaths. Occasional links are found with hospitalisations, but the direction of the relationships tends to alternate from positive to negative, suggesting that the information from hospitalisations has only short-term market relevance.

Some general conclusions can be drawn from the empirical findings. Bond and equity markets display strong relationships with COVID-19 cases and deaths at long horizons in the early stages of the pandemic. The direction of the relationship is not always consistent; however, with positive and negative links are indicated. This points to lead-lag relationships between the different COVID-19 metrics and financial markets. Deaths from COVID-19 tend to lag positive cases by a couple of weeks, helping to explain these differences. From summer 2020, the dependency between COVID-19 and financial markets begins to weaken, with only limited bands of high coherency evident. This coincides with the swift recovery in financial markets which can be attributed to fiscal and monetary stimulus programs, optimism about prospects for a vaccine, strong performance from sectors benefiting from the pandemic such as technology, and perhaps an initial overreaction to the virus.

Some important takeaways arise from the findings detailed. Throughout the asset classes examined, there is a strong overlap between the strength of the COVID-19 relationship and policy interventions to support the market. This highlights the fragility of financial markets to significant shocks and the key role that central banks and governments play in ensuring stability. A second important takeaway is the acceleration in digital transformation which occurred rapidly during the crisis. In many regards, technology-related companies benefited from the pandemic, with a shift from the traditional in-person working model to remote working. While this has been curtailed to an extent in the post-pandemic period, the ability to scale technology rapidly will facilitate advancing technologies such as artificial intelligence. Finally, the variation in findings recorded for Treasuries, corporate bonds, commodities and stocks once again highlights the vital role that diversification plays in terms of limiting investment losses.

Further research might examine the response of international markets to the COVID-19 pandemic, especially in light of the evidence that Chinese domestic stocks present significant relevant information flows prior to international markets (Corbet et al., 2020d). The analysis could also be extended to other asset classes, such as cryptocurrency, where the market reacted very swiftly to the pandemic (Corbet et al., 2020c; Conlon et al., 2024g).

8 COVID-19 and Equity Markets

Global equity markets were severely impacted by the onset of the COVID-19 pandemic, losing almost one-third of their value over a short period. This chapter examines the potential for equity diversification across regions, sectors and factors using global data. Empirical findings indicate very limited opportunities for diversification, pointing to challenges in avoiding large losses. The chapter also examines the sudden and rapid recovery in global equity markets which occurred from mid-March 2020. In contrast to the downturn, the recovery was heterogeneous across regions, sectors and factors. As equity markets become increasingly connected, the downturn instigated by the COVID-19 pandemic highlights the challenges in achieving meaningful downside risk diversification.

8.1 Introduction

The acute respiratory syndrome coronavirus 2 (SARS-CoV-2), commonly referred to as COVID-19, was first identified in Wuhan, China, where public health restrictions were introduced on December 23, 2020. The World Health Organisation (WHO) declared COVID-19 a global public health emergency on January 30, 2020. Given the speed at which the virus spread worldwide and its high mortality rate, COVID-19 was declared a pandemic on March 11, 2020. By this point, considerable economic harm had already been inflicted by the spread of the virus, with public health restrictions and business shutdowns having a particular impact.

Equity markets were initially slow to respond to the growing crisis. Between December 31, 2019 and February 12, 2020, the MSCI World index, a broad market index representative of global stocks, rose by over 3 percent, despite strong evidence of worldwide contagion. Over the following 29 trading days, the index fell by 34 percent, among the swiftest and most extreme stock market declines on record. The severe impact felt by equity investors gives rise to many research questions. Would diversification help in avoiding some of the downside risk? Were investors able to reclaim their losses from the pandemic? Do any segments of the equity market outperform the broad index during this period?

Diversification is a central principle in finance, both across and within asset classes. An equity investor can obtain diversification by spreading their capital across a range of companies within the same economy. They can also expand the diversification benefits by investing in different sectors. Investments in international markets can likewise provide diversification gains, given their distinct economic fundamentals. A further diversification tool being popularised by the asset management sector is factor investing, allowing investors to allocate to a range of apparently unrelated alternative company characteristics. By taking advantage of these different diversification opportunities, an investor might be able to protect their investments against substantial losses better than if they were allocated to a single region or sector.

https://doi.org/10.1515/9783111707990-008

This chapter assesses the performance and risk characteristics of global equity markets during the COVID-19-related bear market and follows their subsequent recovery. Using MSCI data on global equity markets, aggregate, regional, sectoral and factor indices are examined and contrasted. Losses during the initial pandemic-led bear market are calculated, seeking to quantify the extent to which diversification helped in reducing losses. The performance achieved during the swift upturn is examined to get an idea of the winners and losers from the pandemic. This provides guidance to investors as to the capacity for diversification in increasingly interconnected global markets.

Our empirical findings corroborate the magnitude of the downturn and indicate that no sector, region or factor was spared. Taking global equity sectors as an example, the best performer during the brief bear market was consumer staples, which lost 24 percent. For context, the World Market Index lost 34.2 percent. The only index found not to lose more than 20 percent during this period was Chinese A Shares, perhaps a consequence of swift and emphatic restrictions. In the period from March 23, 2020, when the market reached its nadir, a widespread and rapid recovery occurred. This was felt most vibrantly among the Information Technology, Materials and Industrials sectors, alongside Latin American, North American and Emerging Markets. Evidence for benefits from diversification during the downturn is limited, and challenges in avoiding laggard stocks in the upturn abound.

Our assessment of the implications of the COVID-19 pandemic on global equity markets is timely and provides important insights for risk management. Increasing global corporate connectedness has resulted in few respite options for equity investors during downturns. Although the benefits of diversification may still be present during more normal times, large systematic losses during a crisis may increase pressures on policymakers to continue to invoke monetary and fiscal tools to support the economy. Despite substantial support through two major crises, equity markets are no closer to weaning themselves off the 'Greenspan Put' (Miller et al., 2002).

8.2 Previous Literature

The literature focuses heavily on bear markets, typically defined as a stock market decrease of 20 % or more (Pagan and Sossounov, 2003). Gonzalez et al. (2005) document 65 bear market periods between January 1800 and September 2000, with only 15 of these occurring after 1950. Much of the attention given to bear markets can be attributed to loss aversion, the notion that investors feel losses more than the equivalent gain (Kahneman and Tversky, 1979). This has led to a detailed literature focusing on the notion of downside risk, referring to the potential for large losses, often estimated using measures such as value at risk (VaR) (Kuester et al., 2006; Duffie and Pan, 1997).[12] To reduce

12 Downside risk can also be estimated using conditional value-at-risk and lower partial moments, such as semi-variance (Conlon and Cotter, 2013). A range of parametric and non-parametric approaches can be used to estimate the extent of tail losses (Conlon et al., 2024g; Bredin et al., 2017).

risk, investors often turn to international diversification (Moerman, 2008), but the benefits of the former have been shown to be negated in the long run (Conlon et al., 2018a) especially for emerging and frontier markets (Jain et al., 2024). Moreover, when considered from a downside risk perspective, international diversification may not provide the benefits frequently touted (You and Daigler, 2010).

The range of risk factors to be considered in creating an internationally diversified portfolio includes currency, industry and country effects (Eiling et al., 2012). Industry investment may provide greater protection from losses, relative to country-level diversification, during periods of high volatility (Marcelo et al., 2013). These gains, however, may be limited by high sectoral correlations during bear markets (Meric et al., 2008). Following an optimisation approach, industry-based allocation outperforms relative to country-based optimisation (Bessler et al., 2021). The gains from sectoral diversification can be realised using an optimisation approach employing stochastic dominance constraints, even after transaction costs (Conlon et al., 2023c).

Building on the early three-factor model of Fama and French (1992), over three hundred different characteristic factors have been identified in the literature (Chen and Zimmermann, 2021). Often indicated as proxies for macroeconomic risks (Adcock et al., 2022; Aretz et al., 2010), factor investing has become mainstream (Dichtl et al., 2019; Blitz and Vidojevic, 2019). Crash risk has been identified in factors (Chabi-Yo et al., 2022; Daniel and Moskowitz, 2016), perhaps limiting their ability to provide diversification benefits during periods of extreme correlation (Christoffersen and Langlois, 2013). Equity indices purporting to capture factor performance tends to rely on long-only exposures, in line with suggestions that most of the added value is extracted from the long legs of factor portfolios (Blitz et al., 2020).

The COVID-19 pandemic affected companies through both the demand and supply channels, with demand impacts leading to a collapse in corporate investment (Hassan et al., 2023). Companies with greater financial flexibility (Fahlenbrach et al., 2021), higher environmental and social ratings (Goodell et al., 2024; Albuquerque et al., 2020), lower exposure to COVID-19 through supply chain and customer location channels (Ding et al., 2021), and firms with a strong corporate culture (Li et al., 2021b), have relative outperformance compared to their peers. These characteristics notwithstanding, the aggregate performance of the stock market over a brief period in February and March 2020, was unprecedented, losing about 34 % (Gormsen and Koijen, 2023). These losses have been attributed to government restrictions on commercial activities and social distancing (Baker et al., 2020). The role of the Federal Reserve also cannot be understated, announcing a willingness to provide trillions of dollars in support (Cox et al., 2020). The importance of sentiment in driving market movements is highlighted by the limited ex-post requirement for this promised infusion.

The effects of the pandemic were not limited to the US markets, with the United Kingdom, China, the US and Germany are the sources of sentiment shocks to other global financial markets (Huynh et al., 2021). Investors seeking to hide from the crisis through diversification were impeded by instant financial contagion to global markets (Samitas et al., 2022). This contagion spread across markets, making it difficult for investors to find any safe haven from the market turmoil (Bei et al., 2024; Conlon et al., 2024g). Much of this negative global impact has been attributed to national lockdown restrictions introduced, to one extent or another, in most countries (Scherf et al., 2022). The Chinese market was particularly impacted, with crash risk reacting swiftly to confirmed cases (Liu et al., 2021a; Corbet et al., 2021).

8.3 Data

8.3.1 Data

Morgan Stanley Capital International (MSCI) World Data for this study are obtained from Eikon, a division of LSEG Data and Analytics. Daily price data from December 31, 2019 through December 31, 2021 are extracted and returns calculated. In the period surrounding the outbreak of the COVID-19 pandemic, the MSCI World index peaked on February 12, 2020 and bottomed out on March 23, 2020. This period, the subsequent period from March 23, 2020 until December 31, 2020, along with the full three-year period, are examined. World data are examined to assess the global impact of the pandemic, alongside three sets of subindices. All data are in US dollar terms to ensure that findings are not impacted by currency fluctuations.

Regional data allows for a breakdown of the effects of the COVID-19 pandemic by geography. Given differences in timing and response to the pandemic, we might expect that market returns, and associated diversification benefits, would differ between regions. Specifically, MSCI World data for the G7 group of advanced economies, emerging markets, Asia, Europe, Latin America, North America and China (A shares) are examined.

The COVID-19 pandemic impacted global industries through increased uncertainty (Szczygielski et al., 2022). The extent to which this uncertainty varies across different sectors and the diversification opportunities available are critical to investors attempting to navigate crises. In this chapter, return data for 11 different MSCI World sectors are examined, namely Communication Services, Consumer Discretionary, Consumer Staples, Energy, Industrials, Information Technology, Materials, Real Estate and Health Care.

A further avenue available to investors seeking diversification is to allocate across equity factor portfolios, seeking to take advantage of alternative fundamental drivers (Christoffersen and Langlois, 2013). MSCI World provide indices on a number of single-sorted factors, examined here: Momentum, Enhanced Value, Quality, Minimum Volatility, Growth Target, High Dividend. While not factor-based, the equally weighted portfolio is also commonly examined as an alternative to market capitalisation weighting and is assessed here.

8.4 Results

The performance and risk characteristics of equity markets throughout the COVID-19 pandemic is assessed. These are reported across a variety of different World equity tranches and for three intervals surrounding the crisis: the two-year period starting December 31, 2019 and ending December 31, 2021, a window starting February 12, 2020 and ending on March 23, 2020 containing the bear market after the onset of the pandemic and, finally, a window from March 23, 2020 until December 31, 2020 corresponding to the swift recovery from the bear market. Summary statistics on mean returns, standard deviation, skewness, kurtosis, and 1 percent and 5 percent value at risk (VaR) are reported. The latter represents an estimate of the expected losses at a particular threshold over a given period.[13]

8.4.1 Regional Performance

Rebased MSCI regional indices are presented in Figure 8.1. All indices were adversely affected by the onset of the COVID-19 pandemic, with substantial decreases observed from February 2020. The associated bear market across most regions was short-lived, with a rapid recovery observed in equity markets. For the majority of markets, the index had regained all losses by December 2020 and showed further upside into 2021.

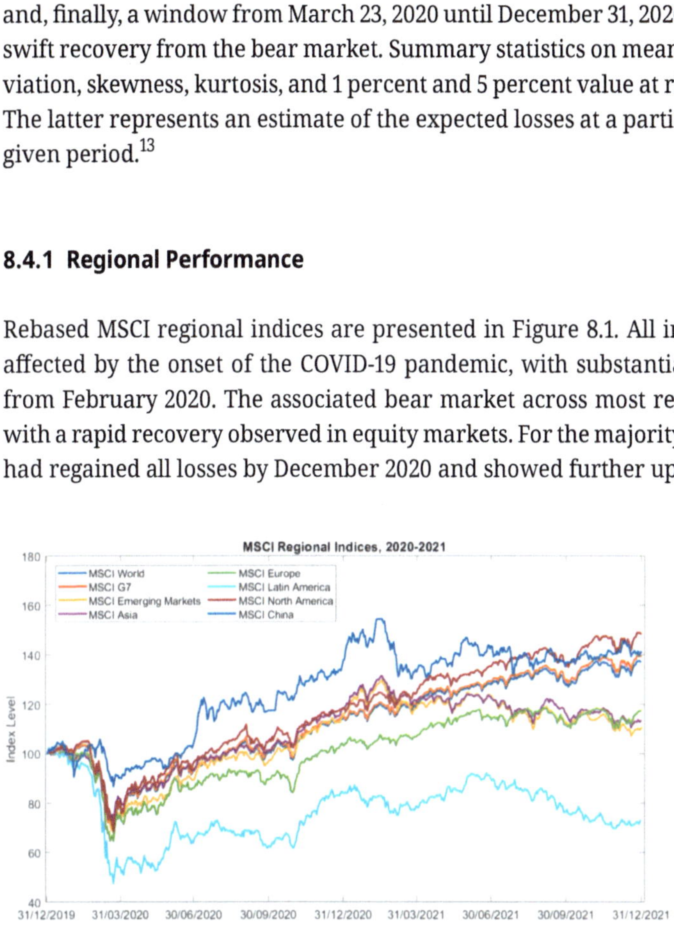

Figure 8.1: Regional Market Indices, December 2019–December 2021.
Note: MSCI regional indices are shown for the period from December 31, 2019 to December 31, 2021. All indices are rebased to a value of 100 on December 31, 2019.

13 VaR is estimated as $VaR_p(1-\alpha) = \mu_p - \sigma_p z(\alpha)$ where $z(\alpha)$ is the α quantile of the standardized distribution, and μ_p and σ_p are the mean and standard deviation of returns, respectively. In this study, historical simulation is used to estimate the α quantile, corresponding to a non-parametric estimate of risk (Conlon et al., 2023a).

The rebased indices also indicate that the response of regional markets to the pandemic was divergent. The Chinese market, perhaps surprisingly, given that the pandemic originated there and the extent of the restrictions imposed by government, is found to be the best performer in the months after the onset of the pandemic. This may reflect the success of the strong containment measures put in place not long after the original outbreak, limiting the wide-scale spread of the virus and allowing the economy to reopen and recover quicker than was the case in other regions. The worst-performing market during the crisis is Latin America. Although this market did recover rapidly, it failed to recoup the total losses experienced during the initial phases of the crisis.

These initial findings point towards limited benefits of diversification during the initial phase of the crisis. All markets suffered losses, some worse than others. Investors in Chinese A shares avoided the bear market felt in other regions, but still lost 13.3 percent at the market low. Recovery from the market low was swift across all markets. Taking the G7 as an example, it lost 32.1 percent by March 23, 2020, but recovered to above its pre-crisis level by August 6, 2020. By December 31, 2021 the World market was 37 percent higher than just before 2020 and had gained over 100 percent from its low point.

Further details are provided in Table 8.1, where summary statistics and risk characteristics for each index are provided. Over the full period, the MSCI World market has annualised returns of 19 percent per annum, remarkable in the context of ongoing economic and health challenges. Returns across the regions were more varied, with low, and even negative, average returns for Emerging Markets, Asia, Europe and Latin America. North America and China were the leading markets, both returning in excess of 20 percent per annum. Asia presents the lowest standard deviation and least skewed returns, pointing to limited risk. Downside risk is also quite dispersed across the market, with Latin America having the largest VaR.

Focusing on the short bear market period between February 12, 2020 and March 23, 2020, the Latin America region is, again, the worst performer, experiencing a 50.8 percent loss in just over 5 weeks. The World Market lost 34.2 percent over the same time. This is further captured by the risk statistics. Europe, for example, had a standard deviation of almost 50 percent, negative skewness of −2 and excess kurtosis of 5.684, pointing to wide distribution of returns with substantial potential for losses. This is borne out by the VaR estimates, with a 1 percent VaR of 11.3 percent, suggesting that in this period one could expect one day in one hundred with losses of this magnitude.

The market recovery was sufficient to recover losses across almost all markets. Over the 21-month period, the World market recovered 68 percent, while the standard deviation was only 11.9 percent. Skewness, pointing to the prospect for losses, was positive during this period, with similar findings documented across other markets. A substantial decrease in downside is also indicated, with 1 percent VaR of between 2.4 percent (Asia) and 5.8 percent (Latin America) during the recovery period.

Table 8.1: MSCI Regional Indices – Summary Statistics.

	World	G7	Emerging markets	Asia	Europe	Latin America	North America	China A shares
2020–2021								
Mean	0.190	0.201	0.069	0.077	0.107	−0.083	0.247	0.208
STD	0.216	0.225	0.196	0.167	0.225	0.355	0.255	0.217
Skewness	−1.141	−1.033	−0.831	−0.165	−1.539	−1.112	−0.771	−0.800
Kurtosis	15.830	15.343	5.993	3.449	17.818	10.624	14.722	5.231
1 % VaR	−0.047	−0.049	−0.043	−0.031	−0.041	−0.073	−0.054	−0.043
5 % VaR	−0.018	−0.019	−0.019	−0.018	−0.023	−0.032	−0.022	−0.022
Feb–Mar 2020								
Aggregate Return	−0.342	−0.343	−0.317	−0.270	−0.357	−0.508	−0.345	−0.128
STD	0.574	0.605	0.429	0.280	0.499	0.903	0.711	0.340
Skewness	−0.508	−0.392	−0.494	−0.274	−2.009	−0.354	−0.086	−0.232
Kurtosis	0.761	0.695	0.281	−0.004	5.684	1.188	0.774	−0.376
1 % VaR	−0.098	−0.101	−0.067	−0.048	−0.113	−0.146	−0.114	−0.046
5 % VaR	−0.086	−0.088	−0.064	−0.039	−0.061	−0.134	−0.090	−0.042
Mar–Dec 2020								
Aggregate Return	0.679	0.688	0.703	0.623	0.596	0.773	0.724	0.591
STD	0.119	0.122	0.111	0.105	0.127	0.152	0.128	0.117
Skewness	0.955	0.940	−0.088	0.561	0.499	0.212	0.843	−0.149
Kurtosis	7.989	7.965	3.914	3.616	4.307	1.502	7.184	3.076
1 % VaR	−0.031	−0.032	−0.027	−0.024	−0.038	−0.058	−0.036	−0.044
5 % VaR	−0.022	−0.022	−0.018	−0.017	−0.026	−0.031	−0.024	−0.015

Note: This table shows summary statistics for a series of MSCI Regional Indices over three periods: December 31, 2019–December 31, 2021, February 12, 2020–March 23, 2020, and March 23, 2020–December 31, 2021. Mean returns are annualised, STD corresponds to the standard deviation of returns, 1 % and 5 % VaR correspond to historical simulation value at risk estimated at a 1 % and 5 % threshold, respectively.

8.4.2 Sectors

The COVID-19 crisis did not impact all sectors of the economy equally. For example, companies in tourism, travel and entertainment were among the most impacted, while those in e-commerce and remote working technologies benefited from the crisis. From the perspective of an equity investor, this may present opportunities to curtail downside risk by investing across multiple global sectors. Figure 8.2 shows the performance of the various MSCI sector indices rebased to 100 on December 31, 2019.

Very considerable differences in both the level of tail risk and aggregate performance are clear. The MSCI World Information Technology sector was the best performer over the two-year period, providing gains of 142 percent from the low point in mid-March. Consumer discretionary and communication services also provided investors with strong performance, quickly regaining any losses experienced in the early phase of the pandemic.

Figure 8.2: MSCI Sector Indices – Summary Statistics.
Note: This table shows summary statistics for a series of MSCI Sector Indices over three periods: December 31, 2019–December 31, 2021, February 12, 2020–March 23, 2020, and March 23, 2020–December 31, 2021. Mean returns are annualised, STD corresponds to the standard deviation of returns, 1 % and 5 % VaR correspond to historical simulation value at risk estimated at a 1 % and 5 % threshold, respectively.

Energy stocks were the laggards during this period, with oversupply of crude oil having a large impact on the sector (Corbet et al., 2021a, 2020b). The initial price drop was also most substantial for this sector, severely impacting the aggregate performance. Other poorly performing sectors include Utilities, Real Estate and Consumer Staples. The latter index is comprised of stocks which tend to have low systematic risk, borne out by this sector experiencing limited losses but also bounded in terms of upside performance.

Further details are provided in Table 8.2, where the sectorial returns are broken out according to time periods. Over the entire period, a substantial dispersion in returns is evident, ranging from 2.5 percent for Energy to 39.6 percent for Information Technology.[14] Further variation is evident across all other summary statistics reported. For example for 5 percent VaR, the level of downside risk varies from 3.7 percent (Consumer Staples) to 7.6 percent (Energy).

Over the short bear market period from February to March 2020, it is difficult to find respite for investors from COVID-19-related losses. The best performing sector, Consumer Staples, lost 23.9 percent, while most other sectors lost at least one-third of their value in just a few weeks. While not one of the worst performers in terms of aggregate returns, the Information Technology sector is found to have the second-highest standard deviation, illustrating the considerable uncertainty surrounding even the more robust sectors. The level of downside risk is substantial across all sectors, with the lowest tail

14 The difference evident for the aggregate energy sector in Figure 8.2 where the index does not recover to its original level and the positive returns seen in Table 8.2 can be explained by the aggregation of average returns which does not account for compounding. This is of particular relevance when extreme returns are evident.

Table 8.2: MSCI Sector Indices – Summary Statistics.

	World	Communication services	Consumer discretionary	Consumer staples	Energy	Financials	Industrials	Information technology	Materials	Real estate	Utilities	Health care
2020–2021												
Mean	0.190	0.195	0.279	0.092	0.025	0.130	0.150	0.396	0.167	0.107	0.072	0.164
STD	0.216	0.220	0.226	0.163	0.402	0.281	0.228	0.288	0.222	0.237	0.230	0.190
Skewness	−1.141	−0.829	−1.046	−1.048	−0.699	−0.743	−0.695	−0.458	−0.988	−1.655	−0.471	−0.449
Kurtosis	15.830	9.554	11.881	16.964	14.125	13.219	13.339	10.222	13.568	18.458	15.703	11.139
1 % VaR	−0.047	−0.040	−0.045	−0.037	−0.076	−0.064	−0.051	−0.052	−0.041	−0.051	−0.051	−0.039
5 % VaR	−0.018	−0.021	−0.020	−0.012	−0.032	−0.026	−0.019	−0.025	−0.022	−0.021	−0.018	−0.014
Feb–Mar 2020												
Aggregate Return	−0.342	−0.281	−0.332	−0.239	−0.539	−0.431	−0.394	−0.310	−0.362	−0.387	−0.327	−0.272
STD	0.574	0.551	0.599	0.496	1.072	0.789	0.609	0.801	0.603	0.677	0.699	0.541
Skewness	−0.508	−0.345	−0.271	−0.100	−0.190	0.150	0.186	0.136	0.026	−0.579	0.248	0.158
Kurtosis	0.761	0.820	1.411	0.815	2.403	1.334	2.035	0.687	2.146	1.542	0.933	0.198
1 % VaR	−0.098	−0.090	−0.098	−0.079	−0.178	−0.116	−0.096	−0.118	−0.098	−0.120	−0.104	−0.079
5 % VaR	−0.086	−0.077	−0.082	−0.045	−0.140	−0.106	−0.079	−0.088	−0.077	−0.082	−0.073	−0.063
Mar–Dec 2020												
Aggregate Return	0.679	0.622	0.953	0.370	0.542	0.651	0.772	0.881	0.898	0.449	0.429	0.495
STD	0.119	0.119	0.109	0.088	0.153	0.124	0.111	0.120	0.104	0.110	0.100	0.098
Skewness	0.955	0.428	−0.629	−0.388	0.857	0.178	−0.105	−0.926	−0.366	−0.299	−0.138	−0.259
Kurtosis	7.989	3.573	1.747	1.784	4.560	3.519	3.200	2.203	2.410	2.222	1.322	4.379
1 % VaR	−0.031	−0.035	−0.032	−0.021	−0.049	−0.031	−0.030	−0.044	−0.032	−0.030	−0.026	−0.026
5 % VaR	−0.022	−0.020	−0.016	−0.011	−0.035	−0.020	−0.016	−0.023	−0.015	−0.017	−0.014	−0.012

Note: This table shows summary statistics for a series of MSCI Sector Indices over three periods: December 31, 2019–December 31, 2021, February 12, 2020–March 23, 2020, and March 23, 2020–December 31, 2021. Mean returns are annualised, STD corresponds to the standard deviation of returns, 1 % and 5 % VaR correspond to historical simulation value at risk estimated at a 1 % and 5 % threshold, respectively.

risk sector, Health Care, is still expected to experience daily losses of 7.9 percent every one hundred days and 6.3 percent every twenty days during this period.

As found for the regional indices, the recovery was rapid and swift. By the end of 2020, all sectors rose by at least 37 percent (Consumer Staples) to a maximum 95.3 percent (Consumer Discretionary). A cross-sector increase of this magnitude is almost unprecedented, comparable with the recovery in markets which occurred as the Global Financial Crisis drew to a close in 2009. Throughout this recovery period, risk, in all forms examined here, was minimal. The standard deviation, or volatility, or stock index returns varied from 9.8 percent to 15.3 percent, while the maximum downside was 4.9 percent (Energy) at a 1 percent tolerance level.

Two features of the COVID-19 pandemic on equity markets are highlighted by these sectoral results. First, during the downturn, even well-diversified equity investors would have experienced hefty losses. Moreover, as these indices are globally diversified, even investors trying to take advantage of the diversification opportunities offered ex-ante by geographic heterogeneity were subject to large losses. Second, the extent of the recovery was rapid, presented limited risk of loss and was also diversified across sectors, even those, such as consumer discretionary, where companies were scarcely able to operate.

8.4.3 Factors

In this Section we assess the performance of portfolios formed using characteristic factors throughout the pandemic. We include many of the most common factors, including momentum, value, quality, growth, minimum volatility and high dividend yield. The MSCI World Equally Weighted index is also shown, represented a thoroughly diversified portfolio. Notably, the MSCI indices are long-only, not the long-short characteristic factors prevalent in the literature. This is representative of the investment opportunity set available to retail investors.

Figure 8.3 shows rebased factor indices from December 31, 2019 through December 31, 2021. The initial decrease in value from February 2020 is clearly visible and common to all factors. The smallest loss was experienced by the value portfolio (–36.3 percent) followed closely by the equally weighted portfolio (–36.19 percent). Given the level of diversification in the latter portfolio, this provides strong evidence that the downturn was pervasive, impacting upon all companies globally.

While all factor portfolios experienced extreme losses, the recovery was more dispersed. Quality and momentum portfolios performed best, strongly surpassing their starting value by mid-2020. The equally weighted portfolio underperformed the MSCI world portfolio, echoing the sectoral-based results, showing that the recovery was strongest in certain sectors of the economy. The remaining factor portfolios, value, high dividends and minimum volatility, only marginally surpassed their starting value at the end of the two year period.

Figure 8.3: MSCI World Factor Indices, December 2019–December 2021.
Note: MSCI factor indices are shown for the period from December 31, 2019 to December 31, 2021. All indices are rebased to a value of 100 on December 31, 2019.

Table 8.3 shows the associated summary statistics for the factor porftolios. While there is a sharp contrast in the mean returns for the factors over the entire window, the risk levels are tightly clustered, with standard deviation ranging from 17.3 percent to 23.9 percent and downside risk at a 1 percent level ranging from 3.6 percent to 4.7 percent. This highlights the difficulties for investors in using long-only factor portfolios in an attempt to diversify risk.

Findings across the cohorts are akin to those found for regions and sectors. All factors lost about one-third of their value in a small number of weeks in early 2020. They all displayed high, correlated risk levels, making diversification difficult. The recovery up to the end of 2020 was rapid, lifting all factor portfolios back to at least the level they were at before the downturn. Moreover, risk was muted during the recovery phase.

While factor portfolios may be looked upon as a mechanism to allow investors to load on alternative, potentially uncorrelated risks, this is found to be of limited assistance during the downturn. Given that these are long-only portfolios, investors were exposed to a dominant market effect when investing in these portfolios. This highlights a key risk for retail investors. In contrast to long-short hedge fund equity strategies, often utilised by sophisticated investors and using downside risk-protected strategies, retail investors bore the brunt of the downturn. This highlights the need to ensure that such investors are aware of the substantial risks associated with investing, even when creating a diversified portfolio, a tenet of modern investing strategies. Allowing investors access to the full plethora of downside risk-protected strategies, normally restricted to sophisticated investors, would help in protecting against systematic risk. This would be of particular benefit to pension funds where a small allocation to such assets could provide diversification benefits.

Table 8.3: MSCI Factor Indices – Summary Statistics.

	World	Equally weighted	Momentum momentum	Enhanced value	Quality	Minimum volatility	Growth target	High dividend
2020–2021								
Mean	0.190	0.119	0.226	0.066	0.244	0.077	0.174	0.063
STD	0.216	0.196	0.239	0.205	0.222	0.173	0.206	0.193
Skewness	−1.141	−1.326	−0.629	−1.211	−0.549	−1.027	−1.431	−1.209
Kurtosis	15.830	16.215	9.472	13.850	13.059	17.703	16.560	16.499
1 % VaR	−0.047	−0.044	−0.042	−0.042	−0.041	−0.036	−0.044	−0.042
5 % VaR	−0.018	−0.016	−0.024	−0.017	−0.019	−0.014	−0.019	−0.016
Feb–Mar 2020								
Aggregate Return	−0.342	−0.367	−0.308	−0.362	−0.304	−0.291	−0.343	−0.331
STD	0.574	0.462	0.570	0.455	0.592	0.483	0.542	0.506
Skewness	−0.508	−1.226	−0.416	−1.362	−0.072	−0.297	−0.789	−0.553
Kurtosis	0.761	1.484	0.698	2.460	0.742	0.708	0.951	1.166
1 % VaR	−0.098	−0.092	−0.096	−0.094	−0.093	−0.082	−0.097	−0.092
5 % VaR	−0.086	−0.074	−0.080	−0.071	−0.080	−0.064	−0.085	−0.066
Mar–Dec 2020								
Aggregate Return	0.679	0.686	0.731	0.468	0.650	0.369	0.690	0.458
STD	0.119	0.117	0.123	0.121	0.120	0.107	0.115	0.116
Skewness	0.955	0.895	0.862	0.674	1.079	1.258	1.010	0.737
Kurtosis	7.989	6.182	6.687	4.414	8.110	8.674	7.383	6.246
1 % VaR	−0.031	−0.031	−0.037	−0.030	−0.034	−0.030	−0.030	−0.032
5 % VaR	−0.022	−0.016	−0.020	−0.017	−0.020	−0.014	−0.018	−0.015

Note: This table shows summary statistics for a series of MSCI Factor Indices over three periods: December 31, 2019–December 31, 2021, February 12, 2020–March 23, 2020, and March 23, 2020–December 31, 2021. Mean returns are annualised, STD corresponds to the standard deviation of returns, 1 % and 5 % VaR correspond to historial simulation value at risk estimated at a 1 % and 5 % threshold, respectively.

8.5 Concluding Comments

The onset of the COVID-19 pandemic presented unprecedented challenges for investors in global equities, characterised by extreme volatility, sectoral divergence, and an absence of liquidity. As shown in this chapter, markets experienced a swift decline in the region of 30 percent, and this was felt across regions, sectors and factor portfolios globally. This was among the fastest market declines in history, forcing policymakers into promises of unprecedented monetary and fiscal support. Highlighting the extent to which the crisis was driven by sentiment, much of the promised support was not required to bolster the market.

The swift and homogeneous decline in stock prices was followed by an equally rapid recovery. While the recovery was, to some extent, preceded by promises of fiscal and monetary support, the potential for a COVID-19 vaccine was also a factor in the recovery. As shown in this chapter, the extent of the recovery was heterogeneous across sectors and regions, reflecting the positive impact of the pandemic on some industries and divergent policy responses across countries. While navigating this landscape was difficult for investors, a simple globally diversified strategy provided strong capital gains for investors.

The traditional diversification benefits of global investing were challenged as correlations, especially during extreme downside price moves, between markets increased during the crisis. The increased prominence of factor investing, partly a result of the introduction of low-cost exchange-traded funds, was also insufficient to avoid large losses early in the pandemic. During the recovery phase, there was a heterogeneous upturn. Although risk, measured through one- and two-sided measures, was minimal, returns varied greatly between factor approaches.

The empirical findings detailed in this chapter highlight the challenges of achieving financial diversification during periods of systemic crisis. While the literature decries the benefits of international diversification in reducing country-level exposures, our findings indicate limited differences between the returns or risk experienced at a global level during the bear market, relative to those indicated by region. Similarly, sectoral diversification provided limited downside protection, relative to holding the individual sectors. This may be explained by a flight-to-quality, whereby investors exited equities, shifting towards perceived safe-haven assets such as government Treasury bills and bonds. Moreover, history did not act as a reasonable guide to markets, given the unprecedented nature of the pandemic. In summary, the findings presented emphasise the need for a better understanding of risk management during downturns, supporting approaches which can better account for tail risk and systemic shocks in an increasingly interconnected global financial landscape.

9 Lessons from COVID-19: Which Asset Classes Really Are Safe-Havens?

The COVID-19 pandemic, characterised by a swift and substantial decrease in stock prices, provided a stern test for the capacity of safe-haven assets to mitigate risk. In this chapter, the risk reduction potential of gold, bitcoin, currencies, commodities and Treasury Bonds is assessed during the COVID-19 pandemic. Gold, Treasury Bonds and the Euro are shown to reduce substantial downside risk, especially during the bear market in equities. While this reduction is also associated with improved portfolio returns during the crisis period, there is a cost in terms of reduced returns over a longer window for investors holding safe-haven assets. This highlights a tradeoff for risk-averse investors seeking to reduce downside risk.

9.1 Introduction

The COVID-19 pandemic had widespread implications for public health, education, social behaviours and the economy. The latter impact was, perhaps, best observed through the lens of the stock market. Once confirmation for the severity of the disease and the rate of transmission became clear, the stock market displayed one of the swiftest and most dramatic declines in financial history (Gormsen and Koijen, 2023). For equity investors, diversification across sectors or countries provided limited benefits. All markets were severely impacted simultaneously, echoing the limited equity market diversification gains available during previous crises (Bartram and Bodnar, 2009).

Safe haven assets have long been documented in the literature (Erb and Harvey, 2013; Hillier et al., 2006; Jaffe, 1989). They are identified as assets which provide limited or negative correlation with traditional assets during periods of market turmoil (Baur and Lucey, 2010). Ideally, by holding a small allocation to these assets, investors will mitigate some of their losses during market downturns. Many different assets have been suggested as safe havens, including gold (Baur and Lucey, 2010), Treasury Bonds (Flavin et al., 2014), currencies (Ranaldo and Söderlind, 2010) and, most recently, cryptocurrencies (Shahzad et al., 2019).

Whether these safe havens provided benefits during the COVID-19-induced market turmoil is, despite much research, still an open question. Gold, for example, was found not to be a safe haven during the crisis, while also found to offer safe haven benefits during the period (Cheema et al., 2022; Gomis-Porqueras et al., 2022). Similarly, while some literature suggests that Bitcoin was a safe haven during the crisis, others indicate that it actually added to portfolio risk (Corbet et al., 2020b; Conlon and McGee, 2020a). This chapter seeks to resolve these apparent contradictions in the literature.

The contribution of this work is twofold. First, we reassess the safe haven benefits of a range of assets during the crisis using a downside risk framework, which quantifies the relative risk improvement found. This analysis is provided over two timeframes:

https://doi.org/10.1515/9783111707990-009

a longer one from 2018 to 2021 and a shorter window surrounding the COVID-19-related bear market in equities. Second, the cost of refuge is examined by evaluating the impact on portfolio returns from investing in safe-haven assets. This analysis allows for an assessment of whether there is a price to be paid for investing in safe-haven assets during normal times and whether this cost is rewarded with positive changes in returns during market turmoil.

The empirical results show that traditional safe-haven assets provided consistent risk-reduction capacity during the COVID-19-related downturn in equity markets. Treasury bonds and the Euro provide the strongest downside risk reduction, followed closely by gold. Bitcoin, in sharp contrast, is shown to be consistently associated with increased portfolio risk. Over the longer window from 2018 to 2021, safe haven investments have a cost, which is a reduction in returns relative to holding the S&P 500 in isolation. Over the brief bear market stemming from the COVID-19 pandemic, however, holding safe-haven assets results in increases in returns, especially for gold. During the period of maximum dislocation, gold also shows considerable risk reduction capacity, highlighting its strong portfolio benefits.

The findings detailed in this chapter give rise to a conundrum for investors. Safe-haven assets can reduce some of the risk experienced during market turmoil, but this comes at a cost in terms of reduced medium-term returns. Are investors willing to pay to get a marginal reduction in downside risk, or are they mainly concerned with expected returns? Only limited literature has considered this tradeoff, which should form an important consideration in portfolio assessment, rather than an isolated analysis of risk reduction.

9.2 Previous Literature

Investors' aversion to losses (Kahneman and Tversky, 1979) leads them to seek safe haven assets which are (almost) always valued at face value (Gorton, 2017). A strong safe haven should be negatively correlated during times of market turmoil, with the assets the investor is seeking to protect (Baur and Lucey, 2010), while a weak safe haven possesses low correlation.[15] A further criterion is that the safe haven asset possesses significant liquidity, allowing investors to trade it during periods of market volatility.

Much of the literature on safe haven assets focuses on the ability to hedge against losses in equity markets (Baur and McDermott, 2010). There has also been some focus on the ability to hedge against adverse price movements in bond markets (Baur and Lucey, 2010; Ranaldo and Söderlind, 2010). Further research has examined the potential to hedge against extreme price fluctuations in the US dollar (Reboredo, 2013b). Beyond

15 The literature also considers the cross-hedging properties of various assets, with a view to reducing portfolio risk. This is distinct from the notion of financial hedging, which refers to risk management to remove or reduce currency, interest rate and commodity risk at a corporate level (Bessler et al., 2019).

financial hedging, investors also worry about severe losses as a result of inflation (Conlon et al., 2018b).

Gold has received significant attention as a safe-haven asset, especially for equity markets. Gold is found to be a short-lived safe haven in extreme stock market conditions (Bredin et al., 2015; Baur and Lucey, 2010). Baur and McDermott (2010) demonstrate that these safe haven characteristics of gold are echoed across European markets, but not for other stock markets, including Canada, Japan, Australia and some emerging markets. Applying a smooth transition model, Berkman and Malloch (2023) find further evidence for hedging and safe haven properties of gold, but also indicate that this is market-specific. Investigating the conditionality of the safe haven properties of gold, Ryan et al. (2024) show that the effectiveness is strongest during crises triggered by macroeconomic news. In contrast to earlier work, He et al. (2018) show that gold is not a safe haven for UK or US markets when a Markov switching approach is used to model the different states. Gold is also a safe haven for crude oil (Reboredo, 2013a) and for currencies (Reboredo, 2013b). In comparison to gold, the hedging properties of silver and platinum are shown to be muted (Bredin et al., 2017).

Government bonds are often purchased by investors during periods of flight-to-quality, with evidence suggesting that it is liquidity rather than credit quality that is demanded (Beber et al., 2009). Decreased equity market sentiment results in increased in-flows to bond funds, consistent with bonds responding positively to equity turmoil (Islam, 2021). The strength of the flight to safety to bond markets is, however, a function of the yield, weakening for low bond yields (Boucher and Tokpavi, 2019). Mixed evidence for the safe-haven properties of bonds exists, nevertheless. Bonds are found to be a hedge, but not a safe haven for stocks (Ciner et al., 2013). Long-dated bonds may, however, provide stronger safe-haven properties than their one-year Treasury bond counterparts (Flavin et al., 2014).

An expansive literature also looks at the possibility of currencies acting as a safe-haven asset. Global equity volatility is associated with positive currency co-skewness in the US dollar, Japanese Yen and Swiss Franc (Chan et al., 2018). Similarly, the Swiss Franc and Japanese Yen have been shown to appreciate against the US Dollar conditional upon US stock prices decreasing and US bond and FX volatility increasing (Ranaldo and Söderlind, 2010). During periods of elevated global risk, the Swiss Franc demonstrates safe haven properties against a limited set of currency rates (Grisse and Nitschka, 2015). The Japanese Yen provides the most consistent safe haven properties (Cho and Han, 2021; Wong and Fong, 2018; Fatum and Yamamoto, 2016), but this may be a consequence of unwinding of carry trades rather than genuine safe haven qualities (Hossfeld and MacDonald, 2015).

Recently, the literature has added an additional set of possible safe haven assets, namely cryptocurrencies. As many cryptocurrencies have a fixed total supply, are not affected by monetary policy, and are decentralised, they have been hypothesised to be a means to protect investors against adverse movement in traditional assets. Early literature found mixed results, with much of the focus on the safe haven properties of Bitcoin.

Bouri et al. (2017) find diversification properties for Bitcoin but limited hedging or safe haven characteristics in a sample from 2011 to 2015. Expanding this sample up to 2018, Shahzad et al. (2019) show that Bitcoin may have some weak safe haven qualities for stock markets. Wang et al. (2019) assesses a much wider sample of cryptocurrencies and equity indices and indicates that cryptocurrencies are not a hedge but do act as a safe haven for equities.

These empirical findings were, however, documented in the absence of a severe global downturn in equity markets. The COVID-19 pandemic provided a stern review of the safe haven qualities of cryptocurrencies. During the initial bull market phase of the pandemic, the major cryptocurrencies showed no safe haven properties, in fact adding to risk when held with stock indices (Conlon and McGee, 2020a; Conlon et al., 2024g). Using a longer window incorporating some of the recovery in cryptocurrency prices, Mariana et al. (2021) indicate that Bitcoin and Ethereum have short-run safe haven qualities, but note their high volatility as an impediment. Similarly, Corbet et al. (2020c) suggest that cryptocurrencies acted as a store of value during the COVID-19 pandemic. Correlations between Bitcoin and stock markets were found to increase in the period after the COVID-19 pandemic was declared, pointing to difficulties in reducing portfolio risk using cryptocurrencies (Corbet et al., 2020e). Wen et al. (2022) contrasts the safe haven performance of gold and bitcoin during the COVID-19 crisis, highlighting that only the former acts as a safe haven. Employing a regime switching model, Li and Miu (2023) find evidence of high correlation between stocks and Bitcoin during high volatility states, consistent with limited hedging or safe haven characteristics. The literature has also considered the hedging and safe haven properties of cryptocurrency more widely, examining their capacity to hedge currency risk (Conlon et al., 2024d; Urquhart and Zhang, 2019) and inflation (Conlon et al., 2024g; Blau et al., 2021).

An extensive literature also examines the potential for safe havens more generally during the COVID-19 crisis. Firm evidence for a simultaneous global flight-to-quality from equity markets to bond markets exists (Papadamou et al., 2021). Cheema et al. (2022) suggests that gold lost its position as a safe-haven asset during the pandemic, while the Swiss Franc retains its role as a store of value. In sharp contrast, Salisu et al. (2021) find that gold is a safe haven during the pandemic. Resolving this apparent contradiction, Akhtaruzzaman et al. (2021) establish that gold is a safer haven during the first phase of the pandemic up to March 16, 2020 and loses this property subsequently.

9.3 Data and Methodology

9.3.1 Data

Data for this study are obtained from Eikon, a division of LSEG Data and Analytics. Daily price data from December 31, 2018 through December 31, 2021 are extracted and returns calculated. Six possible safe havens are examined as follows. The Goldman Sachs Commodity Index (GSCI) is selected as representative of the broad commodity market, and selected due to the evidence that important constituents such as precious metals and soft commodities have some safe haven properties (Rubbaniy et al., 2022; Bredin et al., 2015). The USD–EUR exchange rate is considered as a safe haven (Cho and Han, 2021), under the assumption that an investor holds Euro during crisis periods seeking appreciation versus the USD. Treasuries are represented by the S&P US Treasury Bond Index, a broad, market-weighted index measuring the performance of the US Treasury Bond market. The price of gold in USD is from the London Bullion Market (LBM) and is examined due to the long history of gold being shown to have safe haven properties (Baur and Lucey, 2010; Baur and McDermott, 2010). Bitcoin prices are taken from Bitstamp, a leading cryptocurrency exchange and are also in USD. Bitcoin, accounting for about half of the market value of all cryptocurrencies, is examined due to the mixed evidence for its safe haven properties and due to its role as a central node in the cryptocurrency markets (Conlon et al., 2024a). Finally, an equally weighted portfolio of the previous five assets is constructed, providing a viewpoint on the level of risk reduction achievable for an investor who wishes to diversify across potential safe-haven assets.

The S&P 500 is taken as representative of the US stock market and is the asset for which an investor is attempting to reduce downside or tail risk. In this chapter, we take a portfolio approach, assessing the reduction in risk of the portfolio for differing allocations to the respective safe-haven asset. Two periods are examined: The first, from December 2018 to December 2021, is included to capture the long-run safe haven performance. The second is from December 2019 to March 2021, representing the period of maximum market turmoil due to the COVID-19 pandemic.

9.3.2 Methodology

The potential for losses in a portfolio is estimated in two related ways in this chapter. The value at risk (VaR) of a portfolio is defined as the maximum expected loss on a portfolio over a given time period, while the conditional value at risk (CVaR) is the expected loss, given that the loss is greater than the VaR (Conlon and Cotter, 2013). VaR is estimated as:

$$VaR(1-\alpha) = \mu - \sigma z(\alpha). \tag{9.1}$$

α is the confidence level considered, $z(\alpha)$ is the α quantile of the standardised distribution, while μ and σ are the estimated mean and standard deviation of returns. In this chapter, a parametric approach to estimating VaR and CVaR is adopted. Specifically, the Cornish-Fisher expansion, an adjustment to the quantiles of the distribution to account for skewness and excess kurtosis, common to financial returns, is employed. Using the Cornish-Fisher expansion, a four-moment VaR is estimated as proposed by Favre and Galeano (2002),

$$\hat{Z}(\alpha, S_p, K_p) = z(\alpha) + \frac{1}{6}(z(\alpha)^2 - 1)S_p + \frac{1}{24}(z(\alpha)^3 - 3z(\alpha))K_p - \frac{1}{36}(2z(\alpha)^3 - 5z(\alpha))S_p^2. \quad (9.2)$$

$z(\alpha)$ is the α quantile of the standard normal distribution. S_p and K_p are the skewness and kurtosis of portfolio P. Four-moment modified VaR is then measured using:

$$MVaR_p(1 - \alpha) = \mu_p - \sigma_p \hat{Z}(\alpha, S_p, K_p). \quad (9.3)$$

The four-moment modified VaR accounts for the tail characteristics of financial returns and has been used extensively to estimate downside risk in financial markets (Conlon et al., 2023a; Conlon and Cotter, 2013).

The level of downside risk reduction achieved by including the safe haven asset in a portfolio alongside the S&P 500 is then calculated by estimating the level of downside risk of the portfolio relative to holding just the S&P 500. Value at risk portfolio reduction is estimated using:

$$RR_{p,\epsilon} = \frac{MVaR_{p,\epsilon}}{MVaR_{S\&P500}} - 1, \quad (9.4)$$

where ϵ is the weight of the safe haven asset in portfolio p. $RR_{p,\epsilon}$ provides the proportion of risk reduced by investing some proportion of capital in the safe haven asset. A positive number indicate that risk is increased by allocating to the safe haven.

9.4 Results

9.4.1 Risk Reduction

The safe haven properties of each of the assets described in Section 9.3 are now examined over two windows. The first, from December 31, 2018 to December 31, 2021 is used to assess the level of risk reduction over a longer period, which includes the COVID-19 pandemic announcement and the subsequent rapid market recovery. The second, from December 31, 2019 to March 31, 2021, includes the rapid and steep decline in equity markets, losing over 34 percent in a small number of weeks (Gormsen and Koijen, 2023). Downside risk is measured at a 1 percent level throughout, corresponding to the worst losses expected on a one-in-one-hundred day basis.

Risk reduction results are provided in Figure 9.1. A negative risk reduction corresponds to a drop in the level of downside risk relative to holding just the S&P 500, while a positive value corresponds to increased portfolio risk. For an asset to act as a safe haven, we require a reduction in risk.

Assessing first the risk reduction capacity of commodities, the level of risk reduction for the GSCI commodity index is reported. Over the longer period, 2018–2021, investing in the GSCI is consistently associated with risk reduction. The maximum level of reduction is achieved with a 55 percent allocation to the GSCI, with the level of risk reduction increasing again for any allocation greater than this. During the 2020 period surrounding the equity bear market, results are more mixed. VaR reduction is minimal, with up

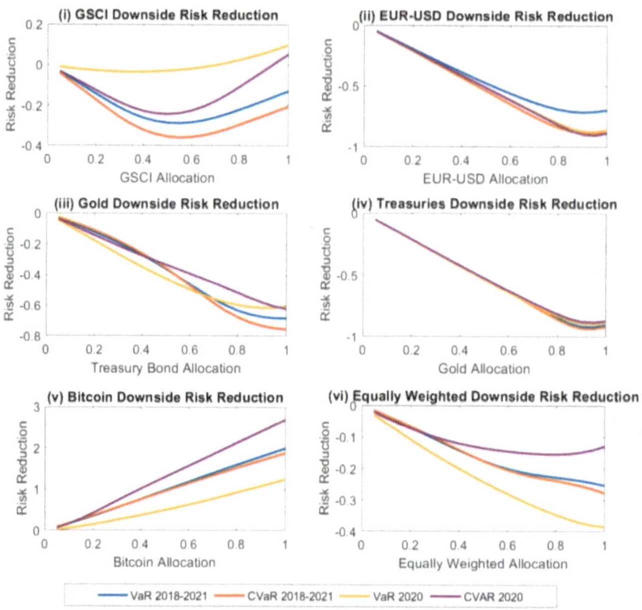

Figure 9.1: S&P 500 downside risk reduction from safe haven assets during the COVID-19 pandemic. *Note*: This figure illustrates the proportion of S&P 500 downside risk removed by allocating a proportion of wealth to safe haven assets. Downside risk is measured using value at risk (VaR) and conditional value at risk (CVaR) at the 1 percent threshold. Risk reduction is plotted on the vertical axis, while the proportional allocation to the safe haven is shown on the horizontal axis. Six different allocation approaches are explored: i) Goldman Sachs Commodity Index (GSCI) representing commodities, ii) EUR–USD exchange rate, iii) Gold, iv) US Treasury Bonds, v) Bitcoin, vi) Equally weighted portfolio containing all of these assets.

to 3.5 percent of S&P 500 risk removed through an allocation to commodities. For large allocations, those greater than 70 percent, portfolio risk is greater than holding the S&P 500 in isolation. In contrast, CVaR risk reduction during this period is considerable, with a reduction of up to 24 percent of S&P risk removed. This contrast with results found for VaR is a consequence of the focus of CVaR on extreme tail risk losses. In other words, the GSCI is able to provide refuge against very extreme downside risks associated with a fat-tailed distribution, but not against those observed using VaR, which just focuses on a level rather than an average.

Findings for the EUR–USD exchange rate are emphatic. A Euro allocation reduces risk in an almost linear manner up to a weight of between 90 and 100 percent. Over the 2018 to 2021 period, VaR risk reduction was smaller than during the later period or when estimated using CVaR. During the turbulent 2020 period, an investor holding a position in the Euro could reduce risk by up to 90 percent. This analysis, however, ignores the tradeoff with returns, with investors potentially surrendering expected returns to reduce risk, which may not be in keeping with their preferences. We later examine the impact on returns in Section 9.4.2.

Gold is also found to have strong downside risk reduction properties when held with equities. There are some differences, however, between the periods and downside risk measures. In the 2018–2021 period, the level of risk reduction, while monotonic, is not strictly linear. Moreover, further risk reduction is achieved at high allocations from a CVaR perspective. In the shorter 2020 window, a small allocation provides stronger risk reduction for lower Gold weights. At higher weights, the level of risk reduction begins to taper off, especially for VaR. It is noteworthy that even a small allocation to Gold adds risk reduction capacity, with a 25 percent allocation accounting for between 14 and 22 percent reduction in downside risk.

US Treasury bonds also provide a strong risk reduction capacity, with a smaller amount of heterogeneity in performance among all the options considered. The performance, for a small allocation, is better than that observed for gold and the EUR–USD exchange rate. For a 25 percent allocation to Treasury Bonds, an investor can reduce downside risk exposure to the S&P by around 27 percent. Furthermore, risk reduction continues linearly up to a 90 percent allocation to bonds, with between 88 and 93 percent risk reduction. Of course, this may also result in a considerable reduction in expected returns, something we examine in the following Section.

One of the frequently touted attractions of Bitcoin is its ability to act as a safe haven for traditional markets. As with other assets, we look at a mix portfolio of Bitcoin and the S&P 500 for different allocation weights. Findings are emphatic. For all allocations, Bitcoin results in greater portfolio risk than the S&P held alone. A 25 percent allocation to Bitcoin increases risk by between 20 and 57 percent. CVaR, or extreme tail risk, is particularly impacted. Over the short bear market window, an allocation of 39 percent to Bitcoin is sufficient to increase portfolio CVaR by 100 percent. This supports the earlier findings of Conlon and McGee (2020a) and Conlon et al. (2024g), that cryptocurrencies do not provide hedging capacity when investors need it most.

Finally, the risk reduction characteristics of the safe haven assets examined may differ in terms of their timing and capacity. Holding a selection of different secure assets may help in optimising the benefits. As a simple test, we examine an equally-weighted portfolio consisting of a 20 percent allocation to each of GSCI, gold, Treasuries, EUR–USD and Bitcoin. While the equally-weighted portfolio does provide some risk reduction benefits, these are much reduced relative to holding a position in gold, Treasuries or EUR–USD alone. The implication is that holding any quantity of Bitcoin has the effect of downsizing the potential risk reduction benefits possible.

Contrasting the various proposed safe havens, it is clear that gold, Treasuries and the EUR–USD rate all provide benefits for risk-averse investors. At the 25 percent allocation rate previously discussed, commodities provide between 3 and 18 percent risk reduction, gold provides between 14 and 22 percent, EUR–USD provides between 24 and 27 percent, and Treasuries provide 27 percent. In contrast, Bitcoin increases risk by between 20 and 57 percent. This highlights that the traditional safe-haven assets retained their lustre during the COVID-19 crisis. We next examine the extent to which investors had to surrender expected returns in order to benefit from these safe-haven properties.

9.4.2 Risk-Return Tradeoff

A majority of the literature on safe haven assets, with the exception of a small number of papers (Bredin et al., 2017), focus on the risk reduction properties of safe haven assets but without considering the impact on expected portfolio returns. In this Section, we reconsider the earlier findings but assessing the impact a partial allocation to a safe-haven asset has on the expected returns of the portfolio relative to holding the S&P 500 in isolation. Three allocation weights are examined: 0.1, 0.2 and 0.3 of wealth allocated to the safe haven.

Empirical results are detailed in Table 9.1. Considering first the entire period, December 2018 to December 2021, there is firm evidence that allocating to safe-haven assets reduces expected returns. Taking an allocation of 0.1 to the safe haven asset, the returns of GSCI, USD–EUR, gold and Treasury Bond mixed portfolios decrease relative to the S&P 500. The returns on the portfolio consisting of an equally weighted set of safe haven assets alongside the S&P 500 have no change in returns, but reduce risk by between 3.1 and 3.4 percent. Bitcoin, in sharp contrast, increases portfolio returns but results in a step-up in risk. While this increase in returns may compensate investors for the added risk, it does not meet the requirement of a safe haven.

Findings at higher safe haven allocations echo those found for a 0.1 allocation. The decrease in returns, and associated reduction in risk, for USD–EUR and Treasury Bonds are of the same magnitude, indicating that, throughout the full cycle, there is a cost to holding these as a safe-haven asset. Gold also has a cost, in terms of reduced returns, but this is lower. Finally, the change in returns for the equally-weighted set of assets is negligible while there is still a reduction in risk. This finding is, however, a result of the strong positive returns of Bitcoin. In essence, a small investment in this asset, while not providing safe haven properties, is helping to fund the investment in bona fide safe haven assets. Whether bitcoin retains such high positive returns in future is an open question, but if it is to become an accepted asset, lower volatility and stable returns will be a minimum criterion.

Over the bear market period coinciding with COVID-19, some of these findings are reversed. Only an allocation to the GSCI results in a reduction in expected returns, while still decreasing risk. Although USD–EUR and Treasury Bonds have similar risk reduction properties; the latter provided a substantially larger increase in returns. Bitcoin provides the largest increase in returns, but increases portfolio risk throughout, again disqualifying it as a safe haven asset. Gold shows strong prospects as a safe haven asset, providing an improvement in returns, which is twice that of the next nearest rival (Treasury Bonds) and strong risk reduction properties, particularly for smaller allocations. For all allocations, the change in return to change in risk ratio is strongest for gold.

Taking the findings detailed here, there are a number of important implications. First, for risk-averse investors seeking risk reduction during a period of financial turmoil, all assets, with the exception of Bitcoin, provide benefits. Second, the picture changes when one accounts for expected returns. While an investor will, generally, pay

Table 9.1: S&P 500 downside risk reduction and expected returns from safe haven assets during the COVID-19 pandemic.

Allocation		GSCI	USD EUR	Bitcoin	Gold	Treasury bonds	EW
December 2018–December 2021							
0.1	Δ mean	−0.014	−0.021	0.064	−0.010	−0.019	0.000
	VaR 1 % reduction	−0.069	−0.108	0.170	−0.060	−0.107	−0.034
	CVaR 1 % reduction	−0.083	−0.109	0.184	−0.053	−0.106	−0.031
0.3	Δ mean	−0.040	−0.063	0.206	−0.028	−0.057	−0.001
	VaR 1 % reduction	−0.210	−0.325	0.553	−0.192	−0.320	−0.106
	CVaR 1 % reduction	−0.257	−0.331	0.559	−0.178	−0.320	−0.102
0.5	Δ mean	−0.066	−0.102	0.366	−0.047	−0.094	−0.002
	VaR 1 % reduction	−0.285	−0.547	0.976	−0.362	−0.533	−0.175
	CVaR 1 % reduction	−0.354	−0.559	0.958	−0.357	−0.534	−0.176
December 2019–March 2020							
0.1	Δ mean	−0.079	0.009	0.058	0.041	0.021	0.009
	VaR 1 % reduction	−0.017	−0.102	0.060	−0.090	−0.108	−0.055
	CVaR 1 % reduction	−0.055	−0.154	0.290	−0.109	−0.160	−0.056
0.3	Δ mean	−0.218	0.026	0.185	0.128	0.065	0.027
	VaR 1 % reduction	−0.034	−0.306	0.260	−0.264	−0.324	−0.156
	CVaR 1 % reduction	−0.030	−0.507	0.498	−0.426	−0.538	−0.242
0.5	Δ mean	−0.336	0.044	0.327	0.222	0.111	0.046
	VaR 1 % reduction	−0.114	−0.358	0.868	−0.243	−0.372	−0.111
	CVaR 1 % reduction	−0.123	−0.560	1.433	−0.364	−0.580	−0.141

Note: This table illustrates the proportion of S&P 500 downside risk removed by allocating a proportion of wealth to safe haven assets, alongside the change in expected returns during each of the periods examined. Downside risk is measured using value at risk (VaR) and conditional value at risk (CVaR) at the 1 percent threshold. Δ Mean corresponds to the change in expected returns from holding the portfolio with a safe haven allocation relative to just holding the S&P 500. Six different allocation approaches are explored: i) Goldman Sachs Commodity Index (GSCI) representing commodities, ii) EUR–USD exchange rate, iii) Gold, iv) US Treasury Bonds, v) Bitcoin, vi) Equally weighted portfolio containing all of these assets.

a cost over the full cycle, many of the assets provide increases in returns during the bear market relative to holding the S&P in isolation. Third, during the crisis, an allocation to gold provides the best risk-to-return benefits.

9.5 Concluding Comments

The bear market associated with the COVID-19 pandemic was one of the swiftest on record, with a very substantial decrease in global equity markets in the space of weeks. In the face of such dramatic losses, investors often include assets in their portfolio which have limited correlation to equity markets during crisis periods. A strong safe-haven asset will display negative correlation during turmoil, increasing in price while the stock market is decreasing. Assets which have been suggested as safe havens include gold, government bonds, currencies, commodities and, most recently, cryptocurrencies. In this paper, we employ a downside risk framework to quantify the risk reduction properties of these asset classes, while also assessing the cost of holding the safe haven asset in terms of the impact on portfolio returns.

The findings documented in this chapter indicate that equity investors could reduce their risk during the COVID-19 pandemic by investing in safe haven assets. From a risk reduction perspective, US Treasury bonds and the USD–EUR rate provide the strongest benefits, followed by Gold. A 10 percent allocation to Treasury Bonds reduces risk by about 10.6 percent. Bitcoin has the effect of increasing portfolio risk regardless of the time window examined or the allocation made. The cost of the risk reduction is a decrease in returns, with the exception of an allocation to Bitcoin, across the full cycle. During the period of maximum market dislocation, however, all safe havens, except commodities, provide positive returns improving the performance of the hedged portfolio. During the market downturn, gold provides particularly strong benefits, having the highest portfolio returns while still retaining strong risk reduction properties.

The provides further evidence that traditional safe haven assets maintained their role throughout the COVID-19 pandemic. A small allocation, however, only has the effect of reducing a limited amount of risk. In other words, safe haven assets, held as part of a portfolio, do not have the effect of eliminating risk. A further critical finding of the study is that Bitcoin is not a safe haven asset. While it may provide performance gains from a portfolio perspective, these are at the expense of increased downside risk. This is counter to the requirements of a traditional safe haven, specifically that holding the asset reduces risks during periods of market turmoil.

Risk-averse investors should also be aware that, in order to temporarily reduce portfolio risk, they may have to give up something in terms of returns. In other words, there is a non-trivial cost involved. While most of the literature has focused on the risk reduction characteristics of safe haven assets, there has been limited focus on the costs associated with reducing risk. A wider perspective, examining the implications for portfolio risk and return throughout the entire cycle, alongside the benefits gained during bear market periods would help investors in assessing whether safe haven investments are a useful and worthwhile component of their portfolios.

Finally, while the current chapter focuses on the capacity of safe-haven assets to reduce risk when held with equity investments, the marginal investor will hold a wider array of assets. In this sense, the present analysis should be repeated for a range of assets, including corporate bonds, hedge funds and private equity, reflective of the investments made by institutional investors such as pension funds. Moreover, an analysis of the benefits of holding safe-haven assets as part of a portfolio diversified across asset classes is warranted. This will help well-diversified investors to understand what they gain from further diversification with safe havens.

10 The Impact of COVID-19 on Firms' Risk Appetite and Risk Assessment Practices

The COVID-19 pandemic has significantly influenced firms' expectations and has a direct influence on future risk assessment practices and strategies across various industries due to the broad lack of preparation exhibited for such an exceptional black swan event. This chapter examines how companies had to develop financial strategies when confronting a global pandemic of unknown depth and duration. Such primary tasks, including attempts to increase liquidity in a highly competitive and fractured market without the intervention of third-party and government support, in what had deteriorated into an extremely desperate situation. A rapid digital transformation, combined with the broad-sweeping adoption of remote working arrangements, introduced cybersecurity risks, some of which corporations were largely unprepared for, necessitating robust data protection measures. Additionally, changes in supply chain management and credit risk models highlight the need for adaptive and resilient risk management frameworks.

10.1 Understanding the Impact of COVID-19 on Risk Appetite and Tolerance

The COVID-19 pandemic has directly affected the risk tolerance of firms across various industries (Zhang and Sogn-Grundvåg, 2022; Klöckner et al., 2023; Bai et al., 2024), many of whom were diligently prepared for a range of potential market-moving events, but largely did not adequately prepare for a global shutdown as a result of a pandemic. Due to such unprecedented economic threats and uncertainties, many businesses have become increasingly risk-averse (Cepel et al., 2020; Liguori and Pittz, 2020; Leng and Sun, 2024). As an immediate response, a strategic focus on survival and long-term resilience rather than aggressive growth reflects the considerable changes in approach. The firm's primary concern in the initial stages of the pandemic was ensuring operational continuity amidst widespread lockdowns and supply chain interruptions. Consequently, there was a notable shift towards maintaining higher levels of liquidity and building substantial cash reserves (Qin et al., 2020; Zheng, 2022; Hoang et al., 2022b; Nguyen et al., 2024). This emphasis on liquidity is driven by the need to protect corporations and buffer against potential revenue shortfalls and unforeseen expenses, largely protected and provided by government bailouts and assistance packages (Khan, 2022; Apergis et al., 2023; Smales, 2024).[16] Such decisions have been further reinforced when consider-

16 Companies have recognised that robust cash reserves are crucial in weathering periods of reduced income and sustaining essential operations without resorting to high-risk borrowing, particularly when confronted with such incredible uncertainty due to such an exceptional black swan event.

https://doi.org/10.1515/9783111707990-010

ing the volatility observed in global markets, where rapid shifts in demand and supply have created an unpredictable business environment. In such a context, liquidity acts as a safeguard, allowing firms to adapt to rapidly changing circumstances without compromising their financial stability.

The increased focus on cash reserves also responds to the tightening credit conditions many businesses faced during the pandemic. With lenders becoming more cautious, access to external financing became more constrained. Specifically, credit providers also had to rely on their risk-mitigating strategies, in which they had to consider the probability of default calculations within a globally-influencing scenario where governments and other market-protecting forces were implementing regulatory changes and support structures, with substantial effects upon risk profiles and market competition. More specifically, in response to the COVID-19 pandemic, as presented in Table 10.1, governments worldwide enacted substantial fiscal and monetary measures to alleviate economic distress. China implemented liquidity injections, infrastructure spending, and loan relief, while Japan expanded quantitative easing and provided zero-interest loans to businesses. European nations, including Germany, France, and Italy, introduced fiscal packages with loan guarantees, direct payments, and tax deferrals. At the same time, the United States rushed legislation through government decision-making levels and implemented several relief packages, including direct stimulus payments, enhanced unemployment benefits, and small business loans. Central banks globally, including the ECB and BoE, undertook significant asset purchases and established lending facilities to maintain market liquidity. These diverse strategies aimed to support businesses, individuals, and healthcare systems amid the pandemic's economic disruptions.

In addition to increasing corporate liquidity, firms have also re-evaluated their investment strategies, with some opting for less aggressive and more calculated investments (Shen et al., 2020; Hoang et al., 2022b; Yan et al., 2023; Zhuang et al., 2023). The pandemic-induced economic slowdown highlighted the specific risks associated with over-leveraging and speculative investment, and the effects of black swan and outlier events on such. As a result, some companies have shifted their investment focus towards projects with shorter payback periods and more predictable returns (Hameiri, 2021; Gultekin et al., 2022). This strategic realignment not only helps in preserving capital but also ensures that investments contribute directly to enhancing operational resilience and core business capabilities. This shift towards a more conservative risk appetite is also evident in the changes to corporate governance practices. Firms have enhanced their risk management frameworks, incorporating more rigorous scenario planning and stress testing to better anticipate and respond to potential future shocks. Some of these measures are now required by government and regulatory authorities, where such measures are designed to provide a clearer understanding of the firm's risk exposure and to develop robust contingency plans. By doing so, companies are better equipped to manage both the immediate and long-term impacts of similar disruptions, ensuring sustained resilience (Seshadri and Kumar, 2023; Florio and Brotto, 2024; Azizah et al., 2024).

Table 10.1: Select fiscal measures in response to the COVID-19 pandemic, 2020 (% GDP).

	A. Above-the line measures		B. Below the line measures		C. Contingent liabilities	
Country	**Tot**	**Add spend and forgone rev (health)**	**Tot size**	**Equity injections, asset purchases, loans, debt assumptions**	**% GDP**	**Guarantees (on loans, deposits etc.)**
Australia	8.8	Additional spending (CAD 4 bn): Support to the health system, including increased testing, vaccine development, medical supplies, mitigation efforts, and greater protection of Indigenous communities	0.8	Farm Credit Canada will receive support from the government that will allow for an additional CAD 5 bn in lending capacity to producers, agribusinesses, and food processors	1	A loan guarantee arrangement between the Government and participating banks to cover the immediate cash flow needs of SMEs
Brazil	6.5	Additional spending (RMB 147 bn): Expenditure to improve epidemic prevention and control and the national public health emergency management system. Forgone revenue: Tariffs were exempted for the import of medicines, medical supplies, and other vehicles used to fight against the outbreak	1.1	Road tolls and some service fees charged by airports and railways were exempted or reduced; the price of electricity was cut by 5 percent. The authorities estimated the cost of the toll exemption to be about RMB 140 bn. Railway logistic fee lowered by 50 % until Jun 30 with an estimated cost of RMB 350 mn. From March 1 to December 31, the port construction fee will be exempted, and some fees will be cut. Allow China's state-funded infrastructure projects to use up to 15 percent of investment for a project to pay wages. The central government transfer payment rate to provinces was increased from 3 % to 4 % for pensions	0	

Table 10.1 (continued)

	A. Above-the line measures		B. Below the line measures		C. Contingent liabilities	
Country	**Tot**	**Add spend and forgone rev (health)**	**Tot size**	**Equity injections, asset purchases, loans, debt assumptions**	**% GDP**	**Guarantees (on loans, deposits etc.)**
Canada	5.6	Additional spending (€0.05 bn): The European Commission redirected funding of €47.5 million towards research on COVID-19 vaccine development, treatment, and diagnostics	0.2	A new and temporary EU unemployment reinsurance fund (SURE) will provide up to €100 billion in loans on favourable terms to governments in support of national unemployment and short-time work schemes. Loans will be guaranteed by the EU budget and EU Member States. The ESM will provide Pandemic Crisis Support to its members to finance crisis-related health spending of up to 2 percent of a requesting member's 2019 GDP. Should all 19 countries draw from the credit line, this would amount to around €240 billion	3.1	Newly established Business Credit Availability Program (BCAP) and Canada Emergency Business Account (CEBA) will provide CAD 65 bn of additional support for businesses in the form of loan guarantees and shared financing arrangements through the Business Development Bank of Canada and Export Development Canada, including in sectors such as oil and gas, air transportation, exportation, and tourism
China	4.1	Additional spending (Rs150 bn): Additional spending on health infrastructure, including COVID-19 testing facilities, personal protective equipment, isolation beds, ICU beds, and ventilators	0.1	Equity infusion for micro, small, and medium-sized enterprises (Rs 500 bn)	0.4	The national guarantee fund will work with banks providing loan guarantee services, planning to increase re-guarantee business by RMB 400 bn in 2020. Local government-backed guarantee/re-guarantee agencies are required to lower guarantee service costs to below 1 percent for SMEs

Table 10.1 (continued)

	A. Above-the line measures		B. Below the line measures		C. Contingent liabilities	
Country	**Tot**	**Add spend and forgone rev (health)**	**Tot size**	**Equity injections, asset purchases, loans, debt assumptions**	**% GDP**	**Guarantees (on loans, deposits etc.)**
EU	0.3	Additional spending (€8 bn): Support for streamlining and boosting health insurance (paid sick leave) for the sick or their caregivers, higher spending on health supplies, and bonuses for health workers	3.1	The authorities announced potential direct equity support in strategic companies (around €21 bn)	0.6	The EU Council agreed on a new guarantee fund of €25 billion for the European Investment Bank, which is estimated to provide bank financing of around €200 billion to firms, particularly SMEs, across the EU. The guarantee fund comes on top of an earlier support package of up to €40 billion announced in March, and both packages are likely to be funded by voluntary contributions from Member States
France	2.7	Additional spending (€23 bn): on hospital capacity, medical equipment, research, and information campaigns	1	An economic stabilization fund (WSF) of €600 bn is established with three components: (i) €100 bn for government equity investments in significantly affected companies; (ii) €100 bn loan to state development bank KfW for financing affected firms that do not have access to KfW's existing programs;	15.2	State guarantees for liquidity bank loans to companies and credit reinsurance schemes

Table 10.1 (continued)

	A. Above-the line measures		B. Below the line measures		C. Contingent liabilities	
Country	**Tot**	**Add spend and forgone rev (health)**	**Tot size**	**Equity injections, asset purchases, loans, debt assumptions**	**% GDP**	**Guarantees (on loans, deposits etc.)**
Germany	9.4	Additional spending (€6 bn): including on medical equipment and staff. Forgone revenue (€0.5 bn): zero VAT rate on targeted medical equipment	6.2	Equity injection to Alitalia (€3.3 bn)	25.3	€400 bn to provide additional state guarantees to non-financial corporations to alleviate liquidity bottlenecks and support refinancing. For the new expansion of the existing KfW programs, the guarantee framework of the federal government was increased by €357 billion. Total guarantees provided by state governments to be increased by €63 bn
India	1.2	Additional spending (IDR 76 tn): IDR 1 tn was initially allocated to cover various outlays, including personal protective equipment, enhanced surveillance at entry gates to Indonesia, hospital treatment, and hospital infrastructure. On March 31, 2020, the government announced a third larger fiscal package, including IDR 75 tn, to boost testing and treatment capability, including the acquisition of personal protective equipment, test kits, ventilators, and the upgrade of 132 referral hospitals to handle COVID-19 patients	0.2	Capital injection to SOEs (IDR 35.2 tn)	4.2	Full guarantees for a collateral-free lending program (Rs 3 tn). Liquidity provision and partial credit-guarantee schemes for non-bank financial companies (Rs 750 bn). Subordinate debt provision for the MSME sector (Rs 200 bn). Credit provisions are to be guaranteed by the government to farmers on concessional terms (Rs 3 tn), for street vendors, and for other miscellaneous measures (Rs 160 bn). The government is to provide a guarantee for credit under a new infrastructure fund for agriculture (Rs 1 tn) and for micro-food enterprises (Rs 100 bn). Numerous miscellaneous guarantee items (Rs 321 bn)

Table 10.1 (continued)

	A. Above-the line measures		B. Below the line measures		C. Contingent liabilities	
Country	**Tot**	**Add spend and forgone rev (health)**	**Tot size**	**Equity injections, asset purchases, loans, debt assumptions**	**% GDP**	**Guarantees (on loans, deposits etc.)**
Italy	3.5	Additional spending (JPY 4.1 tn): Production, procurement, and distribution of critical equipment such as masks and ventilators (JPY 0.6 tn). Transfers to local governments to be used for their health- and long-term care-related measures, including cash handouts to medical and long-term care practitioners (JPY 2.4 tn). Other health-related measures, e. g., vaccine development, etc. (JPY 1.1 tn)	0.2		33.8	Budget allocation of €35 bn to guarantee loans, with total guarantees estimated at about €530 bn. Guarantees cover up to 30 % of the value of SME loans subject to moratorium (€70 bn) and between 70 % and 90 % of the value of loans for all businesses (€200 bn). SME Guarantee Fund is enhanced from €40 bn to over €100 bn. A guarantee of €0.5 bn for the state development bank Cassa Deposit e Prestiti will provide liquidity support to banks financing medium to large enterprises. Co-insurance scheme to guarantee loans to exporters (€200 bn)
Japan	11.3	Additional spending: First supplementary budget (KRW 2.1 tn): Epidemic prevention and treatment, support for medical institutions and quarantined households. Third supplementary budget (KRW 2.5 tn): Expanding diagnostic and treatment facilities and smart medical centres; promoting treatment and vaccine development; promoting test-trace-treatment to be a global standard; and increasing official development aid of K COVID-19 response kits and tools	0		3	Guarantees on bonds/borrowing by the Development Bank of Japan and the Japan Finance Corporation (JPY 7.6 tn). Guarantees on external bonds issued by the Development Bank of Japan and Japan Bank for International Cooperation (JPY 1.1 tn). Guarantees on bonds/borrowings by other public financial institutions for their equity injection programs. (JPY2.5 tn). Expanded the guarantee cap on the capital injection scheme into banks (JPY 3 tn). Expanded the insurance capacity of the Nippon Export and Investment Insurance (JPY1.5 tn)

Table 10.1 (continued)

	A. Above-the line measures		B. Below the line measures		C. Contingent liabilities	
Country	**Tot**	**Add spend and forgone rev (health)**	**Tot size**	**Equity injections, asset purchases, loans, debt assumptions**	**% GDP**	**Guarantees (on loans, deposits etc.)**
Korea	3.1	Additional spending (€4.3 bn): Budget support from the contingency fund to the Ministry of Health (€1.4 bn); advance transfer to the regions for health services (€2.9 bn); additional funding for research related to the development of drugs and vaccines (€0.05 bn). An emergency management process for the procurement of all goods and services needed by the public sector to implement any measure to address the pandemic	0	Loans for the industrial sector to promote digital transformation and modernization	1.8	Special guarantee for SMEs and small merchants (KRW 5.5 tn), guarantee for small businesses (KRW 3 tn). Guarantees for SMEs and middle market enterprises with unfavourable credit history (KRW 7.9 tn). Korea Credit Guarantee Fund (KODIT) to support corporate bond issuance by primary collateralized obligations (KRW 11.7 tn). Guarantees/loans related to trade financing and overseas projects (KRW 6 tn)
New Zealand	21.3	Additional spending: Transfers to municipalities that have large health expenses due to the pandemic. Various other measures to strengthen the health care sector. Forgone revenue: The financial situation in the hospital trust is strengthened through increased appropriations and temporarily reduced employer tax	2.1	The reinstatement of a government fund that buys bonds issued by Norwegian companies to increase liquidity and access to capital in the Norwegian bond market, with a ceiling of NOK 50 bn	2.1	A loan guarantee scheme for firms with a turnover of between NZ$250 thousand and NZ$80 million per annum, with the Government carrying 80 % of the credit risk. The loans will be limited to NZ$500 thousand for a maximum of three years and are expected to be provided by the banks at competitive, transparent rates
Norway	5.6	Additional spending: to contain the outbreak, provided mainly to the Ministry of Health	1.7	S$20 billion in loan capital was set aside to help businesses and individuals facing cash flow challenges with loan obligations and insurance premium payments	4.5	Establish a government guarantee and loan scheme which includes loan guarantees for SMEs (NOK 50 bn) and a scheme for re-insurance of private credit insurance providers (NOK 20 bn)

Table 10.1 (continued)

Country	A. Above-the line measures		B. Below the line measures		C. Contingent liabilities	
	Tot	**Add spend and forgone rev (health)**	**Tot size**	**Equity injections, asset purchases, loans, debt assumptions**	**% GDP**	**Guarantees (on loans, deposits etc.)**
Russia	1.9	Additional spending (SAR 47 bn): Budget reallocation within the Ministry of Health budget [and other budget items] for emergency spending to fight COVID-19	0.1	Off-budget support provided by the National Development Funds (NDF): SAR 22 bn distributed as follows: (i) loan rescheduling/restructuring and different loan programs to SMEs: SAR13 bn. (ii) support to employment programs in the private sector: SAR 5 bn. (iii) social loans to families with low incomes: SAR4 bn	0.5	The federal government announced guarantees of up to RUB 500 bn on bank lending to firms, including RUB 220 bn in guarantees to VEB to guarantee bank credit to systematically important enterprises
Singa-pore	15.4	Additional spending: includes SEK 1 bn to the Public Health Agency to increase testing for COVID-19; 10,000 persons will be able to undergo training in health and social care in the fourth quarter if they study half-time, expanded adult vocational training focusing on health and social care. Funding of extraordinary costs associated with Covid-19 for municipalities and regions	4.2		0	

Table 10.1 (continued)

	A. Above-the line measures		B. Below the line measures		C. Contingent liabilities	
Country	**Tot**	**Add spend and forgone rev (health)**	**Tot size**	**Equity injections, asset purchases, loans, debt assumptions**	**% GDP**	**Guarantees (on loans, deposits etc.)**
Spain	3.4	Additional spending: Funding for the National Health Service, including expanding the number of hospital beds, medical staff and equipment. Forgone revenue: Waiver of VAT and customs duties on critical medical imports, including ventilators, testing kits, and protective gear	0	The government has put in place a £1 bn program to support firms driving innovation and development through grants and loans	9.7	Up to €100 bn government guarantees for firms and self-employed, covering both loans and commercial paper of medium-sized companies that participate in Spain's Alternative Fixed Income Market (MARF) Additional guarantees of up to €2 bn for exporters through the Spanish Export Insurance Credit Company Introduction of a special credit line for the tourism sector through the ICO (€400 mn) Guarantees for loan maturity extensions to farmers using the special 2017 drought credit lines A line of guarantees to provide financial assistance on housing expenses for vulnerable households (€1.2 bn) Additional loan guarantees for SMEs and self-employed through the Compañía Española de Reafianzamiento (€1 bn) An ICO line of guarantees for the automotive sector (€500 mn)

Table 10.1 (continued)

	A. Above-the line measures		B. Below the line measures		C. Contingent liabilities	
Country	**Tot**	**Add spend and forgone rev (health)**	**Tot size**	**Equity injections, asset purchases, loans, debt assumptions**	**% GDP**	**Guarantees (on loans, deposits etc.)**
Sweden	5.2	Additional spending: Includes army pharmacy (CHF2.55 billion), medication (CHF30 million) and health protection (CHF10 million)	0		4.8	Credit guarantees for Swedish airlines. Expansion of the Swedish Export Credit Agency's credit guarantee framework and the programs under the Swedish Export Credit Corporation
Switzer-land	4.8	Additional spending: Additional funding for the health sector. The Lk2.5 bn does not include additional allocation from the Reserve Fund (another Lk0.5 bn)	0		6.4	Guarantees for Covid-19 bridge loans (for firms with annual turnover up to CHF500 million) (CHF40 billion) Guarantees for startups (CHF0.1 billion) Guarantees for airlines (CHF1.275 billion)
Turkey	0.2	Additional spending (€2.1 bn): on medical equipment, tests, administration etc.	0.4		6.5	Credit Guarantee Fund (TBCG) guarantees to SMEs, large firms, and individuals

Table 10.1 (continued)

	A. Above-the line measures		B. Below the line measures		C. Contingent liabilities	
Country	**Tot**	**Add spend and forgone rev (health)**	**Tot size**	**Equity injections, asset purchases, loans, debt assumptions**	**% GDP**	**Guarantees (on loans, deposits etc.)**
UK	6.2	Additional spending ($304 bn) Coronavirus Preparedness and Response Supplemental Appropriations Act (March 6, 2020) approved with $6.8 bn for treatments, drugs, and public health measures. Families First Coronavirus Response Act (March 18, 2020) includes health provisions that increase outlays in Medicare, Medicaid, and other programs with federal matching by an estimated $59 bn. Coronavirus Aid, Relief, and Economic Security Act (March 27, 2020) approved $138 bn for additional health spending, which includes funding for hospitals ($100 bn), the Centers for Disease Control ($4.3 bn), and vaccine development ($27 bn); expansion of Medicare payments and provision of tax advantages for certain medical expense. Paycheck Protection Program and Health Care Enhancement Act (April 23, 2020) includes $75 bn for hospitals and $25 bn for testing	0	Coronavirus Aid, Relief, and Economic Security Act (March 27, 2020) includes $56 bn in loans for distressed businesses (e. g., passenger and cargo air carriers, postal service)	16.8	The Coronavirus Business Interruption Loan Scheme (CBILS) launched with the British Business Bank supports SMEs with access to loans of up to £5 mn and for up to 6 years. The government provides lenders with a guarantee of 80 % on each loan and covers the first 12 months of interest payments and any lender-levied fees. The Coronavirus Large Business Interruption Loan Scheme (CLBILS) provides a government guarantee of 80 percent to enable banks to make loans of up to 25 percent of companies' turnover, or up to £200 mn to firms with an annual turnover above £45 mn. Under the new Covid-19 Corporate Financing Facility (CCFF), the Bank of England will buy short term debt from larger companies. The combined size of the CBILS, CLBILS, and CCCF schemes is £330 bn. The Bounce Back Loan Scheme will help SMEs to borrow between £2K and £50K for up to 6 years, with the government guaranteeing 100 percent of the loan and SMEs not paying any fees or interest in the first 12 months. Trade credit Insurance for business-to-business transactions will receive up to £10 billion of government guarantees through the Trade Credit Reinsurance scheme

Table 10.1 (continued)

	A. Above-the line measures		B. Below the line measures		C. Contingent liabilities	
Country	**Tot**	**Add spend and forgone rev (health)**	**Tot size**	**Equity injections, asset purchases, loans, debt assumptions**	**% GDP**	**Guarantees (on loans, deposits etc.)**
US	12.3	Additional spending (AR $33 bn): Budget increase for Health Ministry to improve virus diagnostics, purchase hospital equipment, and build temporary emergency treatment centres. Budget transfers to specific hospitals. Four monthly bonuses of AR $5K for healthcare workers (AR $12 bn). Other (non-costed) support for the health sector includes infrastructure spending and discretionary transfers related to healthcare to provinces. Forgone revenue (AR $5.5 bn): Exemption from import duties and statistical tax for medical supplies (April–August). Tax aliquots on credits and debits in bank accounts and other operations of 2.5 and 5 percent for health service operations. 95 percent reduction in the aliquot of employer social security contributions for a period of 90 days for health workers (April–June)	0.3		2.3	Coronavirus Aid, Relief, and Economic Security Act (March 27, 2020) includes $454 bn to backstop section 13(3) Federal Reserve facilities that purchase corporate obligations in the primary or secondary market

Note: Sources: National authorities and IMF staff estimates. Data available from here.

Specifically, the COVID-19 pandemic has significantly impacted various sectors in a largely different manner. In the tourism sector, Baláž et al. (2024) provided a longitudinal analysis demonstrating the stability of risk preferences despite major life events during the pandemic. Their study highlights that while generic risk traits and tolerance for travel-related risks remained stable, situational risk preferences, especially among financially affected individuals became more tolerant over time. From a more physical standpoint, Kim and Liu (2022) investigated the role of social distancing measures and trust in the recovery of purchase intentions in the UK's tourism and hospitality sectors, finding that trust significantly mediated the relationship between social distancing and purchase intentions, with risk tolerance moderating this influence, underscoring the critical role of trust in the sector's post-pandemic recovery. Williams et al. (2022) analysed international travel intentions amid COVID-19, emphasising the impacts of risk tolerance, uncertainty, and ambiguity in decision-making, identifying that intolerance towards uncertainty and ambiguity leads individuals to defer travel plans completely. Aragon et al. (2024) explored how the pandemic influenced cab drivers' risk and time preferences in Lima, Peru, revealing an increase in risk tolerance and patience that varied with age, suggesting a broader behavioural shift potentially affecting socioeconomic outcomes through changes in economic preferences.

Huang et al. (2024) focused on individual investment behaviours during COVID-19 lockdowns in China, identifying a significant reduction in investments in risky mutual funds, attributed to decreased overall assets and increased allocation towards risk-free money market funds. This shift was more pronounced among individuals with lower risk tolerance, indicating a conservative adjustment in wealth strategies. Shachat et al. (2021) presented experimental evidence from China on the evolution of pro-social behaviour and risk attitudes during the early stages of the COVID-19 lockdown. They observe increased altruism and cooperation but decreased trust, with significant shifts in risk tolerance in different domains, suggesting that public health crises can profoundly alter economic preferences. Rafaï et al. (2023) examined compliance with COVID-19 prophylactic measures in France, comparing stated and elicited preferences. Their findings suggest that stated preferences, such as self-reported risk tolerance and trust are better predictors of compliance than experimentally elicited measures, highlighting the importance of perceived risk and trust in public health compliance. Caballero and Simsek (2021) provided a theoretical investigation into how endogenous risk intolerance and large-scale asset purchases (LSAPs) interact following a recessionary shock like COVID-19. They argue that LSAPs can stabilise asset prices and aggregate demand by transferring unwanted risk to the government's balance sheet, demonstrating the significant role of monetary policy in mitigating risk intolerance during economic downturns. Heo et al. (2021b) documented the negative impact of the pandemic on financial risk tolerance among a broad sample of financial decision-makers, noting a general shift away from risk-taking. Their findings highlight the pandemic's role in altering financial attitudes and underscore the need for adaptive risk management strategies, while Heo et al. (2021a) assessed changes in financial risk tolerance during the initial surge of COVID-19 cases in the US. They report a significant reduction in risk tolerance, particularly among younger individuals, indicating that the pandemic disproportionately impacted this demographic's willingness to take financial risks.

Very few situations exemplified changing attitudes to investor risk-taking during the pandemic, the growth of WallStreetBets, which initially began in 2012 as a niche subreddit focused on high-risk trading strategies. Initially attracting a small community, the forum's user base exploded during the COVID-19 pandemic, growing from 1 million in early 2020 to over 10 million by mid-2021 (Corbet et al., 2022e). The pandemic's economic uncertainty and lockdowns led to increased retail investor participation, in some cases driven by the provision of stimulus checks and increased free time due to shifting employment arrangements. WSB became a hub for meme stocks, where users shared investment strategies presented with humorous intentions, irreverence, and a touch of nihilism, epitomised by phrases like "YOLO" (you only live once). The COVID-19 pandemic and subsequent government stimulus measures fostered risk-taking among retail investors, particularly on platforms like Reddit and WallStreetBets. Stimulus checks provided many with disposable income, and lockdowns offered the time to engage in trading activities. Economic policies, often referred to as "helicopter money" increase liquidity in the market, leading to higher trading volumes and volatility. Many inexperienced investors turned to social media for guidance, often getting swept up in the collective enthusiasm and herd behaviour seen in forums like WSB. The combination of accessible trading platforms like Robinhood, zero-commission trades, and the sharp growth in retail investor participation created an environment conducive to speculative trading. WallStreetBets capitalised on this by orchestrating massive rallies in stocks like GameStop and AMC, driven by the collective buying power of its users. These events often resulted in significant price distortions and highlighted the influence of social media on financial markets.

In response to the pandemic, companies have accelerated their digital transformation initiatives and adopted remote working policies (Almeida et al., 2020; Grimm, 2021; Hiziroglu et al., 2024). Evidence of such development is presented in Table 10.2. The necessity to continue operations amidst lockdowns and social distancing measures has pushed businesses to invest heavily in digital technologies (Amankwah-Amoah et al., 2021; Guimarães et al., 2022; Mammaev et al., 2023; Dyba and Di Maria, 2024), with evidence of such dynamic shifts presented in Table 10.3 through elevated IT risks and the increased use of AI. This shift has not only ensured business continuity but has also opened new avenues for innovation and efficiency. The healthcare sector, for instance, has rapidly integrated telemedicine and digital health solutions to meet the surge in demand for remote consultations and services (Cui et al., 2023). Similarly, the manufacturing sector has leveraged automation and digital tools to streamline operations and reduce dependency on physical presence.

The impact of the pandemic on risk appetite varies significantly across industries. The healthcare sector has exhibited a higher risk appetite compared to others, driven by the urgent need to address the health crisis and the opportunities arising from increased

Table 10.2: Remote working dynamics, United States % of population teleworking.

Month	Total	Men	Women
10/2022	17.9	16.5	19.4
11/2022	18.5	17.2	20.1
12/2022	19.0	17.8	20.3
01/2023	19.4	18.2	20.8
02/2023	20.0	18.7	21.3
03/2023	19.5	17.9	21.4
04/2023	18.5	16.7	20.6
05/2023	18.9	17.3	20.8
06/2023	19.0	17.2	21.0
07/2023	19.9	17.8	22.5
08/2023	19.5	17.7	21.6
09/2023	19.8	18.0	21.8
10/2023	19.8	18.1	21.7
11/2023	20.5	18.8	22.4
12/2023	21.9	19.8	24.3
01/2024	22.9	21.3	24.8
02/2024	22.7	21.1	24.5
03/2024	23.0	20.9	25.3
04/2024	21.5	19.5	23.8
05/2024	21.7	19.9	23.9
06/2024	22.3	20.1	25.0
07/2024	23.0	20.2	26.3

Note: Data obtained from the U. S. Bureau of Labor Statistics, Labor Force Statistics from the Current Population Survey. BLS added new questions to the Current Population Survey (CPS) starting in October 2022 that focus on telework or work at home for pay. These questions ask whether people had teleworked or worked at home for pay in the survey reference week and the number of hours teleworked. In our analyses, telework or work at home for pay is frequently referred to simply as "telework." From October 2022 to November 2023, questions asked whether people had teleworked in February 2020, before the COVID-19 pandemic started. People who telework are those who indicated they teleworked or worked at home for pay at any time during the survey reference week. The telework question is asked about people who were employed and at work in the survey reference week, which is generally the calendar week that contains the 12th day of the month. It is not asked about people who were employed but not at work due to vacation, illness, or other reasons. The term "at work" does not refer to where people work, but rather that people performed some work for pay or profit during the survey reference week. The telework rate is the number of people who telework or work at home for pay as a percentage of those who were employed and at work during the survey reference week. The term "at work" does not refer to where people work, but rather that people performed some work for pay or profit during the survey reference week.

demand for medical services and products. In contrast, the automotive, aerospace, and defence sectors have shown a more conservative approach. These industries, heavily reliant on global supply chains and facing substantial disruptions, have prioritised risk mitigation and operational stability (Ewertowski and Butlewski, 2022; Fatani et al., 2024; Martinez et al., 2024). For example, automotive companies have focused on enhancing supply chain resilience by diversifying suppliers and increasing inventory levels to safe-

Table 10.3: International ICT dynamics.

	Businesses experiencing ICT incidents (security breaches)		Businesses having performed big data analysis only with own employees		Businesses that offered positions for ICT specialist		Businesses using artificial intelligence (AI)
	2012–2019	2020–2023	2012–2019	2020–2023	2012–2019	2020–2023	2020–2023
Australia	18.78	20.76	5.49	15.49	n/a	10.22	3.32
Austria	11.68	15.39	n/a	n/a	8.54	11.33	7.81
Belgium	22.38	23.24	21.95	37.50	12.87	15.39	9.86
Canada	17.00	18.10	n/a	n/a	20.10	5.60	4.70
Colombia	11.94	9.92	4.33	5.34	n/a	n/a	7.18
Czechia	20.93	29.33	7.48	17.57	6.68	7.45	5.29
Denmark	10.09	26.45	14.42	39.50	12.49	19.12	16.12
Estonia	8.31	25.83	9.76	18.90	7.91	8.30	4.15
Finland	17.99	43.79	14.11	31.69	10.49	12.93	13.48
France	15.49	25.63	13.20	28.70	8.17	9.72	5.79
Germany	11.18	26.19	16.57	31.86	8.92	11.03	9.24
Greece	6.61	17.80	10.10	22.78	6.58	9.99	3.30
Hungary	15.47	13.41	5.19	34.22	10.26	8.25	3.24
Ireland	17.58	14.96	19.60	29.74	10.11	9.55	12.05
Italy	10.08	15.67	7.06	24.95	5.27	4.88	6.22
Japan	45.49	56.30	n/a	n/a	n/a	n/a	3.52
Korea	4.45	2.27	2.70	n/a	n/a	n/a	11.11
Latvia	12.21	18.99	6.80	32.94	4.97	5.07	3.46
Lithuania	15.99	16.00	9.82	36.55	8.38	8.40	5.43
Luxembourg	17.36	16.08	12.13	26.52	12.05	11.79	10.76
Netherlands	11.51	30.11	20.52	41.22	10.55	15.24	10.27
New Zealand	11.96	7.10	n/a	n/a	n/a	n/a	9.02
Norway	10.64	16.80	12.91	9.52	6.86	8.09	8.33
Poland	12.85	29.70	5.94	18.00	5.06	5.10	3.56

Table 10.3 (continued)

	Businesses experiencing ICT incidents (security breaches)		Businesses having performed big data analysis only with own employees		Businesses that offered positions for ICT specialist		Businesses using artificial intelligence (AI)
	2012–2019	**2020–2023**	**2012–2019**	**2020–2023**	**2012–2019**	**2020–2023**	**2020–2023**
Portugal	8.50	11.47	10.21	28.17	6.39	6.17	7.56
Slovak Republic	14.60	12.31	6.39	27.39	5.61	5.41	6.03
Slovenia	13.60	14.89	8.12	15.85	6.82	8.76	8.42
Spain	12.44	16.72	6.91	32.18	11.73	13.45	8.09
Sweden	34.86	21.11	9.15	31.19	9.11	11.99	9.08
Switzerland	24.16	10.45	34.30	26.69	n/a	n/a	9.56
Türkiye	n/a	28.51	8.76	12.33	5.28	6.87	4.59
United Kingdom	5.72	n/a	19.51	n/a	10.95	n/a	4.11
United States	n/a	n/a	n/a	n/a	n/a	n/a	5.65
European Union (27 countries)	13.30	22.16	9.35	28.22	8.09	9.49	7.22

Note: Data obtained from the OECD, where ICT investment is defined as the acquisition of equipment and computer software that is used in production for more than one year. ICT has three components: information technology equipment (computers and related hardware); communications equipment; and software. Software includes the acquisition of pre-packaged software, customised software, and software developed in-house. This indicator is measured as a percentage of total non-residential gross fixed capital formation. Based on the 2nd revision of the OECD Model Survey on ICT Access and Usage by Businesses.

guard against future disruptions. The healthcare industry's relatively higher risk tolerance can be attributed to the critical nature of its services and the immediate necessity to respond to the pandemic. Investment in innovative solutions and rapid scaling of operations were essential to meet the unprecedented demand. Conversely, the automotive, aerospace, and defence sectors, facing plummeting demand and significant operational challenges, have adopted a more cautious stance. These industries have concentrated on preserving capital, reassessing investment plans, and ensuring continuity of essential operations.

10.2 Changes in Risk Assessment Practices

The COVID-19 pandemic has underscored the critical need for robust supply chain resilience, leading firms to implement significant changes in their risk assessment practices (Moosavi et al., 2022). One of the primary adjustments has been the increase in inventories to buffer against potential disruptions, evidence of which is presented in Figure 10.1. This strategic move aims to create a safety net that allows businesses to continue operations even when supply chains face unexpected hurdles. By maintaining higher levels of essential materials and products, companies can mitigate the impact of delays or shortages, thereby ensuring a more stable supply chain.

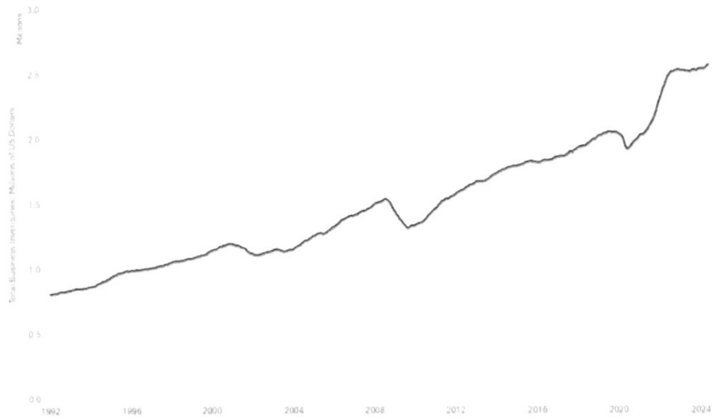

Figure 10.1: Total business inventories, United States.
Note: Millions of Dollars, Seasonally Adjusted. U.S. Census Bureau, Total Business Inventories [BUSINV], retrieved from FRED, Federal Reserve Bank of St. Louis; https://fred.stlouisfed.org/series/BUSINV, August 22, 2024.

Another key strategy has been the diversification of supply bases. Firms have recognised the risks associated with over-reliance on single suppliers or specific geographic regions, which can become bottlenecks during crises. Diversifying suppliers across different regions reduces dependency on any single source and spreads risk more evenly.

This approach enhances supply chain resilience and allows firms to leverage competitive advantages from different suppliers, such as cost benefits or specialised capabilities. Regionalisation of supply chains has emerged as a prominent strategy to bolster resilience further. Companies can reduce the logistical complexities and vulnerabilities associated with long-distance supply chains by localising production and sourcing closer to end markets. This shift is particularly evident in sectors where timely delivery and local market responsiveness are crucial. Regionalisation not only shortens lead times but also reduces exposure to international trade disruptions, tariffs, and political uncertainties. In addition to these supply chain strategies, firms have placed a heightened emphasis on liquidity and cash reserves.[17]

The COVID-19 pandemic has profoundly challenged traditional credit risk models, necessitating their recalibration to incorporate new macroeconomic scenarios and data sources effectively. Existing models, primarily built on historical data and designed to predict gradual economic shifts, struggled to adapt to the sudden halt in economic activity induced by the pandemic. The unique nature of the COVID-19 crisis rendered many traditional assumptions and predictive relationships inoperative. As a result, risk modelling teams were forced to reconsider how historical data could be relevant to forward-looking credit analysis in this new context. Government stimulus programs and payment holidays have generated further distorting effects. These interventions, while necessary to mitigate immediate financial distress, have masked the true extent of credit risk by temporarily suppressing indicators such as days-past-due metrics. Consequently, credit models that rely heavily on these indicators to forecast future losses have produced skewed results. The short-term relief provided by these measures has delayed the manifestation of financial distress, making it challenging for existing models to predict long-term creditworthiness accurately. Additionally, the varied responses to the pandemic across different geographies and sectors have introduced significant heterogeneity in risk assessment. The pandemic's impact on consumer behaviour and economic activity has varied widely, influenced by factors such as local infection rates, government policies, and sector-specific dynamics. This variability necessitates more granular and adaptive modelling approaches that can account for the asynchronous recovery patterns and sector-specific risks.

The COVID-19 pandemic has significantly accelerated the adoption of digital technologies, with many businesses transitioning to remote work environments almost overnight. This rapid shift has expanded the digital footprint of organisations, exposing

17 The economic uncertainty brought about by the pandemic has highlighted the importance of maintaining financial flexibility. By increasing cash reserves, businesses can better weather financial shocks, invest in necessary adaptations, and seize opportunities that may arise in a volatile market environment. Overall, these changes in risk assessment practices reflect an approach to building resilience against future disruptions. The combination of increased inventories, diversified supply bases, regionalisation of supply chains, and a focus on liquidity and cash reserves represents a strategic recalibration to ensure continuity and stability in an unpredictable global environment.

them to heightened cybersecurity risks. The increased dependency on digital platforms and online communication tools has made systems more vulnerable to cyberattacks. Phishing, ransomware, and other forms of cyber threats have surged as malicious actors exploit the expanded attack surface created by remote working arrangements and increased online activity (Muthuppalaniappan and Stevenson, 2021; Lallie et al., 2021; Corbet et al., 2022e). Organisations have had to respond swiftly by bolstering their cybersecurity measures to protect sensitive data and ensure business continuity. The implementation of robust data protection strategies has become paramount in this hybrid work environment. Companies invest in advanced security technologies, such as multi-factor authentication, encryption, and endpoint security solutions, to safeguard their digital assets. Additionally, there is a greater emphasis on employee training and awareness programs to mitigate human error, which remains a significant vulnerability in cybersecurity defence.

The complexity of managing cybersecurity risks in a hybrid work model also necessitates a robust approach to risk assessment. Regular security audits, penetration testing, and continuous monitoring of network activities are critical to identifying and addressing potential threats. Organisations are increasingly adopting zero-trust architectures, which operate on the principle that no entity, whether inside or outside the network, should be trusted by default. This approach helps to ensure that access to resources is continuously verified and limited to only those with a legitimate need. Further, regulatory development surrounding data protection has become more stringent globally, compelling businesses to comply with diverse legal requirements across different jurisdictions. In the European Union, the General Data Protection Regulation (GDPR) has set a high standard for data protection, mandating strict protocols for handling personal data and imposing hefty fines for non-compliance. Similarly, the California Consumer Privacy Act (CCPA) in the United States has introduced rigorous privacy requirements, granting consumers greater control over their personal information and ensuring transparency in data practices. Beyond these well-known regulations, numerous countries have enacted or are implementing their own data protection laws. For instance, Brazil's Lei Geral de Proteção de Dados (LGPD) mirrors many aspects of the GDPR, requiring organisations to adopt strong data governance practices and protect data subjects' rights. In Asia, countries like Japan and South Korea have strengthened their data protection frameworks with the Act on the Protection of Personal Information (APPI) and the Personal Information Protection Act (PIPA), respectively. These regulations emphasise the importance of data security and enforce significant penalties for breaches. In addition to national regulations, regional frameworks are also emerging. For example, the African Union has introduced the Malabo Convention, which sets out data protection and cybersecurity principles for member states. Similarly, the Association of Southeast Asian Nations (ASEAN) has developed the ASEAN Framework on Personal Data Protection, aiming to harmonise data protection standards across the region.

Compliance with these varied regulations poses a complex challenge for multinational corporations. Each regulatory framework has its own specific requirements, timelines, and enforcement mechanisms. Businesses must overcome these complexities to avoid severe penalties and reputational damage. This often involves conducting thorough data audits, implementing robust data management systems, and continuously monitoring compliance across different jurisdictions. The global nature of data flows further complicates compliance efforts. Organisations must ensure that data transfers between countries meet the stringent requirements set by regulations like the GDPR, which restricts data transfers to countries without adequate data protection standards (Li et al., 2019). Mechanisms such as Standard Contractual Clauses (SCCs) and the EU-US Privacy Shield (recently invalidated and replaced by the EU-US Data Privacy Framework) are critical for maintaining compliance in international data transfers.

Broadly, the global regulation of data protection has become increasingly stringent and complex, requiring businesses to stay vigilant and proactive in their compliance efforts. Failure to adhere to these diverse regulations can result in severe penalties, highlighting the critical need for adaptive data protection strategies. The shift to a more digitally dependent and remote working environment due to the COVID-19 pandemic has necessitated significant enhancements in cybersecurity measures.

10.3 Sector-Specific Risk Management Adjustments

The COVID-19 pandemic has reshaped global health systems and profoundly impacted financial institutions and supply chain management. Banks, in particular, have faced unprecedented challenges in assessing credit risk amidst economic turbulence and government interventions. Simultaneously, businesses have been compelled to revolutionise their supply chain strategies to maintain operational resilience. More specifically, banks have had to adapt their credit risk models significantly in response to the new economic realities imposed by COVID-19 and the various government interventions that followed. Traditional credit risk models, which relied heavily on historical data and presumed a gradual economic impact, became inadequate almost overnight. The sudden halt in supply chains and demand across various sectors meant that the assumptions underpinning these models no longer existed. As a result, banks had to quickly recalibrate their models to account for unprecedented levels of uncertainty and economic disruption. One major challenge financial institutions faced was the distortion of typical credit risk indicators due to widespread government stimulus programs and payment holidays. While necessary to alleviate immediate financial distress for individuals and businesses, these interventions obscured traditional delinquency indicators such as days-past-due metrics. Consequently, banks had to look beyond these conventional measures to assess credit risk accurately. This has led to an enhanced focus on early warning indicators that leverage alternative data sources, providing a more real-time and nuanced view of borrower health. Integrating alternative data sources has become critical to modern credit risk assessment. Transactional data, for instance, offers valuable insights into the financial behaviour of both retail and non-retail borrowers. Banks can gauge credit quality and detect early signs of financial distress by analysing the nature and frequency of incoming and outgoing payments. This approach is particularly useful in monitoring the performance of small and medium-sized enterprises (SMEs) during the recovery period, enabling targeted interventions where necessary.

Furthermore, banks are increasingly utilising advanced analytics and machine learning to enhance their risk assessment capabilities. These technologies allow for processing vast amounts of data, including non-traditional sources such as e-commerce activity, geolocation data, and electronic tax filings. By integrating these diverse datasets, banks can develop more robust predictive models that better account for the dynamic and interconnected nature of the current economic environment. The shift towards these sophisticated analytical tools reflects a broader trend within the financial services sector towards greater reliance on data-driven decision-making. Banks have also had to invest in their technological infrastructure to adapt to these new methodologies. High-frequency big data platforms have become essential to managing and analysing the influx of alternative data. Institutions previously hesitant to invest in such technology have been compelled to accelerate their spending to remain competitive. This investment supports the immediate need for improved risk assessment and positions banks to better handle future crises by providing a more agile and responsive framework for credit risk management.

Further, the COVID-19 pandemic has necessitated a significant shift in how companies manage their supply chains, prompting the adoption of advanced analytics and increased digitisation to enhance visibility and planning (Kohl et al., 2022; Khan et al., 2023; Sharma and Rai, 2024). As businesses grappled with unprecedented disruptions, the need for real-time data and predictive analytics became paramount. These tools have enabled companies to monitor supply chain performance closely, predict potential disruptions, and respond swiftly to changing conditions. Advanced analytics facilitate more accurate demand forecasting, inventory management, and logistics planning, which is crucial for maintaining operational continuity during volatile periods. Integrating these technologies has improved supply chain resilience and fostered a culture of proactive risk management. Simultaneously, the pandemic exposed a critical talent gap in digital skills within supply chain management (Chae et al., 2024). The demand for professionals with expertise in these areas surged as the reliance on digital tools and data analytics increased. Companies have had to invest in re-skilling and up-skilling their existing workforce to bridge this gap. Training programs focused on digital literacy, data analysis, and advanced supply chain technologies have become essential components of corporate strategies. In addition to internal training initiatives, partnerships with educational institutions and industry-specific certifications have emerged as effective methods to develop the necessary skill sets. The emphasis on digital skills is crucial for immediate pandemic response, long-term strategic planning, and competitive advantage in a digital economy. These strategic adjustments in supply chain management reflect a broader recognition of the interconnected nature of modern business risks.

10.4 Compound Risks and Financial Resilience

The COVID-19 pandemic has had a complex and often detrimental impact on global green initiatives and environmental efforts while also revealing the interconnectedness of various risks and the need for strengthened risk management strategies. As governments and organisations diverted resources and attention to managing the public health crisis, many sustainability projects and climate action plans were delayed or deprioritised. Economic pressures led some countries to relax environmental regulations to stimulate industrial recovery, potentially reversing emissions reduction and conservation progress. The pandemic also disrupted supply chains and funding for renewable energy projects, slowing some regions' transition from fossil fuels.

The concept of a compound risk multiplier has emerged, quantifying how the combined effects of different risks can produce a total impact that exceeds the sum of individual shocks. This is particularly relevant in the pandemic, where health crises have cascaded into broader economic and financial shocks, amplifying the overall impact. The simultaneous disruptions in multiple sectors, these have led to significant declines in GDP across many countries, as illustrated in Figure 10.2 of the provided document, exacerbated by concurrent events such as war and geopolitical instability (Ahonen et al., 2022; Conlon et al., 2022; Corbet et al., 2020c, 2022a,b,d; Meehan and Corbet, 2023; Kyriazis et al., 2023; Hu et al., 2024; Lang et al., 2024). These economic disruptions have not only strained public health systems but also disrupted supply chains, reduced workforce productivity, and increased the financial burden on governments through emergency response and recovery expenditures (Xu et al., 2020; Fu et al., 2022; Gamal et al., 2022; Zaerpour et al., 2023; Ivanov, 2024).

As a result, other environmental threats, such as deforestation, plastic pollution, and biodiversity loss, received less attention and resources, potentially exacerbating these issues. The focus on pandemic response meant governments faced reduced revenues from diminished economic activity while simultaneously experiencing increased expenditure demands. This dual financial strain underscores the importance of robust financial resilience frameworks that can accommodate the unpredictability and severity of compound shocks.

While the pandemic did lead to temporary reductions in global emissions due to decreased economic activity, these gains were largely offset as economies reopened, highlighting the need for more systemic changes to achieve lasting environmental progress. The situation has triggered a reevaluation of risk management strategies, emphasising the necessity to account for compound risks that span health, climate, and economic domains.

Moving forward, integrating compound risks into financial frameworks is crucial for enhancing overall financial resilience. This includes the development of climate-resilient financial instruments and policies, such as green bonds and climate risk insurance, designed to provide financial protection against climate-related risks that often intersect with other types of risks, like those posed by pandemics (Monasterolo, 2020;

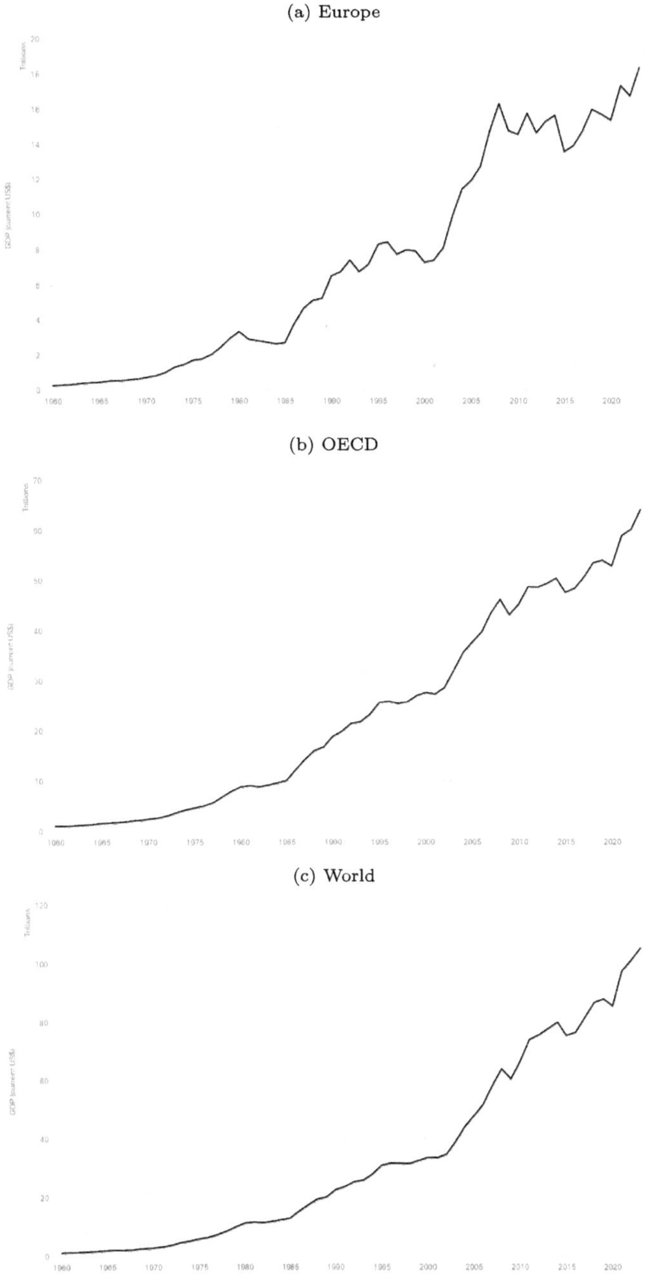

Figure 10.2: GDP (current US$).
Note: GDP (current US$), World Bank national accounts data, and OECD National Accounts data files.

Bhattacharyay, 2021; Mhlanga, 2022). By investing in, and promoting these instruments, businesses and governments can enhance their capacity to absorb shocks and maintain financial stability in the face of compound risks while supporting the continuation and advancement of green initiatives in a post-pandemic world.

10.5 Concluding Comments

The COVID-19 pandemic has significantly altered risk management for firms in multiple sectors. The importance of adaptive and resilient risk management strategies is a key lesson learnt from the global crisis. Traditional risk management models, which consider risks in isolation, have been inadequate during the unprecedented disruptions of the pandemic. Firms must adopt advanced models that include diverse variables, such as forward-looking indicators and scenario analyses, to forecast and address potential impacts on financial stability. Developing and adopting innovative financial instruments and policies is essential for enhancing resilience in this integration. Instruments like green bonds and climate risk insurance offer financial protection against various risks, including those from pandemics. Investing in and promoting these instruments enables firms to absorb shocks better and sustain financial stability. Policies promoting sustainable practices and resilience are essential for mitigating long-term impacts.

Emphasising liquidity and cash reserves is now fundamental to financial resilience strategies. The liquidity crises during the pandemic highlighted the necessity of sufficient liquidity for firms to manage financial stress. Strong cash reserves allow organisations to maintain operations and fulfil obligations without resorting to drastic actions like asset liquidation or excessive borrowing. This emphasis on liquidity guarantees that firms possess the resources needed to tackle major financial issues.

Effective risk management necessitates ongoing monitoring and reassessment of strategies. This involves routine stress testing and scenario analysis to assess the potential effects of different risk scenarios. Adopting a proactive approach to risk management enhances firms' resilience and prepares them for global crises. The COVID-19 pandemic has expedited business digital transformation. The rapid shift to remote work highlights the essential role of digital technologies in ensuring business continuity. This shift has introduced numerous cybersecurity risks, increasing the necessity for strong data protection measures and effective cybersecurity frameworks. Organisations must continue to invest in advanced security technologies like multi-factor authentication, encryption, and secure cloud services to protect their digital assets. Alongside technological upgrades, enhanced cybersecurity training programs for employees are essential. Human error is a major vulnerability in cybersecurity, necessitating firms to foster a culture of security awareness. Ongoing training and updates on cybersecurity best practices can reduce risks related to phishing, ransomware, and other cyber threats. In a hybrid work environment, keeping employees informed and alert can greatly minimise security breach risks.

Adopting zero-trust architectures based on continuous verification and least-privilege access is increasingly important. This method ensures continuous verification of resource access, restricting it to those with legitimate needs. Implementing these frameworks effectively safeguards against unauthorised access and data breaches, ensuring the integrity of the organisation's digital infrastructure. The pandemic-driven digital transformation has underscored the significance of regulatory compliance in data protection. Firms must manage a complex landscape of global data protection regulations, including GDPR in the EU and CCPA in the US. Adhering to these regulations is essential to prevent significant fines and foster trust with customers and stakeholders by showing a commitment to data protection.

The pandemic underscored the significance of effective supply chain management. Global supply chain disruptions have led firms to boost inventories, diversify suppliers, and regionalise production to improve resilience. These strategies mitigate supply chain disruptions and ensure a stable flow of essential materials and products, enhancing operational stability. The crisis has highlighted the necessity for stricter corporate governance practices. Firms have improved risk management frameworks by integrating more rigorous scenario planning and stress testing to anticipate potential future shocks better. These measures clarify the firm's risk exposure and aid in developing effective contingency plans, ensuring resilience in a volatile environment.

11 How Has COVID-19 Shifted Our Understanding of Traditional Finance?

The COVID-19 pandemic has fundamentally shifted our understanding of traditional finance and financial theory by exposing the limitations of several established financial frameworks. Further, we must consider how finance will be affected by the accelerating adoption of digital financial solutions and social media. Specifically, this chapter focuses on how the COVID-19 pandemic challenged conventional, traditional financial systems, generating exceptional geopolitical and sectoral uncertainty and episodes of the most exceptional market volatility experienced in recent times, which necessitated unprecedented fiscal and monetary responses and the rapid integration of fintech innovations. Specifically, we discuss the shift towards more resilient, adaptable, and inclusive financial systems and the long-term implications of these changes, suggesting that the lessons learned during the pandemic will shape the future of finance, emphasising the need for agility, digital transformation, and a re-evaluation of financial stability mechanisms.

11.1 Introduction

The onset of COVID-19 and the pandemic's rapid contagion led to widespread lockdowns and social distancing measures, bringing economic activities to a near halt across various sectors. Although essential to curb the virus's transmission, these measures triggered a sharp decline in consumer demand and industrial production, leading to severe contractions in global GDP. The sudden decline in economic activity caused significant disruptions in supply chains, both domestically and internationally, exacerbating the economic fallout. Financial markets reacted swiftly to the pandemic's escalation, with global stock indices plummeting and volatility indices, such as the VIX as presented in Figure 11.1 (Baker et al., 2020; Conlon et al., 2020, 2024i; Corbet et al., 2021b, 2022a,c, 2024). Investors sought financial safety through elevated cash reserves and the purchasing of government bonds, causing substantial capital outflows from emerging markets and increasing pressures on vulnerable economies and sectors therein. The abrupt repricing of assets and heightened market uncertainty underscored the interconnectedness of global financial markets and highlighted the fragility of financial systems when faced with such acute economic shocks. Nasir et al. (2023), Bernstein et al. (2024), Conlon et al. (2024b) was compounded by a dramatic increase in corporate and household debt defaults as income collapsed. Businesses, particularly small and medium-sized enterprises (SMEs), faced liquidity crises, struggling to meet operational costs due to diminished revenues. Simultaneously, households experienced unprecedented financial stress, with rising unemployment and reduced income levels. The financial strain on businesses and house-

https://doi.org/10.1515/9783111707990-011

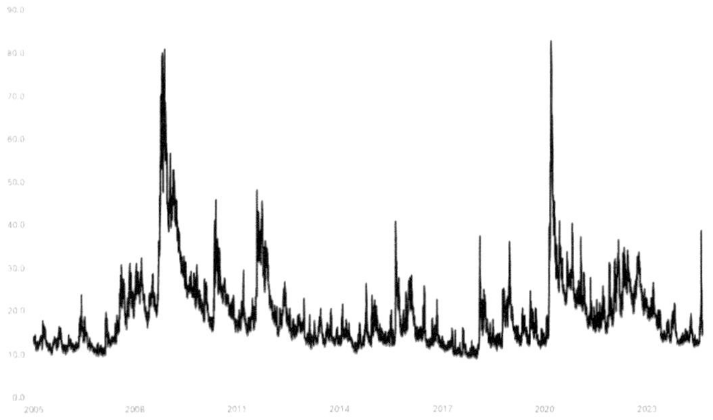

Figure 11.1: The volatility index (VIX).
Note: The VIX Index, commonly known as the "fear gauge," is a real-time market index representing the market's expectations for volatility over the coming 30 days. It was introduced by the Chicago Board Options Exchange (CBOE) in 1993 and is derived from the prices of S&P 500 index options. By measuring the implied volatility of these options, the VIX provides insight into the level of uncertainty or risk perceived by investors in the stock market. A higher VIX value typically indicates increased investor anxiety and the anticipation of market turbulence, while a lower VIX suggests relative calm and stability. The VIX is widely used by traders, analysts, and portfolio managers as a tool for risk management and market timing and as a component in constructing derivative products. Its role as a leading indicator of market sentiment makes it a key barometer in financial markets globally.

holds further strained banking systems as non-performing loans surged, as presented in Figure 11.2, threatening financial stability.

Governments introduced substantial fiscal stimulus packages, encompassing direct financial support to individuals and businesses, loan guarantees, and tax reliefs to mitigate the immediate economic impact and foster recovery. The pandemic also exposed significant weaknesses in global supply chains and the over-reliance on specific regions for critical goods and services. The disruption in manufacturing and logistics highlighted the need for greater diversification and resilience in supply chains to withstand future shocks. Furthermore, the crisis presented evidence of the importance of robust public health infrastructure and the need for substantial investments in healthcare systems to manage such pandemics effectively. The COVID-19 pandemic has broadly redefined global finance, revealing vulnerabilities and areas necessitating substantial and direct reform. The rapid policy responses provided crucial lessons on the importance of financial system resilience and the role of coordinated global actions in mitigating the impacts of such unprecedented shocks. The following chapter discusses such themes in more detail, exploring the specific impacts on various financial sectors and the critical lessons learned from the pandemic.

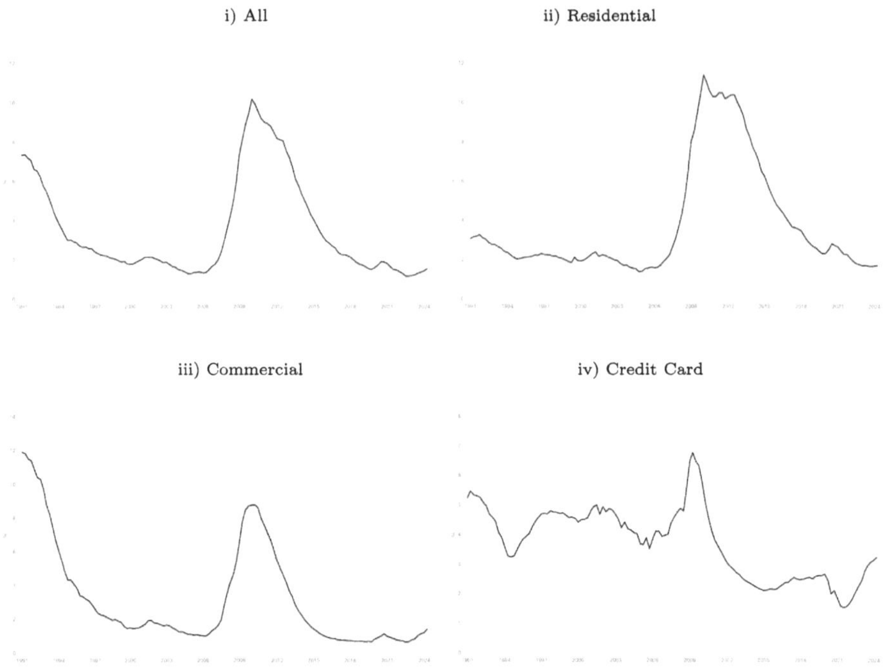

Figure 11.2: Charge-off and delinquency rates on loans and leases at commercial banks.
Note: Charge-offs, the value of loans removed from the books and charged against loss reserves, are measured net of recoveries as a percentage of average loans and annualised. Delinquent loans are those past due thirty days or more, still accruing interest, and those in non-accrual status. They are measured as a percentage of end-of-period loans. Banks are insured U. S.-chartered commercial banks. Size, where used, is measured by consolidated assets adjusted for mergers; where used, "other" banks are those smaller than the 100 largest. Data obtained from the following source.

11.2 COVID-19: The Initial Economic Shock and Broad Financial Stability

The onset of the COVID-19 pandemic triggered an unprecedented economic shock, causing extreme volatility in global financial markets. Major indices like the S&P 500 and FTSE 100 experienced the steepest falls since the 2008 financial crisis as presented in Figure 11.3. Financial systems, including banks, credit unions, insurance companies, and asset managers, played a crucial role in mitigating the economic shock by channelling savings into investments and facilitating credit flows. Central banks worldwide implemented various interventions to stabilise financial markets and support the broader economy. For example, the European Central Bank (ECB) launched the Pandemic Emergency Purchase Programme (PEPP), which involved significant asset purchases to ensure liquidity and support credit flows (Lane, 2020). Regulatory measures were also key. Central banks and financial regulators provided capital relief to banks, allowing them to use capital buffers to absorb losses and support lending. The reduction of the counter-

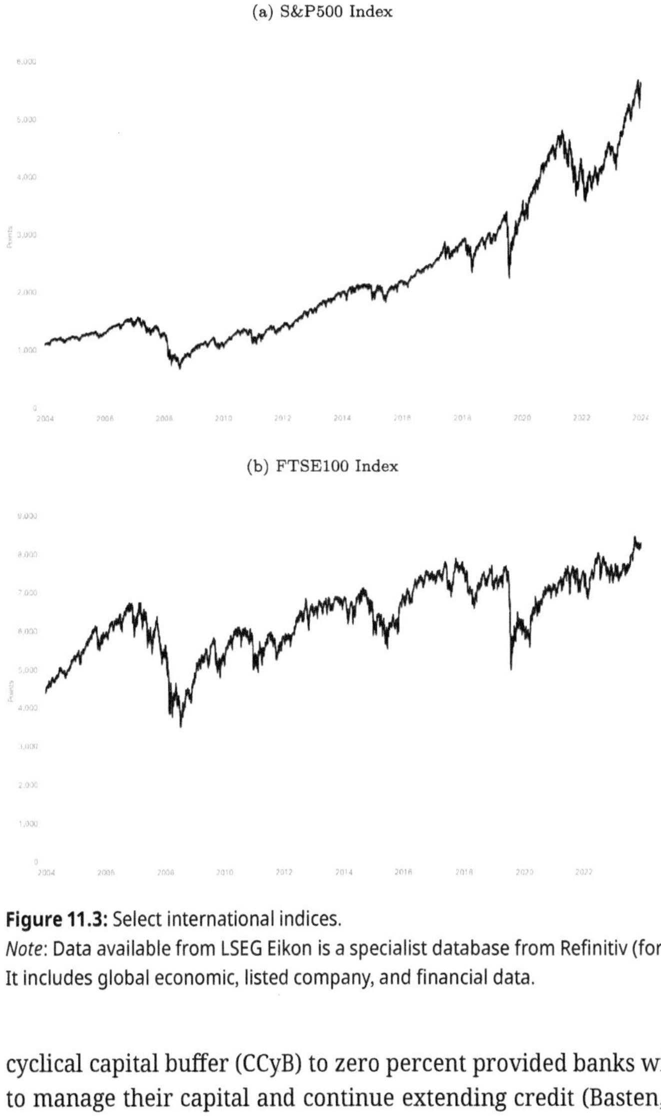

Figure 11.3: Select international indices.
Note: Data available from LSEG Eikon is a specialist database from Refinitiv (formerly Thomson Reuters). It includes global economic, listed company, and financial data.

cyclical capital buffer (CCyB) to zero percent provided banks with additional flexibility to manage their capital and continue extending credit (Basten, 2020; Benbouzid et al., 2022).

The immediate response from central banks and regulatory authorities highlighted the importance of pre-crisis regulatory reforms, such as higher capital and liquidity requirements, which enabled banks to withstand the economic shock better (Li et al., 2020; Berger and Demirgüç-Kunt, 2021; Duncan et al., 2022). In the face of economic uncertainty, swift and decisive action, including large-scale asset purchase programs and targeted financial support, was instrumental in stabilising financial markets and maintaining investor and consumer confidence. Ensuring ample liquidity in the financial system was crucial to prevent a freeze in credit markets, which could have had severe repercussions for businesses and households. Central banks' actions to keep credit flowing, as

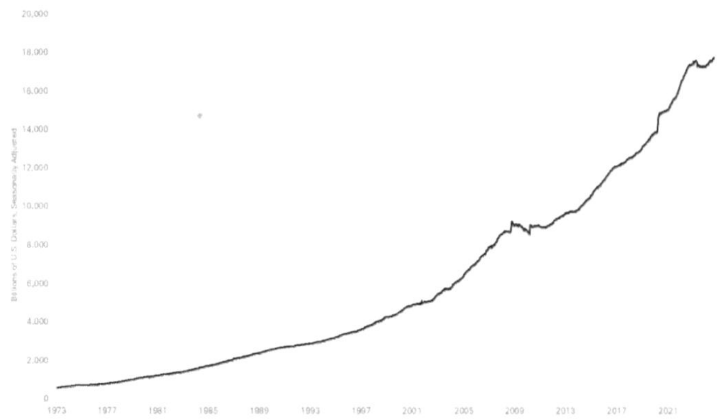

Figure 11.4: Bank credit, all commercial banks, billions of U. S. dollars, weekly, seasonally adjusted.
Note: Data obtained from FRED, "Federal Reserve Economic Data, FRED is an online database consisting of hundreds of thousands of economic data time series from scores of national, international, public, and private sources. FRED was created and is maintained by the Research Department at the Federal Reserve Bank of St. Louis, combining data with a powerful mix of tools that help the user understand, interact with, display, and disseminate the data."

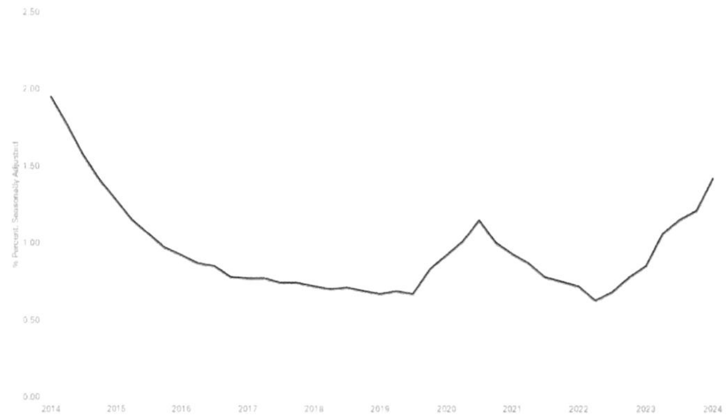

Figure 11.5: Delinquency rate on commercial real estate loans (excluding farmland).
Note: Delinquency Rate on Commercial Real Estate Loans (Excluding Farmland), Booked in Domestic Offices, All Commercial Banks, Percent, Quarterly, Seasonally Adjusted. Data obtained from FRED, "Federal Reserve Economic Data, FRED is an online database consisting of hundreds of thousands of economic data time series from scores of national, international, public, and private sources. FRED was created and is maintained by the Research Department at the Federal Reserve Bank of St. Louis, combining data with a powerful mix of tools that help the user understand, interact with, display, and disseminate the data."

presented in Figure 11.4, helped cushion the economic blow and facilitated a quicker recovery. Forbearance measures, such as payment moratoriums on loans and mortgages, provided temporary relief to borrowers facing financial difficulties, helping maintain the stability of the broader financial system by reducing the potential for widespread loan defaults, evidence of which is presented in Figure 11.5.

Central banks implemented expansive asset purchase programs, buying government bonds and corporate securities to lower yields and encourage borrowing and investment. Some of these programmes are listed in Table 11.1. Refinancing operations played a crucial role in maintaining credit supply, with central banks easing conditions on targeted long-term refinancing operations (TLTROs) to provide low-cost loans to banks, incentivising them to extend credit to SMES and households. Fiscal measures were equally important. Governments implemented direct cash transfers, wage subsidies, and tax reliefs to support individuals and businesses facing income losses. The scale of fiscal interventions varied across countries, reflecting differing fiscal capacities and policy approaches. The EU's Next Generation EU (NGEU) recovery package, detailed in Table 11.2, worth €750 billion, was a significant aspect of Europe's fiscal response. This initiative, financed through joint debt issuance by the European Commission, aimed to support recovery efforts and invest in green and digital transitions. The Recovery and Resilience Facility (RRF) within the NGEU provided grants and loans to member states based on national recovery plans aligned with EU priorities. As outlined in Table 11.3, national fiscal policies complemented EU-level initiatives, with individual member states deploying substantial fiscal resources to address the pandemic's economic fallout. These policies included extensive support for health systems, direct financial aid to businesses and workers, and investments in infrastructure projects to stimulate economic recovery. Investments in green technologies and digital infrastructure were prioritised to drive future growth and job creation, aligning with long-term environmental sustainability goals and technological advancement. Managing fiscal interventions required strategic borrowing, efficient resource allocation, and innovative financing mechanisms to ensure fiscal sustainability. The pandemic also presented the importance of international cooperation in fiscal policy, with cross-border coordination and support mechanisms proving crucial in providing financial stability and supporting recovery efforts. The interconnected nature of global economies highlighted the need for a unified response to global crises.

11.3 COVID-19 Induced Digital Transformation in Finance

The COVID-19 pandemic has acted as a catalyst for digital transformation within the financial sector. As social distancing measures and lockdowns were implemented globally, financial institutions had to adapt to maintain operational continuity rapidly. The acceleration of digital transformation became evident as remote working, digital banking, and fintech solutions were swiftly adopted (Bao and Huang, 2021; Fu and Mishra, 2022). Financial services providers leveraged technology to transition from traditional brick-and-mortar setups to virtual environments, ensuring seamless service delivery amidst unprecedented constraints. Remote working emerged as a necessity, prompting financial institutions to invest in robust digital infrastructure. This shift required significant upgrades in IT systems to support secure and efficient remote access for employees.

Table 11.1: Central bank asset purchase programs during COVID-19.

Central bank	Program name	Start date	Asset types purchased	Program size	Description and objectives
Federal Reserve (USA)	COVID-19 Quantitative Easing (QE)	Mar-20	U. S. Treasuries, Mortgage-Backed Securities (MBS), Corporate Bonds	Initially unlimited; later targeted at $120 billion per month ($80 billion in Treasuries, $40 billion in MBS)	Aimed at lowering borrowing costs, stabilising financial markets, and ensuring liquidity. The Fed also introduced facilities to buy corporate bonds and support credit markets
European Central Bank (ECB)	Pandemic Emergency Purchase Programme (PEPP)	Mar-20	Eurozone sovereign bonds, corporate bonds, commercial paper	Initially €750 billion, expanded to €1.35 trillion, and later to €1.85 trillion	Designed to counter risks to monetary policy transmission posed by the pandemic, PEPP provided flexible asset purchases across asset classes and countries
Bank of England (UK)	Asset Purchase Facility (APF) and COVID Corporate Financing Facility (CCFF)	Mar-20	UK government bonds (gilts), investment-grade corporate bonds	APF expanded to £875 billion for gilts and £20 billion for corporate bonds	APF aimed at lowering borrowing costs and supporting market functioning. CCFF provided liquidity to large firms to stabilise corporate funding markets
Bank of Japan (Japan)	Special Program to Support Financing in Response to COVID-19	Mar-20	Japanese government bonds (JGBs), corporate bonds, commercial paper	Increased ETF purchases to ¥12 trillion annually; corporate bond and CP purchases to ¥20 trillion	The BOJ expanded purchases of JGBs, ETFs, and corporate bonds to stabilise markets and support corporate financing
Reserve Bank of Australia (Australia)	Bond Purchase Program (BPP)	Nov-20	Australian government bonds, semi-government securities	AUD 200 billion, later expanded to AUD 300 billion	The RBA introduced the BPP to lower funding costs and ensure a smooth functioning of the bond market
Bank of Canada	Government of Canada Bond Purchase Program (GBPP)	Mar-20	Canadian government bonds, provincial bonds, corporate bonds	Initially CAD 5 billion per week, gradually tapered	Aimed at providing liquidity to the government bond market and supporting provincial and corporate financing
Reserve Bank of New Zealand	Large Scale Asset Purchase (LSAP) Program	Mar-20	New Zealand government bonds, Local Government Funding Agency (LGFA) bonds, inflation-indexed bonds	NZD 100 billion	LSAP aimed at keeping interest rates low and ensuring liquidity in government and local government bond markets
Sveriges Riksbank (Sweden)	Asset Purchase Programme	Mar-20	Government bonds, municipal bonds, covered bonds, corporate bonds	SEK 700 billion	Riksbank expanded its asset purchases to include municipal bonds and corporate bonds to stabilise markets and support the economy

Table 11.1 (continued)

Central bank	Program name	Start date	Asset types purchased	Program size	Description and objectives
Swiss National Bank (Switzerland)	COVID-19 Asset Purchase Program	Mar-20	Foreign currency-denominated assets, corporate bonds	Program size not publicly disclosed	SNB conducted interventions in foreign exchange markets and purchased assets to prevent excessive appreciation of the Swiss franc and maintain economic stability
Bank of Korea	Bond Purchase Program	Apr-20	Korean government bonds, special purpose bonds	Initially KRW 1.5 trillion; expanded in subsequent months	The Bank of Korea aimed to stabilise the bond market and support government funding
Reserve Bank of India (India)	Government Securities Acquisition Programme (G-SAP)	Apr-21	Government securities	INR 1 trillion (Q1 FY2021–22), additional rounds followed	The RBI launched G-SAP to ensure orderly market conditions and manage the yield curve
People's Bank of China (PBoC)	Targeted Medium-Term Lending Facility (TMLF) and others	2020	Lending to banks for specific purposes	Various targeted measures, not specified as a single large-scale asset purchase	PBoC focused on targeted lending facilities to support SMEs and other priority sectors, rather than outright bond purchases

Note: The data presented in the table regarding central bank asset purchase programs during the COVID-19 pandemic were compiled from multiple authoritative sources. Information on the Federal Reserve's programs, including the COVID-19 Quantitative Easing measures and the Secondary Market Corporate Credit Facility (SMCCF) was sourced from the Federal Reserve Board's official press releases and policy announcements. The details on the European Central Bank's Pandemic Emergency Purchase Programme (PEPP) were obtained from the European Central Bank's official website, including their monetary policy statements and updates published between March 2020 and 2021. For the Bank of England's Asset Purchase Facility (APF) and the Covid Corporate Financing Facility (CCFF), data was extracted from the Bank of England's official announcements, monetary policy summaries, and financial stability reports. The information related to the Bank of Japan's Special Program to Support Financing in Response to COVID-19, including ETF purchases, was sourced from the Bank of Japan's monetary policy statements and financial market reports. Details of the Reserve Bank of Australia's Bond Purchase Program were drawn from the Reserve Bank of Australia's monetary policy meeting minutes and statements, which outlined the objectives and expansion of the bond purchases. Information on the Bank of Canada's Government of Canada Bond Purchase Program (GBPP) was gathered from the Bank of Canada's official publications and policy statements. The Reserve Bank of New Zealand's Large Scale Asset Purchase (LSAP) Program details were sourced from the Reserve Bank of New Zealand's official announcements and monetary policy reviews. Information on Sveriges Riksbank's Asset Purchase Programme was compiled from Sveriges Riksbank's financial stability reports and press releases. The Swiss National Bank's COVID-19 asset purchases, the Bank of Korea's Bond Purchase Program, and the Reserve Bank of India's Government Securities Acquisition Programme (G-SAP) details were obtained from their respective central bank reports, press statements and monetary policy documents. For the People's Bank of China, the data on targeted lending facilities were sourced from PBoC's monetary policy implementation reports and official government releases.

Table 11.2: EU's Next Generation EU (NGEU) recovery package.

Component	Fund/instrument	Billion €	Objectives	Impl. timeline
Recovery and Resilience Facility (RRF)	Grants and Loans	723.8	Support member states' reforms and investments focusing on green and digital transitions, economic resilience, job creation, and long-term economic growth.	2021–2026
React-EU	Cohesion Policy Funds	50.6	Provide additional funding to existing Cohesion Policy programs to support healthcare systems, job preservation, SMEs, and social services.	2021–2023
Horizon Europe	Research and Innovation	5	Enhance EU's research and innovation capabilities in fields such as health, green energy, and digital technologies, driving scientific breakthroughs.	2021–2027
InvestEU	Investment Programme	6.1	Stimulate private and public investment in sustainable infrastructure, research and innovation, SMEs, and social investment to foster economic recovery.	2021–2027
Rural Development	Agricultural and Rural Funding	7.5	Promote the sustainability of the agricultural sector and rural development, support farmers, and boost the digital transformation of rural areas.	2021–2027
Just Transition Fund (JTF)	Transition Support	10	Assist regions heavily reliant on fossil fuels in transitioning to a greener economy by investing in job retraining, diversification, and technological innovation.	2021–2027
RescEU	Civil Protection Mechanism	1.9	Strengthen EU-wide disaster response, enhance preparedness, and provide rapid deployment of resources in emergencies such as pandemics and natural disasters.	2021–2027
Other EU Programs	Various	1.9	Provide additional funding to enhance resilience and recovery in various sectors, including health, security, and digital transition.	2021–2027

Note: The information presented in this table is based on official documents and announcements from the European Commission, including the detailed breakdown of the Next Generation EU (NGEU) package as outlined in the European Council conclusions, the European Parliament's briefings, and the European Commission's financial and economic reports. Specific funding allocations and program objectives were cross-referenced with the Multiannual Financial Framework (MFF) 2021–2027 and subsequent revisions introduced in response to the COVID-19 crisis. Additional data and clarifications were derived from publications by the European Central Bank, academic analyses, and reputable financial news outlets such as the Financial Times and Bloomberg, ensuring a comprehensive and accurate portrayal of the NGEU recovery package.

Table 11.3: National-level European fiscal policies in response to COVID-19.

Country	Policy/measure	Start date	Fiscal impact (billion €)	Description and objectives
Germany	Economic Stabilisation Fund (Wirtschaftsstabilisierungsfonds – WSF)	Mar-20	600	Established to support large companies facing liquidity issues; includes guarantees, recapitalisation, and credit lines to stabilise firms and protect jobs
	Short-Time Work Scheme Expansion (Kurzarbeit)	Mar-20	40	Extended wage subsidies to companies to reduce hours instead of laying off workers, supporting millions of employees
	Immediate Assistance Program for SMEs	Mar-20	50	Provided direct grants to small and medium-sized enterprises affected by the pandemic
France	Solidarity Fund	Mar-20	30	Created to provide monthly grants to small businesses and the self-employed affected by lockdowns and reduced demand
	State-Guaranteed Loans (Prêts garantis par l'État)	Mar-20	300	Enabled businesses to access credit lines backed by the government to ensure liquidity and operational continuity
	Partial Unemployment Scheme (Chômage partiel)	Mar-20	36	Provided wage compensation for employees on reduced work hours due to business disruptions, covering up to 84 % of net salary
Italy	Cura Italia Decree	Mar-20	25	Offered tax deferrals, increased health funding, and support for workers affected by the pandemic, including temporary unemployment benefits
	Liquidity Decree	Apr-20	400	Provided state guarantees to loans for businesses, ensuring access to capital and safeguarding employment
	Relaunch Decree (Decreto Rilancio)	May-20	55	Introduced measures for business support, health sector funding, and direct aid to families
Spain	Economic and Social Shield (Escudo Social)	Mar-20	100	Included moratoriums on mortgage payments, rental assistance, and energy utility payment deferrals to protect vulnerable households
	Temporary Employment Regulation Schemes (ERTE)	Mar-20	20	Extended furlough schemes that allowed companies to temporarily lay off workers while providing state-funded income support
	ICO Loan Guarantee Program	Mar-20	100	Offered government-backed loans to businesses to maintain liquidity and support economic activity during the crisis

Table 11.3 (continued)

Country	Policy/measure	Start date	Fiscal impact (billion €)	Description and objectives
U. Kingdom	Coronavirus Job Retention Scheme (CJRS)	Mar-20	70	Introduced to provide wage subsidies for employees furloughed due to the pandemic, covering up to 80 % of salaries
	Self-Employment Income Support Scheme (SEISS)	Apr-20	28	Offered grants to self-employed individuals whose businesses were adversely affected by COVID-19 restrictions
	Business Interruption Loan Scheme	Mar-20	330	Provided government-backed loans to small and medium-sized enterprises to ensure business continuity
Netherlands	Emergency Bridging Measure for Employment (NOW)	Mar-20	15	Offered wage subsidies to companies that experienced significant revenue loss, covering up to 90 % of wages to prevent layoffs
	Temporary Support for Self-Employed (Tozo)	Mar-20	4	Provided income support and business loans to self-employed individuals affected by the pandemic
	Business Finance Guarantee Scheme	Apr-20	10	Government-backed loan scheme to ensure SMEs have access to liquidity during economic disruptions
Sweden	Short-Time Work Allowance	Mar-20	7	Introduced subsidies for companies to reduce employees' working hours while maintaining a large part of their salary
	Loan Guarantee for SMEs	Apr-20	5	Offered loan guarantees to banks to facilitate lending to small and medium-sized enterprises facing financial difficulties
	Support for Cultural Sector	Apr-20	0.5	Provided financial support for cultural organizations and artists affected by event cancellations and restrictions

Note: The data and descriptions provided in this table are based on official government releases, legislative documents, and fiscal policy reports from the respective national governments. Information was cross-referenced with publications from national finance ministries, central bank reports, and European Union economic monitoring summaries. Additional verification was conducted through reputable financial news outlets such as Reuters, Bloomberg, and Financial Times to ensure accuracy and comprehensiveness. The fiscal impact estimates represent the initial budget allocations and announced funding levels during the onset of the pandemic in 2020 and subsequent adjustments in 2021. These figures reflect direct fiscal measures and may not capture subsequent revisions or additional funding allocated in later phases of the pandemic response.

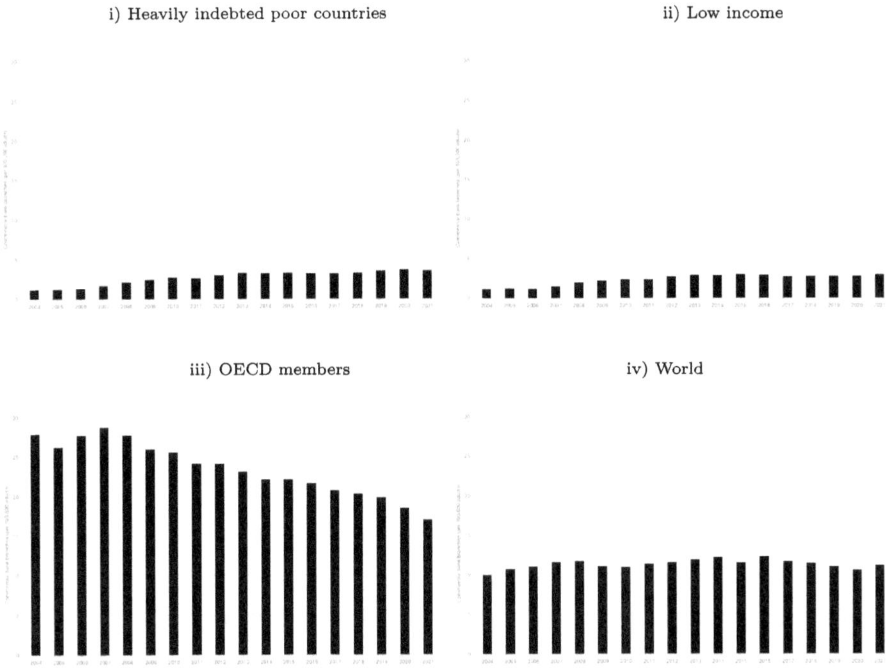

Figure 11.6: Commercial bank branches (per 100,000 adults).
Note: Data obtained from International Monetary Fund, Financial Access Survey.

Virtual private networks (VPNs), cloud computing, and collaborative tools became integral to the financial industry's operations. These technological advancements enabled business continuity during the pandemic and demonstrated the potential for long-term operational efficiencies.

The growth of digital banking adoption was driven by customers seeking safe and convenient ways to manage finances without visiting physical branches, as shown in Figure 11.6. The increased use of mobile banking apps and online platforms facilitated digital payments, fund transfers, and loan applications (Daragmeh et al., 2021; Tut, 2023; Al-Khawaja et al., 2023). This shift emphasised the need for user-friendly digital interfaces and ongoing innovation to meet changing consumer demands. Financial institutions enhanced their digital capabilities by focusing on personalised and intuitive customer experiences. Fintech companies played a key role in this digital transformation, offering alternatives like peer-to-peer lending, digital wallets, and blockchain-based transactions (Lee et al., 2021a, 2023). These technologies gained popularity during the pandemic, promoting financial inclusion by providing access to banking services for underserved populations, thus demonstrating the potential of technology to bridge gaps within the financial ecosystem (Bollaert et al., 2021; Erel and Liebersohn, 2022).

The COVID-19 pandemic amplified financial inequalities, disproportionately impacting vulnerable groups, including low-income households, women, and minorities

(Kantamneni, 2020; Connor et al., 2020). Economic instability, limited access to financial services, and increased debt burden heightened these groups' financial vulnerabilities. This situation highlighted the need for more inclusive financial systems and prompted both policymakers and financial institutions to seek strategies that promote financial inclusion. The pandemic exposed systemic flaws in financial access, reinforcing the importance of building resilient, inclusive financial systems capable of withstanding global crises. Digital financial services have proven particularly effective in reaching underserved communities where traditional banking infrastructure is often inadequate. Mobile money services, for instance, enable individuals in remote areas to engage in savings, borrowing, and transfers without needing to visit a bank, significantly benefiting regions with low banking penetration. These digital solutions have empowered marginalised groups by improving their capacity to manage financial risks and access economic opportunities.

Operational efficiencies were realised as financial institutions optimised their processes through automation and artificial intelligence (AI) (Fethi and Pasiouras, 2010; Li et al., 2021a). Robotic process automation (RPA) enables the automation of routine tasks, reducing the burden on human resources and minimising errors. AI-driven analytics offered insights into customer behaviour, risk management, and fraud detection, enhancing decision-making processes. These advancements improved operational efficiency and positioned financial institutions to respond more agilely to market changes. The rise of new customer service models was another significant outcome of the digital transformation. Virtual customer service channels, including chatbots and video conferencing, have replaced in-person interactions. Chatbots, powered by AI, provided instant responses to customer queries, enhancing service efficiency and satisfaction. Video conferencing tools enabled financial advisors to offer personalised consultations remotely, maintaining the human touch in customer relationships. These models presented evidence of the shift towards a more digital-first approach in customer service delivery. Digital readiness became a critical factor for financial institutions, encompassing the ability to quickly adapt to technological advancements and integrate them into existing frameworks. Institutions that had already invested in digital transformation before the pandemic found themselves better positioned to navigate the crisis. Digital readiness was highlighted as a strategic priority, prompting financial entities to continuously evaluate and upgrade their digital capabilities to stay competitive and resilient.

Cybersecurity emerged as a paramount concern as digital transformation accelerated. The increased reliance on digital platforms exposed financial institutions to heightened cyber threats (Corbet and Gurdgiev, 2019, 2020). Ensuring the security of digital transactions, protecting sensitive customer data, and maintaining regulatory compliance became critical challenges. Financial institutions invested in advanced cybersecurity measures, including multi-factor authentication, encryption, and continuous monitoring systems, to safeguard operations and build customer trust. Several countries implemented digital identification systems during the pandemic to streamline access to government aid and financial services. These systems, often integrated with financial platforms, ensured that relief funds reached those in need promptly and efficiently. By linking digital IDs with financial accounts, governments and financial institutions could disburse payments directly, reducing the risk of fraud and ensuring greater transparency. This integration of digital identification with financial services has the potential to significantly enhance financial inclusion, especially for marginalised populations who previously lacked formal identification.

Despite these advancements, the transition to digital financial services has not been without challenges. Digital divides persist, with significant portions of the population lacking internet access, digital literacy, or the necessary devices to utilise these services. Addressing these barriers is crucial to ensure digital financial inclusion is truly inclusive. Governments and private sector stakeholders must invest in digital infrastructure, education, and outreach programs to bridge these gaps and ensure equitable access to digital financial services. Without such efforts, the benefits of digital financial inclusion may remain out of reach for the most vulnerable populations. In response to the increased reliance on digital financial services, regulatory frameworks have had to adapt quickly to ensure consumer protection and system integrity. Regulators have worked to balance innovation with oversight, introducing guidelines to protect consumers from fraud, ensure data privacy, and maintain the stability of financial systems. The pandemic highlighted the need for agile regulatory approaches to keep pace with technological advancements while safeguarding users.

The global response to the COVID-19 pandemic exhibited diverse strategies across regions, reflecting unique economic structures, healthcare capacities, and political frameworks. In Asia, countries like South Korea and Singapore implemented robust testing and contact tracing, minimising economic disruptions and enabling quicker recovery. Conversely, South Asian countries faced challenges due to dense populations and limited healthcare infrastructure, leading to prolonged economic hardships.

International organisations such as the IMF and World Bank played crucial roles, providing financial support and policy guidance. The IMF mobilised emergency financing for over 80 countries, stabilising economies and preventing deeper recessions. The World Bank focused on health interventions and economic recovery projects, emphasising multilateral cooperation. Pre-existing conditions influenced regional adaptations. Latin American countries with prevalent informal employment faced challenges enforcing lockdowns and providing social safety nets. Smaller economies with stronger social protection systems, like Uruguay, managed to contain the virus more effectively.[18]

---

18 Further, low- and middle-income countries (LMICs) encountered unique challenges due to limited fiscal space and weaker health infrastructure. Financial support from the IMF and World Bank was paramount, highlighting the need for resilient financial systems and greater financial inclusion. Digital financial services played a critical role in reaching underserved populations, underscoring the importance of building robust financial systems for economic stability and recovery. The pandemic high-

11.4 Concluding Comments

The COVID-19 pandemic has fundamentally challenged our understanding of finance, exposing vulnerabilities and underscoring the need for resilient financial systems. Key lessons include the importance of strong capital buffers, flexible regulatory frameworks, and strong risk management. Financial institutions must enhance stress-testing scenarios and integrate advanced technologies like blockchain and AI for better transparency and decision-making. Cybersecurity has also become critical in the increasingly digital financial landscape.

Policy reforms should balance regulatory oversight with innovation, promoting financial inclusion and reducing inequality. The development of regulatory sandboxes can help test new financial products safely. Crisis management plans and international cooperation are essential for future preparedness, ensuring coordinated responses and fiscal stability. Digital finance has grown exponentially, and the role of artificial intelligence has become more prominent, highlighting the need for robust digital infrastructure and adaptive regulatory frameworks. Financial institutions must remain agile, leveraging technology and data analytics to respond swiftly to economic changes. Central banks should continue developing innovative monetary policies, including the potential use of digital currencies, to enhance financial inclusion and stability. The pandemic has exacerbated financial inequalities and spurred financial inclusion innovations, particularly through digital services. These advancements are crucial for reaching underserved communities and supporting broad-based economic recovery.

---

lighted disparities in financial resilience between high-income and low-income countries. High-income countries utilised extensive fiscal stimulus packages, while LMICs relied more on international support. Successful strategies involved rapid policy responses, robust financial infrastructure, and targeted fiscal support, whereas delays and inadequate financial infrastructure led to unsuccessful outcomes. The pandemic underscored the need for policy coordination and global cooperation. Effective monetary and fiscal policy coordination facilitated several measures, with international organisations playing key roles in financial support and policy guidance. Strengthening global financial governance frameworks is essential for coordinated responses to future crises.

12 How Will COVID-19 Impact Financial Markets in the Long Term?

Much has been made of the short-term economic and financial impacts of the COVID-19 pandemic, while less has been written about its long-term implications. In this chapter, some of the long-term financial effects are discussed. Starting with the macroeconomic implications, the chapter then considers the rise of digitisation and digital assets during the pandemic and their impact in future decades. The prospects for ESG, at the forefront of policy discussion in the immediate aftermath of the crisis, are then examined.

12.1 Introduction

Emerging as a localised respiratory illness in Wuhan, China in December 2019, the novel coronavirus, titled COVID-19, led to a global pandemic infecting hundreds of millions and costing northwards of 15 million lives (Taylor, 2022). The short-term impacts on the economy were widespread, with lockdowns and restrictions resulting in job losses, company closures and limiting economic trade. These economic ructions led, in turn, to short-term turmoil in financial markets. Taking the stock market as an indicator, this dropped in value by over 30 percent in under two months. Oil prices briefly turned negative during the crisis, highlighting another challenge faced by financial investors (Corbet et al., 2021a). While these short-run downturns reversed rapidly, many long-run implications from the pandemic will be felt in the decades ahead. In this chapter, we take a brief tour of just some of the long-run implications of the COVID-19 crisis which are beginning to emerge.

The macroeconomic implications of the pandemic were rapid and severe. Labour market disruptions, supply chain breakdowns and a global economic recession resulted in large monetary and fiscal responses from policymakers. Already low interest rates meant that policymakers had to rely heavily on non-traditional monetary policy to support the economy. A further challenge then arrived in the form of inflationary pressures, forcing policymakers to hike interest rates. In the long run will central bankers be able to wean financial markets away from a high level of dependency during crises? If not, will central bankers have a sufficient arsenal to fight further crises, in light of already bloated Reserve balance sheets?

Lockdowns and restrictions from the COVID-19 pandemic had the effect of accelerating the rate of digitisation in the economy. While this was immediately felt in the use of videoconferencing tools for work and education, a longer-term move towards cloud computing and artificial intelligence-driven models have been cited as the beginnings of the fourth industrial revolution. While these are the most evident winners from the crisis, which sectors lost out? What are the longer-term benefits to corporations, and society, of the move to digital-first platforms?

https://doi.org/10.1515/9783111707990-012

The crisis, while initially harrowing for cryptocurrency investors, quickly turned to euphoria, with the size of the digital currency asset class increasing substantially. While short-run questions, such as whether cryptocurrencies provided hedging and safe haven properties, have at least been partially answered, many other relevant issues have emerged from the crisis. In this chapter we assess the promise of non-fungible tokens (NFT) and whether they have a longer-term future. The long-term acceptance of digital currencies is also discussed with a focus on Central Bank Digital Currencies. Finally, the longer-term risks to the asset class from under-regulation are detailed.

One of the more promising shoots to emerge from the crisis is the newfound focus on environmental, social and governance (ESG) issues. The crisis appeared to bring a realisation that, for future prosperity and a sustainable planet, a broader view of stakeholder needs must be accounted for rather than the traditional view of shareholder economic welfare. Throughout the crisis, the evidence for improved corporate performance for firms with stronger ESG ratings is mixed. The long-term ESG outlook may be more positive, with calls for economic recovery to be linked to sustainability objectives. In this chapter, we assess the extent to which this ambition for a green recovery has, to date, been met.

Alongside the many public health issues associated with the COVID-19 pandemic, governments globally also had to deal with the unprecedented economic and financial fallout. The rapid recovery by financial markets, albeit with significant monetary support, highlights a level of financial resilience that bodes well for future crises. The boom in credit issuance in the period after the crisis, while perhaps supporting some zombie companies, showed that company quality can be judged on the promise of long-term future cash flows rather than current, liquidity-driven, financial challenges. In this light, the crisis has shown that the structure of financial markets has strengthened substantially since the global financial crisis.

12.2 Macroeconomic Implications

The initial response from Central Banks globally echoed that of previous crises. Interest rate decreases were announced by many Central Banks in an attempt to stimulate spending, increase liquidity and support financial markets. As highlighted for G7 countries in Table 12.1, however, the scope for dropping interest rates was limited in many countries, a long-run implication from the global financial crisis and subsequent sovereign debt crisis (Cukierman, 2013). Furthermore, in the presence of already low interest rates, the scope for monetary policy transmission to real economic activity is low (Ahmed et al., 2024).

With limited capacity to influence monetary policy through the traditional interest rate channel, central bankers were forced to, once again, turn to the so-called new tools of monetary policy, quantitative easing and forward guidance (Bernanke, 2020). Quantitative easing, involving bond-buying operations by central banks, is shown to have had a

Table 12.1: G7 interest rate changes at COVID-19 onset.

Country	Pre-COVID rate (%)	Post-initial COVID(%) response rate (%)	Approximate date of change
United States	1.50–1.75	0.00–0.25	March 15, 2020
Canada	1.75	0.25	March 27, 2020
United Kingdom	0.75	0.10	March 19, 2020
Japan	−0.10	−0.10 (unchanged)	N/A
Germany (ECB)	0.00	0.00 (unchanged)	N/A
France (ECB)	0.00	0.00 (unchanged)	N/A
Italy (ECB)	0.00	0.00 (unchanged)	N/A

substantial influence on available liquidity, resulting in increases in bank lending (Christensen and Gillan, 2022; Rodnyansky and Darmouni, 2017). A further implication was an increase in bond prices and issuance, helping to directly support businesses struggling with liquidity (Todorov, 2020). The effects of quantitative easing on the economy are substantial, with evidence for a peak effect on GDP of 1.5 percent (Kapetanios et al., 2012).

In response to the emerging economic challenges brought about by the COVID-19 pandemic, central banks globally made a series of quantitative easing announcements. Documented in Table 12.2 for G7 countries, the initial announcements coincided with the period of market turmoil. In the US, the first announcement of $700 billion in asset purchases was modest, but rapidly followed by an expansion to unlimited quantitative easing. Remarkably, the date of the announcement, March 23, 2020, coincided with the end of the equity bear market, with the bellweather S&P 500 rising consistently from this point throughout the remainder of 2020.[19] The balance sheet of the Federal Reserve increased markedly during this period, from under 20 percent of GDP to 37 percent at the peak (Wright, 2022).

One significant implication of the pandemic is the surge in inflationary pressures in the post-COVID-19 period. While this was felt globally, it was particularly evident in the US, where inflation jumped to 9 percent in June 2022, the highest observation since 1981 (Amiti et al., 2024). Much debate has centred on the cause of this inflation increase, especially whether it is demand or supply-led. Blanchard and Bernanke (2023) attribute the initial burst of inflation to relative price shocks and sectoral shortages, followed by labour market pressures on inflation. Starting from March 2022, the US Federal Reserve began to increase interest rates, but this was deemed by many economists to be behind the curve. This notwithstanding, the effects of inflation were short-lived, coming back to more normal growth rates by 2024.

19 Although stock markets reacted positively to the announcement of unlimited quantitative easing, the debt channel was also affected, with bond credit spread reductions emerging from reduced default risk (Nozawa and Qiu, 2021).

Table 12.2: G7 quantitative easing announcements in response to COVID-19.

Country	Date	Quantitative easing announcement
United States	March 15, 2020	$700 billion in asset purchases ($500 billion in Treasuries, $200 billion in mortgage-backed securities)
	March 23, 2020	Expanded to unlimited QE, including purchases of corporate bonds
ECB (Germany, France, Italy)	March 18, 2020	Announced €750 billion Pandemic Emergency Purchase Programme (PEPP)
	June 4, 2020	Expanded PEPP by €600 billion to €1.35 trillion
	December 10, 2020	Further expanded PEPP by €500 billion to €1.85 trillion
United Kingdom	March 19, 2020	Increased asset purchase program by £200 billion to £645 billion
	June 18, 2020	Further increased asset purchases by £100 billion to £745 billion
	November 5, 2020	Expanded asset purchases by £150 billion to £895 billion
Japan	March 16, 2020	Doubled annual ETF purchase target to ¥12 trillion
	April 27, 2020	Removed ¥80 trillion cap on government bond purchases
Canada	March 27, 2020	Launched Commercial Paper Purchase Program (CPPP)
	April 1, 2020	Announced plans to purchase C$5 billion in government bonds per week
	October 28, 2020	Adjusted to C$4 billion per week, focusing on longer-term bonds

The COVID-19 pandemic once again highlighted the central role of policymakers in the financial system (Spatt, 2020). Financial institutions that were 'too big to fail' were bailed out during the global financial crisis, setting a precedent for future crises. Although banks were distinctly not at the centre of the COVID-19 financial crisis, policymakers again showed a willingness to support the corporate bond markets broadly (Spatt, 2020). This led to widespread debt issuance during the crisis, largely indiscriminate of credit ratings and supporting firms, which would otherwise have found themselves insolvent rather than suffering from COVID-19-related liquidity problems. The legal and regulatory infrastructure in most developed economies was found to be lacking in the face of COVID-19-related challenges, especially in relation to avoiding unnecessary firm liquidations (Didier et al., 2021). A significant long-term challenge, in this light, is a framework which can distinguish healthy firms which should be placed in hibernation from those which should not benefit from government support during a systemic crisis.

The COVID-19 pandemic demonstrated the capacity of policymakers to counter a serious exogenous threat to the economy. Whether the crisis and the associated increases to Reserve balance sheets leave policymakers more constrained in future remains to be seen. A further successive threat to the economy before deleveraging occurs might limit the extent of possible quantitative easing, but higher interest rates due to inflation leave further room for traditional monetary policy channels. A long-term implication of the crisis is that policymakers have firmly installed non-traditional monetary policy as part of their crisis-fighting ammunition, perhaps adding to the already well-documented 'Greenspan Put' underpinning markets (Miller et al., 2002). Stepping back from far-reaching supports in future crises will be difficult, leaving policymakers in a bind.

12.3 Increased Digitisation

One of the primary long-term impacts of the COVID-19 pandemic is the increasing prevalence of digitisation. With many businesses unable to operate in-person, remote working became commonplace, with the proportion of the workforce working from home more than quadrupling during the peak of the crisis, according to one estimate (Bick et al., 2020). One immediate impact was the almost instant rise in videoconferencing software such as Zoom for business and education. Measuring the implications in terms of stock performance, cloud and software services such as Dropbox, work from home providers such as Zoo,m and online entertainment including Netflix and Spotify were prominent winners (Cirelli and Gertler, 2022).

This outperformance of information technology firms continued in the post-COVID period, driven by a move towards cloud computing and a renewed interest in artificial intelligence spurred by early successes with deep learning. Companies adopting cloud computing are found to have higher accounting returns for the following year, indicating a swift return on investment (Zheng et al., 2023). Digital transformation also reduces company stock crash risk, by decreasing opacity and increasing internal controls (Jiang et al., 2022). Digitisation also positively impacts company investment efficiency, by reducing financial frictions and correcting agency problems (Chen and Jiang, 2024). Finally, increasing corporate digitisation curtails systematic risk by reducing financing costs, reducing operational costs and mitigating crash risk (Jiang et al., 2025). An important long-term implication of sustained digitisation is the potential for substantial reductions in emissions (Zhu et al., 2023).

While there are many observed benefits from enhanced digitisation in the aftermath of the COVID-19 pandemic, commercial real estate, as an asset class has been substantially impacted. An initial geographical effect accounted for a short-term decrease in commercial real estate of up to 0.93 percent (Ling et al., 2020). Similarly, Real Estate Investment Trusts (REITs) experienced strongly negative cumulative abnormal returns surrounding COVID-19-related business closures (Bhargava and Weeks, 2022). The effect of COVID-19 infections on rents was negative for retail real estate, but the pandemic increased prices in Germany (Heiniger et al., 2024). Further heterogeneity is evident in residential real estate markets, where prices in dense locations are found to have dropped, while those in suburban areas increased during shutdowns (D'Lima et al., 2022). The long-run implications for real estate are still uncertain, but a greater prevalence of remote working will likely have a heterogeneous effect on residential property and, largely, a negative effect on office and retail real estate (Van Nieuwerburgh, 2023). The short-term price shocks to housing markets instigated by remote working will give way to smaller long-term effects, corresponding to a 1.8 percent increase in rents (Howard et al., 2023). One implication not yet assessed quantitatively in the literature is the potential for greater flexibility and mixed use for properties originally intended for commercial use.

12.4 Digital Currencies

Cryptocurrencies were among the biggest financial casualties of the early stages of the COVID-19 pandemic. Exemplifying the extent of the losses, Bitcoin, the largest cryptocurrency by a significant margin, lost almost 70 percent of its value in less than one month (Conlon and McGee, 2020a; Conlon et al., 2024g). In keeping with other financial assets, these losses were rapidly recovered, making cryptocurrencies appear to have the characteristics of a safe haven while the virus was still spreading widely (Corbet et al., 2020c). The subsequent surge in inflation provided another test for cryptocurrencies, with the evidence for inflation hedging ability mixed (Blau et al., 2021; Conlon et al., 2021). Despite substantial volatility, cryptocurrencies have flourished in the post-COVID-19 period perhaps marking their widespread acceptance as a financial asset.

One form of digital assets that experienced substantial growth in the period after the COVID-19 pandemic is non-fungible tokens (NFTs). NFTs are digital assets which use blockchain technology to verify their authenticity and ownership (Conlon and Corbet, 2023). In contrast to cryptocurrencies such as Bitcoin, they are not interchangeable or fungible and is considered as collectible items. The strong post-COVID bull market in cryptocurrencies, alongside greater digitisation, innovative use cases and substantial speculation, led to significant growth in NFTs. This bubble in NFTs was, however, short-lived with assets decreasing rapidly in value. The best-known example of this is the NFT of the first tweet on Twitter, originally sold in March 2021 for $2.9 million but only gathering bids of up to $25,000 a year later. While the decrease in value of NFTs coincided with rising interest rates, cryptocurrency volatility, market saturation, environmental concerns and lack of market liquidity were some of the factors which undermined the long-term prospects of the digital asset class.

While cryptocurrencies were introduced as an alternative to fiat currencies, policymakers have begun to look at the potential of Central Bank Digital Currencies (CBDC), a digital form of fiat currency issued by a government similar to cash or deposits, and which can be designed to pay interest (Agur et al., 2022). Such a currency would exist only in digital form, without any physical currency, backed and issued by a central bank (Dionysopoulos et al., 2023). The COVID-19 pandemic, having promoted digitisation, led to increased interest from various governments in CBDC with launches in Jamaica, the Bahamas and Nigeria, alongside pilot projects in 36 countries.[20] The long-term implications of CDBC are not yet fully understood, with potential challenges for monetary policy (Davoodalhosseini, 2022), possible increases in international contagion effects (Minesso et al., 2022), implications for financial stability (Chen and Siklos, 2022; Keister and Monnet, 2022) and the macroeconomy more broadly (Barrdear and Kumhof, 2022). A significant challenge to the adoption of CBDC, in light of the considerable volatility during the

20 https://www.atlanticcouncil.org/cbdctracker/ accessed: July 2024.

COVID-19 pandemic, will be links between digital currencies such as Bitcoin and CBDC (Bas et al., 2024; Conlon et al., 2024e), perhaps acting as a barrier to adoption.

The COVID-19 pandemic acted as a natural experiment to understand the extent of retail trading in Bitcoin. US government economic impact payments were associated with increased trading volume and an uptick in the price of Bitcoin (Divakaruni and Zimmerman, 2024). This echos the previous evidence that cryptocurrency investors tend to be active traders holding investment biases who invest in assets with higher media attention (Hackethal et al., 2022). Retail traders follow momentum-type strategies in cryptocurrencies but contrarian strategies in gold and stocks, pointing to expectations surrounding future widespread adoption (Kogan et al., 2024). This evidence for the scale of retail involvement highlights the importance of regulation to protect such investors. This is supported across many dimensions, given the considerable evidence of malfeasance within the cryptocurrency space, ranging from the collapse of the FTX exchange (Conlon et al., 2023a, 2024e), gambling (Conlon and McGee, 2020b), fraud (Conlon and McGee, 2021), illegal activities (Foley et al., 2019) and cybercriminality (Corbet et al., 2020a). While regulation is undoubtedly required, one urgent challenge is that the responsibility for regulation falls between agencies (Fletcher et al., 2021). For cryptocurrencies to have a long-term future as an accepted investment class, rather than an ephemeral speculative asset, clear rules protecting retail investors are required.

12.5 Pandemic Implications for ESG

The pandemic resulted in a heightened awareness of global risks, how rapidly a crisis can spread in an integrated economy and increased recognition of impending perils such as climate change. At a corporate level, this additional awareness is curious in light of the limited evidence that stronger corporate social responsibility affected stock returns during the COVID-19 market crash (Bae et al., 2021). Similarly, stronger ESG is not found to explain stock returns during the crisis, while internally generated tangible assets predict performance (Demers et al., 2021). Taking a more expansive view of the value of ESG during crises, Long et al. (2024) indicate that high ESG firm underperform both in good and bad times. In contrast, Goodell et al. (2024) indicate the existence of a premium in firms with more substantive ESG preparation before the pandemic, especially in terms of mitigating government interventions such as work-from-home. Eisenkopf et al. (2023) help to resolve this inconsistency, providing evidence that higher ESG scores were associated with improved performance at the start of the crisis, but this effect faded away rapidly. This is in keeping with other findings documented in this book, suggesting that the COVID-19 bear market was very short-lived, with the market rising from its lowest level within about six weeks.

Decomposing ESG into its constituents also helps to improve the outlook somewhat. Firms with greater COVID-19 environmental responsibility have better stock returns, taken as an indication that investors reward climate relevant initiatives (Garel and

Petit-Romec, 2021), but these findings do not carry over to social responsibility. Li and Miu (2023) document that banks with greater environmental and social engagement are more stable during the crisis, attributed to a stakeholder-aligned culture. Using a global sample, Ding et al. (2021) find that greater social responsibility activities, among other factors, is associated with better stock performance during the crisis. Gianfrate et al. (2024) demonstrate that the performance of strong ESG firms varies considerably across countries, pointing to a substitution effect between ESG and factors such as healthcare coverage. For US stocks, Hsu and Huang (2024) find that a greater degree of information asymmetry across the three ESG components is associated with higher COVID-19 stock performance. Finally, other ongoing policy-related and macroeconomic events, such as Brexit and the US–China trade war may have confounded any direct inference relating to ESG during the pandemic (Akyildirim et al., 2024a). These findings highlight the challenges in making any long-term inference with respect to improved ESG on corporate performance.

While there is considerable ambiguity over the benefits of ESG investing during the crisis, there have been attempts to link corporate and public recovery plans to environmental goals. Using G20 survey data, Hepburn et al. (2020) isolate five arenas in which economic recovery could be linked to sustainability goals: clean infrastructure, building efficient retrofits, natural capital investment, clean R&D and educational investment. Calls for long-term commitments of public investment alongside robust pricing of emissions are among the suggestions to reorient the economy post-pandemic (Barbier, 2020). Public funding provided to companies during the crisis was occasionally subject to environmental conditions, such as the carbon reduction obligation was placed on Air France by the French government (Scherf et al., 2022).

The many calls from policymakers, regulators and corporates for a green recovery have only had limited success. Total funds allocated to COVID-19 recovery are shown to be vastly greater than that required for low-carbon investments (Andrijevic et al., 2020), taking as an indication that economic recovery should be linked to a climate-positive investment. In the US, the inflation reduction act, which, despite the name, was targeted at reduced greenhouse gas emissions, has been indicated as sufficient to meet climate goals (Jordan et al., 2023). Moreover, calls for a green recovery are likely to be ignored, with assessments suggesting that fossil fuel producers, in particular, are likely to pursue a dirty recovery (Le Billon et al., 2021). Despite many promises to 'build back better', research indicates that policymakers have not linked the COVID-19 Economic recovery with emissions cuts to the extent promised (Nahm et al., 2022). Given the potential systematic importance of climate risk (Conlon et al., 2024c), these findings point to a missed opportunity, with environmental concerns taking a back seat to economic prosperity in the post-COVID recovery. They also raise the question as to what is required to seriously address the climate challenge, if the exogenous shock of COVID-19 was insufficient to influence future investment.

12.6 Concluding Comments

In this chapter we tour a number of the impacts of the COVID-19 pandemic on financial markets, extrapolating from some of the known implications to the long-run. While there is little doubt that the pandemic influenced financial markets across a broad spectrum, the focus is on a limited set of topical themes, namely the macroeconomy, digitisation, digital currencies and ESG. While the pandemic provided some aspirations for future progress in these areas, many issues remain unresolved, and some missed opportunities can already be flagged.

While the global economy came into the crisis after many years of consistent growth, this period was also associated with low interest rates and inflation. At the onset of the crisis, interest rates in G7 countries were between 0 and 1.75 percent, leaving policy makers with limited wriggle room. The main monetary policy tool employed to support the economy was quantitative easing, an effective continuation of policy from the global financial crisis. A further challenge which emerged from the crisis was inflation levels not seen since the 1980s. At the time of writing, substantially raised interest rates and improved supply lines appear to have dampened inflation back to near pre-pandemic levels. A challenge to policymakers now, given already raised Reserve balance sheets and large government borrowings, is how to best deal with future exogenous shocks to the economy.

One important outcome of the crisis is the rapid acceleration of digitisation, partly resulting from regulations forcing employees, where possible, to work from home, alongside social distancing restrictions. In addition to transforming everyday life, digitisation has significant implications for companies, improving efficiency, reducing costs and providing potential for emissions reductions. One obvious loser from the rise in digitisation is real estate markets, but even here, the effects are heterogeneous. Commercial and retail property is most affected by the move towards home working. In residential property, densely populated urban areas were the initial losers while suburban properties increased in value. While the long-run equilibrium in real estate, it is difficult to forecast; there is little doubt that digitisation is here to stay and will result in greater flexibility for workers and companies alike.

The COVID-19 crisis was both a catastrophe and a bonanza for the nascent digital currency asset class. In the early stages of the crisis, it was among the biggest losers, while, when other markets turned the corner, cryptocurrencies underwent a huge bull market. Cryptocurrencies, however, failed many of the tests from the crisis, providing mixed evidence on their ability to hedge risks, act as a safe haven or as a store of value during inflation. One of the largest bubbles of the modern age, that of NFTs, emerged swiftly in the wake of the crisis and returned to negligible levels just as quickly. The rise and acceptance of CBDC in the post-crisis period is one major implication of the crisis that may impact financial markets for centuries to come. A further implication from the crisis is the need to regulate cryptocurrency markets, to protect retail investors trading a volatile asset which is subject to multiple nefarious use cases.

In the immediate aftermath of the COVID-19 crisis, ESG-related issues came to the fore, giving rise to a new hope for stakeholder-friendly capital. The aggregate effects of ESG, while perhaps differing by geography and industry, were limited when accounting for company performance during the crisis. At a component level, however, there is some evidence that environmental and social engagement are associated with stronger corporate stock returns throughout the pandemic. At a macroeconomic level, much has been made of the opportunity provided by the crisis to redirect the economy towards a more sustainable, environmentally aligned pathway. The outcomes have been generally disappointing, however, with recovery plans not sufficiently linked with climate goals. The long-run goal of climate-friendly capitalism remains a lofty aspiration, one not necessarily helped by the crisis.

Much work remains to be done to understand the long-run implications of the COVID-19 pandemic on financial markets. While some ideas are raised in this chapter, it is also important to understand the long-run impact on other financial institutions, such as banks. The acceleration of digital banking has given rise to low-cost, online-only competitors, forcing incumbent banks to move away from traditional channels. Further, years of low interest rates have been challenging for banks, hurting their profitability and ability to reinvest for future growth. Banks, already burdened by substantial regulation and compliance costs in the wake of the global financial crisis may be subject to additional costs to deal with potential credit, market and operational risks evident during the crisis. At a more macro level, the financial industry requires better risk models capable of providing accurate market risk assessment during exogenous events such as the COVID-19 pandemic. Finally, the pandemic issued a warning to insurance and re-insurance companies that their pricing models are subject to long tail risks, thought to be a thing of the past.

13 The Influence of COVID-19 on Green Finance

In this chapter, we explore the influence of the COVID-19 pandemic on green finance, an asset class that was growing at a substantial speed before facing exceptional challenges as investors sought protection. Governments were, therefore, challenged to identify a path for the continued growth of green finance while simultaneously stimulating economic growth and protecting citizens. One solution that we will discuss is the incorporation of green finance into recovery plans, such as the EU Green Deal and the US Clean Energy Initiatives, alongside several other policies aimed at fostering a green-driven recovery. Central banks have also played a significant role through tailored interventions such as Green Quantitative Easing, which influences investor behaviour towards more sustainable assets.

13.1 Introduction

The COVID-19 pandemic has generated unprecedented global disruption, prompting a substantive reevaluation of financial priorities, with necessity often outweighing thoughts surrounding sustainability alignment. Green and sustainable finance, which incorporates Environmental, Social, and Governance (ESG) criteria into financial decision-making has become quite a central point of focus in recent times. The pandemic has presented quite a significant danger to the area's continued growth, with much division transpiring as many view green finance as an area that can wait until more pressing areas of the economy and financial system are restored to full health. The following chapter considers such views but focuses on how the continued growth of green finance is possible, even when considering how to fix other problems in the system simultaneously.

Green finance, prior to the COVID-19 pandemic, had been developing at an extraordinary pace (Zhou et al., 2022; Khan et al., 2022; Goodell et al., 2022; Goodell and Corbet, 2024; Xu et al., 2024), largely driven by expanding awareness and acceptance of the need for further focus on sustainable investment frameworks. Investment strategies and portfolios had long considered relatively new products such as green bonds and ESG-focused investment funds; however, the onset of the pandemic raised substantial concern regarding the long-term growth of such products, particularly during periods of exceptional crises. Crises provide a unique opportunity to test the resilience and adaptability of such developing financial products. From a short-term perspective, the pandemic generated an incredible shock, and a sharp negative influence upon broad green finance, propagating largely through rapidly-shifting liquidity conditions, flight-to-safety behaviour, and an immediate change of investor preferences to more crisis-proof assets, much of which fell outside green investment products due to their relative youth and untested nature (Sharma et al., 2021; Zhao et al., 2023). Nonetheless, the same period presented evidence of the critical importance of sustainability as the dy-

https://doi.org/10.1515/9783111707990-013

namic interconnectedness between health crises, environmental degradation, and economic stability became a point of increased focus, even more so during periods of lockdown, as populations garnered quite a strong respect for open areas and the ability to travel freely. Consequently, there has been a strong political shift towards integrating sustainability-related investment into economic recovery plans, as presented in Table 13.1, which provides evidence as to how green finance has been playing a central role in these efforts.

The COVID-19 pandemic left policymakers with limited manoeuvrability with respect to green finance, ignoring its role in future projects and planning would significantly damage the substantial work placed in its growth to date. To continue the evolution of the area, ambitious recovery plans were built to directly consider sustainability goals, such as the European Union's Green Deal and the Biden Administration's clean energy initiatives in the United States, which are described in detail in Table 13.2. While attempting to mitigate the substantial damage generated through the pandemic, such government policies were designed to drive a cultural shift towards low-carbon, economically resilient economies. Central banks have had a central role through the implementation of monetary policy. For example, the ECB has implemented non-standard monetary policies such as the Green Quantitative Easing (QE) program, which has sought to direct significant financial resources towards sustainable projects and assets, thereby directly influencing investor behaviour and attempting to restore investor confidence (Cui et al., 2022; Yousaf et al., 2022).

13.2 The Impact of COVID-19 on Green Finance Development

Green finance, supported by substantial corporate and government supports has grown at an exceptional pace (Khan et al., 2022; Yin and Xu, 2022; Xu et al., 2023). For example, green bonds and ESG-related investment funds have acted as tools to generate capital for green initiatives, not only to support the financing of green projects, but also to enhance the transparency and accountability of such funds in an attempt to attract a broader base of investors interested in sustainability. Due to the relative youth of such products, several substantial issues had developed with regard to fraud and criminality; however, the growing presence of government and major corporations had provided reassurance to investors of a rapidly maturing sector. Institutions and investors have progressively incorporated sustainability criteria into their financial decisions due to a combination of incentives and regulatory interventions, recognising the potential long-term financial returns that existed, which could coincide with environmental responsibility goals (Baumgartner and Ebner, 2010; Sheehan et al., 2023; Zhou and Liu, 2023). Such momentum was further supported by major international agreements such as the Paris Agreement, which established clear and, at the time, agreed-upon reasonable targets for reducing carbon emissions while simultaneously promoting green investments. The key components of the agreement are presented in Table 13.3. However, the outbreak of

Table 13.1: Sustainability measures in COVID-19 economic recovery plans.

Country	Measure/initiative	Started	Estimated funding (in billion €/$)	Objectives and key features
EU	Next Generation EU (NGEU) – Green Transition	2020	€250 (out of €750 total)	Dedicated 37 % of RRF to climate initiatives; investments in renewable energy, energy efficiency, sustainable mobility, and biodiversity; alignment with the European Green Deal goals of carbon neutrality by 2050
	EU Green Bond Issuance	2021	€250 (targeted issuance by 2026)	The EU issued green bonds to fund sustainable projects under NGEU, aiming to become the world's largest green bond issuer and set a benchmark for sustainable finance
Germany	Green Recovery Package	2020	€40	Focused on green hydrogen technology, building retrofits for energy efficiency, electric vehicle (EV) infrastructure, and decarbonisation of industry
	National Hydrogen Strategy	2020	€9	Development of a national hydrogen infrastructure; support for research and development of hydrogen technologies to facilitate the transition to a green economy
France	France Relance Plan – Green Investments	2020	€30	Prioritised investments in energy-efficient buildings, low-carbon transportation, green energy projects, and enhancing biodiversity
	Green Loan Guarantee Program	2021	€5	Provided guarantees for loans aimed at financing environmentally sustainable projects, especially in SMEs and renewable energy sectors
UK	Green Industrial Revolution Plan	2020	£12 (approx. €14)	Investments in offshore wind energy, hydrogen production, nuclear power, electric vehicles, energy storage solutions, and carbon capture and storage (CCS) technology
	National Infrastructure Strategy	2020	£600 (total over 5 years, including green projects)	A broader strategy that includes significant investments in sustainable transport, green energy, and digital infrastructure to support the green transition
US	American Rescue Plan and Infrastructure Bill	2021	$100 (green projects; out of $1.9 trillion total)	Funding for clean energy projects, electric vehicle infrastructure, modernisation of the power grid, public transportation improvements, and building energy efficiency retrofits
	Clean Energy for America Act	2021	N/A	Proposed legislation offering tax incentives for clean energy production and electric vehicle adoption, aiming to support long-term sustainability goals
Canada	Climate Action and Recovery Plan	2020	CAD 15 (approx. €10)	Emphasised clean energy, zero-emission public transit, energy-efficient building retrofits, and natural climate solutions (e. g., forest management)
	Canada Infrastructure Bank's Green Initiatives	2020	CAD 10 (approx. €6.5)	Investments in green infrastructure projects, including renewable energy and energy efficiency in public buildings

Table 13.1 (continued)

Country	Measure/initiative	Started	Estimated funding (in billion €/$)	Objectives and key features
Japan	Green Growth Strategy	2020	¥2 trillion (approx. €15)	Focus on renewable energy, hydrogen technology, carbon recycling, and electrification of transportation; targeted at achieving carbon neutrality by 2050
	Renewable Energy Promotion Act	2021	N/A	Aimed at doubling renewable energy capacity by 2030, supporting solar, wind, and geothermal projects
S. Korea	Green New Deal	2020	KRW 73 trillion (approx. €55)	Investments in smart grids, green mobility, renewable energy projects, sustainable urban development, and enhancing digital infrastructure to support eco-friendly industries
	Digital Green Transition	2020	Included in Green New Deal	Combining digital and green technologies, focusing on smart city development, intelligent transportation systems, and green data centres
Australia	Technology Investment Roadmap	2020	AUD 1.9 (approx. €1.2)	Targeted low-emission technologies, including hydrogen, energy storage, and carbon capture, aimed at reducing emissions and fostering economic growth
	Clean Energy Finance Corporation (CEFC) Funding	2020	AUD 1.4 (approx. €0.9)	Additional funding for CEFC to support renewable energy projects, energy efficiency improvements, and clean tech innovation
China	Green Finance Guidelines	2020	No specific funding announced	Encouraged banks and financial institutions to prioritise green loans and investments, focusing on renewable energy, energy efficiency, pollution control, and sustainable agriculture
	Belt and Road Initiative (BRI) – Green Development	2021	N/A	Introduced guidelines to green the BRI, encouraging environmentally sustainable projects in partner countries
Norway	Green Transition Package	2020	NOK 3.6 billion (approx. €0.35)	Support for offshore wind, carbon capture and storage (CCS), and low-emission technology development
Sweden	Fossil-Free Sweden Initiative	2020	SEK 1 billion (approx. €0.1)	Investments in fossil-free technology development, including electrification of transport and industries; part of broader efforts to achieve a climate-neutral Sweden by 2045

Note: Data obtained from related government websites and international media sources.

Table 13.2: EU Green Deal and Biden administration's initiatives.

Feature	European Union's Green Deal	Biden clean energy plan
Launch Date	Dec-19	Jan-21
Main Objective	Achieve climate neutrality (net-zero emissions) by 2050	Achieve net-zero greenhouse gas emissions by 2050
Interim Goals	55 % reduction in greenhouse gas emissions by 2030 (from 1990 levels)	50–52 % reduction in greenhouse gas emissions by 2030 (from 2005 levels)
Key Legislation	European Climate Law, "Fit for 55" legislative package	Inflation Reduction Act (IRA), Bipartisan Infrastructure Law
Renewable Energy	Increase share of renewable energy to at least 40 % by 2030	Achieve 100 % carbon-free electricity by 2035
Energy Efficiency	Renovation Wave for buildings; mandatory energy efficiency targets	Retrofit buildings; promote energy-efficient appliances
Carbon Pricing	Extend Emissions Trading System (ETS); Carbon Border Adjustment Mechanism (CBAM)	Tax incentives for carbon capture; exploring carbon pricing options
Transportation	Phase out internal combustion engine cars by 2035; develop comprehensive EV charging network	Incentives for electric vehicles (EVs); nationwide network of 500,000 EV chargers by 2030
Industry	Support decarbonization with low-carbon technologies; hydrogen strategy	Investment in clean manufacturing; tax credits for industrial decarbonization
Agriculture	Farm to Fork Strategy; sustainable farming practices	Climate-smart agriculture initiatives; research and development funding
Biodiversity	EU Biodiversity Strategy 2030; protect 30 % of EU land and sea areas	America the Beautiful initiative; protect 30 % of U. S. lands and waters by 2030
Circular Economy	Circular Economy Action Plan; focus on recycling and sustainable product lifecycle	Promote waste reduction and recycling initiatives; extended producer responsibility
Research and Innovation	Horizon Europe funding for green technologies; European Innovation Council	Increased funding for clean energy R&D through Department of Energy (DOE)
International Cooperation	Strengthen EU's role in global climate diplomacy; support developing countries	Rejoin Paris Agreement; lead international climate summits and alliances
Just Transition	Just Transition Mechanism (€150 billion support for affected regions)	Clean energy job creation; transition support for coal communities

Table 13.2 (continued)

Feature	European Union's Green Deal	Biden clean energy plan
Public Engagement	European Climate Pact to involve citizens in climate action	Public awareness campaigns; support local climate action plans
Finance and Investment	Mobilise at least €1 trillion in sustainable investments over the next decade	Federal funding and tax incentives to mobilise trillions in private sector investment

Note: Both the EU Green Deal and Biden Administration's initiatives aim for climate neutrality by 2050 through comprehensive legislative measures, economic incentives, and international collaboration. Key focus areas include renewable energy expansion, energy efficiency, sustainable transportation, industrial decarbonisation, biodiversity conservation, circular economy promotion, and just transition mechanisms for impacted workers and communities.

Table 13.3: Key characteristics of the Paris Agreement.

Aspect	Description
Objective	The primary objective of the Paris Agreement is to limit global warming to well below 2 °C above pre-industrial levels, while pursuing efforts to limit the temperature increase to 1.5 °C. This aim is based on scientific research indicating that exceeding these thresholds could lead to catastrophic climate impacts
Carbon Emission Reduction Targets	Each country sets its own nationally determined contributions (NDCs) outlining specific targets for reducing greenhouse gas emissions. These targets are intended to reflect the country's highest possible ambition, adjusted based on national circumstances and capabilities. Countries must submit updated NDCs every five years, with a focus on enhancing their emission reduction commitments over time
Long-term Emission Goals	The Agreement encourages countries to achieve a balance between anthropogenic emissions by sources and removals by sinks of greenhouse gases in the second half of this century. This goal supports the transition to net-zero emissions globally, requiring substantial reductions in carbon emissions across all sectors
Green Investment and Financial Flows	The Paris Agreement promotes making financial flows consistent with a pathway toward low greenhouse gas emissions and climate-resilient development. This includes mobilizing both public and private sector investments in renewable energy, energy efficiency, sustainable agriculture, and other green projects. Developed countries have committed to mobilize at least $100 billion per year by 2020 to support climate action in developing nations, with a focus on enhancing mitigation and adaptation efforts
Global Participation	The Agreement is a legally binding international treaty with nearly universal participation, including 196 parties (195 countries and the European Union). It is the first universal climate agreement that requires all signatory countries to take action on climate change, regardless of their economic status or development level
Transparency and Accountability	The Agreement establishes a robust transparency framework requiring countries to monitor, report, and verify their greenhouse gas emissions and progress towards NDCs. Regular reporting is subject to international review to ensure transparency, accuracy, and accountability. This framework also includes provisions for technical expert reviews and multilateral assessments to promote compliance and track progress
Adaptation and Resilience	The Paris Agreement emphasizes the need for climate adaptation and enhancing resilience to climate change impacts. It calls for strengthening the capacity of countries to deal with climate-related hazards, such as extreme weather events, rising sea levels, and temperature shifts. The Agreement encourages the development of national adaptation plans and provides a platform for sharing knowledge, technology, and best practices in adaptation efforts

Table 13.3 (continued)

Aspect	Description
Support for Developing Countries	Developed countries are expected to provide financial, technical, and capacity-building support to developing countries to help them achieve their climate goals. This includes facilitating access to technology, knowledge transfer, and financial resources to build resilience and reduce emissions. The Green Climate Fund is one of the mechanisms designed to support these efforts
Review Mechanism	A global stocktake is conducted every five years to assess the collective progress towards the long-term goals of the Agreement. This stocktake informs the subsequent NDCs, encouraging countries to enhance their climate actions and commitments over time. The process is designed to be transparent, inclusive, and evidence-based, ensuring that all parties are accountable for their contributions to global climate goals

Note: The information provided in this table is derived from various authoritative sources that discuss the Paris Agreement's objectives, mechanisms, and commitments. Key sources include the United Nations Framework Convention on Climate Change (UNFCCC), which provides official documents and texts related to the Paris Agreement, including the full text of the agreement, decisions adopted by the Conference of the Parties (COP), and updates on implementation progress. Insights from the Intergovernmental Panel on Climate Change (IPCC) reports, such as the Special Report on Global Warming of 1.5 °C, offer scientific evidence on the importance of limiting global temperature rise and the need for greenhouse gas reduction targets. The World Resources Institute (WRI) publications and analyses provide valuable perspectives on the operational aspects of the Paris Agreement, including nationally determined contributions (NDCs), adaptation strategies, and financial commitments. The Green Climate Fund (GCF) serves as a key financial mechanism, providing funding for climate action in developing countries, and its role is detailed on the GCF website. Additionally, the Climate Action Tracker (CAT) independently monitors and evaluates countries' emission reduction commitments, assessing their alignment with the Paris Agreement's goals. The International Energy Agency (IEA) offers analysis of global energy policies and trends, highlighting pathways for countries to transition towards a low-carbon future. Finally, official statements and reports from the annual COP meetings provide updates on the evolving context of the Paris Agreement, including decisions and commitments to enhance ambition, finance climate action, and ensure transparency.

COVID-19 in early 2020 introduced severe disruptions and doubt surrounding such continued adherence to such green targets (Ahonen et al., 2022; Akyildirim et al., 2022, 2023, 2024b; Conlon et al., 2020, 2022, 2023a,b, 2024d,f; Corbet et al., 2022a,d, 2024; Conlon et al., 2024f; Lang et al., 2024). While the initial phase of contagion relating to the pandemic was associated with extreme levels of market volatility (Corbet et al., 2022f; Akyildirim et al., 2024a; Conlon et al., 2024c), liquidity shortages (Corbet et al., 2020d; Conlon et al., 2024g), substantial corrosion to investor confidence, and a broad shift in investor focus towards more risk-averse assets (Conlon et al., 2024b). Within this context, green bonds and other sustainability-related financial instruments experienced a temporary decline in issuance and investment, as market participants contended with more immediate economic uncertainties, prioritising the stabilisation of their portfolios with more traditional financial products. However, the pandemic also presented a strong argument in favour of more obscure, potentially diversifying products such as that relating to cryptocurrency, fintech, and other maturing assets, such as green finance.

As the immediate shock associated with the pandemic began to alleviate, planning shifted in a progressive direction to focus on how green finance could be incorporated into any development planning. Developing several incentives and realistic pathways, recovery plans focused on the integration of green finance from a strategic perspective to build sectoral resilience, such as that in the EU's Green Deal, which ambitiously focused on achieving carbon neutrality by 2050, focusing directly on reducing greenhouse gas emissions, while simultaneously enhancing energy efficiency and promoting the greater usage of renewables. The fund received support from the NextGenerationEU recovery fund and includes initiatives from the Recovery and Resilience Facility (RRF), which has mandated that EU member states allocate at least 37 % of their respective spending on green investments and regulation reform. Similarly, in the US, clean energy and sustainability in economic policy has been central to plans towards a green recovery. The American Jobs Plan, for example, emphasised as a requirement, a significant investment in green infrastructure, including the modernisation of the national electricity grid, the expansion of hybrid and electric public transit, and the retrofitting of buildings so as to improve energy efficiency. Further access to funding for the clean energy technological R&D is also central to such plans, with a core aim of reducing the US carbon footprint while generating employment in distinct green jobs.

Such recovery plans have coincided with a shift in regulatory frameworks and incentivisation plans. The ECB, for example, introduced Green Quantitative Easing (Dafermos et al., 2018; Aloui et al., 2023; Tufail et al., 2024), which enabled the investors to purchase green bonds at discounted yields in an attempt to incentivise investors and train behaviour in a socially responsible manner. Such projects distinctly encourage investment in sustainable projects that the ECB selects. Further, the role of central banks in this area has also incorporated macroprudential regulation, including climate risk assessments within financial stability monitoring frameworks as a signal of the level of priority being afforded to such risk. Such a decision sends a clear signal that central banks consider threats to sustainability and climate change to act as a simultaneous threat to the financial system itself. By establishing requirements upon financial institutions requiring and mandating regular assessment and thorough, clear disclosure of their respective exposure to climate-related risks, central banks thereby promote greater resilience within the financial sector. Central banks are thereby sending a strong signal to financial markets as to their priorities, and simultaneously ensuring that they are adequately prepared for the potential economic impacts of climate change.

In comparison, policy measures implemented elsewhere have varied substantially, signalling the levels of attention and priorities being afforded. The Chinese government integrated green finance into its broader economic strategy in a similar manner to both the EU and the US, with similar points of focus. Similarly, Japan launched the Green Growth Strategy with ambitions to achieve carbon neutrality by 2025, focusing on hydrogen technology, offshore wind power, and a focus on energy savings through smart, energy-efficient buildings. Other countries in South Asia have introduced substantive green finance and green-related recovery plans; however, they are heavily hindered by a lack of available fiscal space and private investment, which could act in a capacity to reduce risk while sharing future rewards. Instead, such countries rely heavily on financing from institutions such as the IMF, the UN and the World Bank, which has focused on development within the Sustainable Development Goals framework, focusing on "building back better". The lack of strong policy frameworks has been a central issue, with many international investors being predominantly concerned about the lack of robustness within such respective green finance sectors. Further assistance has also been provided in the form of policy advice and technical assistance, which are identified to be significant issues in some countries with no previous track records of such development.

There is a growing recognition that ESG factors are critical to long-term financial performance and risk management. Studies have shown that sustainable investments perform better during economic downturns, reinforcing the case for integrating ESG criteria into investment strategies (Eccles and Viviers, 2011; Van Duuren et al., 2016; Chong and Phillips, 2016; Alessandrini and Jondeau, 2020; Akyildirim et al., 2024a). The elevated demand experienced for products such as green bonds and other similar sustainable investment products have presented evidence of quite a sustained, more permanent shift by investors to such products as part of their regular portfolios, signalling evidence of more permanent changes in investor behaviour. The continued growth of new financial products has also generated much-needed funding to support the development of enhanced transparency, which will support accountability with regard to fraud and wrongdoing as the market develops. Such structural development will simultaneously elevate trust in these products, and attract a wider investment group.

Similar to the added security provided through improved transparency, direct regulatory changes and incentives for proper conduct are also central to the growth of wider green finance. Several governments and regulatory bodies have introduced various measures to encourage investments in sustainable projects, evidence of which is presented in Table 13.4, including the provision of tax incentives and subsidies for renewable energy projects. Several governments have focused on revising existing regula-

Table 13.4: Government plans to support investment in sustainable projects.

Country	Measure	Description	Date
EU	Green Bond Standard	A voluntary framework introduced to enhance transparency and integrity in the green bond market. It requires that funds raised by green bonds be allocated to projects aligned with the EU Taxonomy for Sustainable Activities, which defines environmentally sustainable economic activities. The standard also mandates rigorous reporting on the use of proceeds and environmental impact, verified by independent, accredited external reviewers	Jul-19
US	Investment Tax Credit (ITC)	This policy provides tax incentives for solar and wind energy projects, allowing investors to deduct a percentage of the cost of installing renewable energy systems from their federal taxes. Initially focused on solar energy, the ITC has expanded to include other forms of renewable energy. It has been instrumental in driving investment in the U. S. renewable energy sector, particularly in solar power	Aug-05
China	Green Credit Guidelines	Issued by the China Banking Regulatory Commission, these guidelines require banks to integrate environmental risk assessment into their lending processes. The aim is to promote loans to projects with positive environmental outcomes while discouraging funding for industries that cause pollution and environmental degradation. This policy is part of China's broader strategy to reduce air pollution and combat climate change	Feb-12
UK	Green Finance Strategy	This strategy includes the issuance of green sovereign bonds aimed at funding infrastructure projects that reduce carbon emissions, enhance energy efficiency, and contribute to achieving the UK's net-zero emissions target by 2050. The strategy also emphasises mobilising private sector investment in sustainable projects, developing new financial products, and enhancing the UK's green finance capabilities	Jul-19
Japan	Feed-in Tariff (FiT) for Renewable Energy	Japan's FiT scheme guarantees fixed payments to producers of renewable energy, such as solar, wind, and biomass, for the electricity they generate and feed into the national grid. This policy has been a key driver of Japan's renewable energy expansion, especially following the Fukushima nuclear disaster, which increased the country's focus on safe and sustainable energy sources	Jul-12
Australia	Clean Energy Finance Corporation (CEFC)	The CEFC is a government-owned financial institution established to provide funding and investment support for clean energy projects. Its mandate includes renewable energy, energy efficiency, and low-emissions technologies. The CEFC aims to accelerate Australia's transition to a low-carbon economy by leveraging private sector funds through co-investment and providing concessional finance to innovative projects	Jul-12

Table 13.4 (continued)

Country	Measure	Description	Date
Canada	Canada Infrastructure Bank's (CIB) Green Projects	The CIB focuses on funding infrastructure projects that support sustainable energy, public transit, and green buildings. With substantial investments targeted towards low-carbon and climate-resilient initiatives, the CIB plays a crucial role in Canada's efforts to meet its greenhouse gas reduction targets and build resilient infrastructure capable of withstanding the impacts of climate change	Jun-17
Germany	National Hydrogen Strategy	Announced as part of Germany's commitment to carbon neutrality, this strategy includes subsidies and funding for developing hydrogen infrastructure. It focuses on promoting green hydrogen production through renewable energy, supporting research and development, and establishing a hydrogen economy that can integrate into existing energy systems. This strategy is critical for decarbonising sectors that are difficult to electrify, such as heavy industry and transport	Jun-20
India	Renewable Energy Certificates (RECs)	A market-based instrument introduced to promote renewable energy, RECs certify the generation of electricity from renewable sources like solar, wind, and biomass. These certificates can be traded on power exchanges, providing an additional revenue stream for renewable energy producers and creating an economic incentive for investment in clean energy projects. RECs also help companies meet their regulatory compliance and sustainability goals	Jan-11
France	Sustainable Development Goals (SDG) Sovereign Bonds	France issues sovereign bonds linked to the United Nations Sustainable Development Goals (SDGs), channelling funds into projects that promote environmental sustainability, including renewable energy development, clean transportation, biodiversity conservation, and water management. These bonds are part of France's strategy to position itself as a leader in sustainable finance and to align national investment strategies with global sustainability objectives	Jan-17

Note: The measures outlined in this table reflect a global trend towards integrating environmental considerations into financial and regulatory frameworks to encourage investment in sustainable projects. These initiatives are part of broader strategies to combat climate change, promote renewable energy, and achieve long-term economic resilience. The dates provided indicate when these measures were officially announced, highlighting the ongoing evolution of green finance policies across different regions. Data for this table has been sourced from the official government publications, regulatory bodies' announcements, and sustainable finance reports, ensuring a comprehensive overview of the key strategies driving green investments worldwide.

tions so as to reduce, and eventually remove barriers to green investments with an ambition to facilitate a greater flow of capital into sustainable sectors. Further, the mandatory reporting of ESG criteria has become more commonplace, and has dictated to companies to disclose their sustainability practices and impacts (Akyildirim et al., 2022, 2023, 2024b; Scrimgeour et al., 2024). Therefore, investors can make better informed decisions, free of any implicit asymmetric information or moral hazard that could persist, while focusing on issues inherent through the practices of greenwashing and socialwashing.

International financial institutions play a significant role in financing green projects in developing countries. These banks not only provide direct funding for sustainable infrastructure projects but also play a critical role in de-risking investments through guarantees and blended finance mechanisms, while also providing key expertise that may be extremely difficult to obtain in a local market. By providing funding and technical assistance, these institutions are helping to bridge the financial and expertise gap for sustainable development. International cooperation is essential for ensuring that all countries, particularly those with limited resources, can participate in the green transition. Collaborative efforts at the global level are necessary to address the cross-border nature of environmental challenges. More specifically, public-private partnerships (PPPs) have emerged as key in mobilising green finance. By combining public sector resources and private sector expertise, PPPs can deliver large-scale sustainable infrastructure projects more efficiently.

13.3 Challenges and Opportunities

Several distinct financial challenges have continued to hinder the broad adoption and development of green finance. Primarily, the upfront costs of such initiatives have historically required substantial initial capital investments, thereby deterring some investors due to a lack of short-to-medium-term returns. Further, the need for more rigid, standardised measurement systems for evaluating a green project's environmental impact and financial performance can often be quite opaque and sometimes generate substantial division and disagreement. Such discrepancies, while sometimes providing opportunities, have also generated incredible losses for those who did not adequately calculate the true associated costs. A lack of reliable long-term data generates doubt; however, this situation will improve over time as more projects are completed.

In response to such challenges, green finance is benefiting from continued technological innovation in renewables, energy efficiency and sustainable agriculture. Each advancement is reducing costs and thereby increasing project returns, therefore, attracting further investment due to the elevated project probability of success. The incentivisation and development of strong financial products has also generated a strong path to success, with some projects developing on novel technology such as blockchain and AI (Qin et al., 2023), which has been used as a tool to improve transparency and accountability. Specifically, blockchain technology can create immutable records of environmental impact, which can greatly improve trust in any developing system through a reduction of cybercriminality risk. Further, AI and big data analytics offer improved methods for assessing and managing risk, therefore providing a more accurate representation of the fair price of green finance-related products.

Further, impact investing, which places equal importance on social and environmental outcomes alongside financial returns, is driving demand for innovative green finance products (Yu et al., 2021; Shao et al., 2022). Further, the development of specialised lending products has become more common as financial institutions set green initiative-driven caveats as central to repayment terms of certain loan products. Private equity firms and venture capitalists have also focused their investment on startups and technologies that advance sustainability goals.

13.4 Successful Examples of Green Recovery

13.4.1 Germany's Hydrogen Strategy

Germany has positioned itself as a frontrunner in the green hydrogen sector. It has set out to achieve carbon neutrality by 2045, building upon the National Hydrogen Strategy (NHS), which was launched in June 2020 and updated in 2023. The NHS outlined a pathway to incorporating hydrogen into Germany's energy system (Flath et al., 2023), providing key target to increase domestic electrolyser capacity from 5 GW to at least 10 GW by 2030. By doing so, it would ensure that hydrogen is produced predominantly through renewable energy sources like wind and solar power, thereby decarbonising industries that are difficult to electrify, such as steel, chemicals, and heavy transport. The government also includes the development of an extensive hydrogen infrastructure, which is critical for the transportation and storage of hydrogen, presenting a plan to build over 1,800 km of dedicated hydrogen pipelines domestically as part of the European Hydrogen Backbone, which aims to create approximately 4,500 km of hydrogen pipelines across Europe. These pipelines will enable the efficient distribution of hydrogen across national and European networks, supporting industrial clusters and export markets, thereby making Germany a central node in its creation and transportation. International cooperation is a particularly important crucial component of Germany's hydrogen strategy. Recognising that domestic production on its own may not suffice to meet future hydrogen demand, the NHS emphasises diversifying hydrogen imports, therefore identifying a prudent pathway through the exploration of partnerships and international collaboration, which is essential for ensuring energy security while supporting global efforts towards a sustainable energy transition.

13.4.2 Southeast Asia's Green Initiatives

In Southeast Asia, significant steps have been taken towards the promotion of green finance and sustainable development, with a direct focus on renewables, infrastructure, and sustainable agriculture. In particular, the Philippines and Indonesia have been the most progressive to date, instigating plans that are centrally driven by solar, wind and geothermal investment projects. Indonesia, in particular, has set out to become a world leader in geothermal energy, whereas the Philippines has focused on wind energy projects through its Renewable Energy Act, which has incentivised solar and wind projects. Forestry has also been a point of central focus, with attention afforded to sustainable palm oil production, targeting aggressive reductions in deforestation and greenhouse gas emissions, with further simultaneous projects focusing on reforestation to support environmental sustainability. Such progress could enhance rural lives and improve the quality of life, income and food security. The continued incorporation of ESG-related criteria into daily practices has become commonplace, while there has been sharp growth in the issuance of green bonds, which has mobilised substantial capital for environmentally beneficial projects. Specifically, Malaysia and Thailand have introduced initiatives to boost the green bond market, while Indonesia's issuance of green sukuk, Islamic bonds for environmental projects, presents evidence of the region's innovative use of financial instruments to support sustainability. Vietnam's green bond market has focused on projects addressing climate change, in particular, the enhancement of water management projects and the creation of urban resilience.

13.4.3 The United States: Transitioning to Clean Energy

The US green recovery plan has focused on a direct transition to clean energy and has been central to the Biden Administration's commitment to achieving net-zero emissions by 2050. Specifically, the American Jobs Plan has acted as a central node in this strategy, providing substantial investment in clean energy infrastructure, electric transportation, and gains through energy efficiency projects. All of this has been mandated to be achieved while providing millions of jobs during the transition to a low-carbon economy, which will be generated through a series of tax credits and grants designed to directly encourage expansion and corporate commitment to modernisation and expansion. Another major point of focus is the expansion of the electric vehicle infrastructure, where a central directive surrounds the installation of 500,000 EV charging stations nationwide by 2030. This initiative is intended to accelerate electric vehicle adoption and reduce transportation sector emissions in an attempt to sharply reduce emissions while simultaneously boosting job creation through a strong domestic automobile manufacturing industry, which has been challenged substantially through aggressive international competition.

13.5 Concluding Comments

The COVID-19 pandemic has significantly influenced progress in the development of green finance, initially as a shock capable of detailing the maturing asset class, to a new-found point of restoration through central positioning in government stability planning. At first, the crisis caused significant instability and difficulties in accessing funds, which tested the resilience of green finance mechanisms. However, upon the realisation that green finance could be damaged substantially, and possibly fatally, by the evolution of the COVID-19 pandemic, governments have moved towards incorporating sustainability into economic recovery strategies. This decision enabled nations to recover in a manner that continues to centralise green finance within developmental structures.

14 The Influence of COVID-19 upon Global Innovation

This chapter discussed the impact of the COVID-19 pandemic on global innovation, focusing particularly on how the crisis accelerated digital transformation, drove advancement in healthcare, and inspired change in business processes across many sectors. The pandemic underscored the critical role of innovation, especially when responding to such an unprecedented challenge, with rapid developments in telemedicine, e-commerce, and remote work technologies. Further, we discuss how the pandemic influenced regional innovation as borders closed, supply chains slowed, and countries began competing for limited resources.

14.1 Introduction

Innovation across most sectors has been central in providing defensive mechanisms against the challenges created by the COVID-19 pandemic. In a traditional sense, innovation is observed as the introduction of new ideas, products, or processes that significantly improve performance or create value; however, during the pandemic, the importance of innovation was particularly magnified as the need for immediate, effective, and in some cases, unconventional solutions to major problems became central, exacerbating severe episodes of uncertainty and destabilisation (Cioroianu et al., 2024; Corbet et al., 2021b, 2022a; Conlon et al., 2020, 2023a, 2024d,f). COVID-19 presented a situation where agility and creativity became vital when responding to unprecedented problems, particularly when providing a pathway for long-term recovery and improved economic resilience. One of the most significant aspects of innovation during the COVID-19 pandemic was the accelerated digital transformation across various sectors (Gabryelczyk, 2020; Kutnjak, 2021; Soto-Acosta, 2020, 2024). As physical interactions became limited by national legislation, businesses and institutions began to adopt digital tools and platforms to maintain operational ability rapidly. The rapid transition by many sectors to the remote working environment was enabled by adaptive innovation, necessitating advancements in communication technologies and cybersecurity measures, some of which already existed but had to be rapidly expanded. Similarly, the education sector witnessed a swift transition to online learning, prompting innovations in digital content delivery and virtual classroom management (Dhawan, 2020; Paudel, 2021; Adedoyin and Soykan, 2023). These changes, initially driven by necessity, have generated lasting implications for how work and learning are conducted, with some of these changes potentially becoming permanent.

The pandemic called for much-needed innovation within the healthcare sector; simultaneously, researchers, pharmaceutical companies, and governments shared in unparalleled collaboration and resource mobilisation to meet pressing needs for diagnostics, treatments, and vaccine development (Alshrari et al., 2022). More importantly, the

https://doi.org/10.1515/9783111707990-014

development and approval of several COVID-19 vaccines within extremely short timelines were portrayed as landmark successes and a direct testament to the power of scientific innovation under phenomenal pressure.[21] Telemedicine allowed for services similar in nature to an in-person patient experience to continue without risking the transmission of the virus, a very important aspect given the scale of use that such social distancing requirements needed to be able to attain. More importantly, technology played a vital role in integrating AI and data analytics to track the virus's spread, enabling the prediction of outbreaks using such data.

While substantial resources were allocated to pharmaceutical innovation, other sectors were attempting to navigate deteriorating global conditions. Various innovative responses catalysed by the economic consequences directly linked to the outbreak of the pandemic were demonstrated, where companies had to re-imagine their business models and strategy formulation to survive and prosper. Sharp expansion of e-commerce was observed as people moved to online shopping, driving innovation in supply chain logistics and contactless delivery services. European-level data, presented in Table 14.1, presents evidence of substantial growth in online shopping in Europe between 2020 and 2023, with some decline evident during the worst phases of the COVID-19 pandemic. Businesses that could quickly pivot and adapt to meet changing consumer demands or re-purpose their production capabilities, such as manufacturers producing personal protective equipment (PPE), demonstrated the critical importance of adaptability and innovation in times of crisis (Corbet et al., 2022f; Conlon et al., 2024c). Such innovation was not solely limited to medical, technological, educational or corporate practice, but also international governance and policy. Innovation was also central to several support packages, including economic relief devised to ensure social stability. Primarily, such supports were implemented due to the varying influence upon global populations, with particularly sharp negative outcomes experienced by the most vulnerable in society. Some of the major policy innovations involved economic stimulus packages, remote voting systems, and digital health passports. These have underlined the need for agile governance structures capable of responding swiftly to emerging challenges.

21 The rapid development and approval of multiple COVID-19 vaccines represent a landmark achievement, demonstrating the power of global collaboration, unprecedented funding, and technological innovation under pressure. Traditionally, vaccine development is a lengthy process, often taking periods far above ten years from conceptualisation to final stage market approval due to the extensive phases of research, clinical trials, and regulatory reviews required to ensure safety and efficacy. However, the urgency of thc COVID-19 pandemic accelerated this timeline sharply. Leveraging technologies which allowed for quicker vaccine design and production, the timeline for vaccine development fell to less than one year. However, while an incredible achievement, this rapid progress was supported by unprecedented global funding from the public and private sectors, facilitating large-scale manufacturing and distribution preparations even before clinical trial results were finalised. Regulatory agencies also adapted, employing emergency use authorisations to fast-track the approval process while maintaining safety standards.

Table 14.1: Internet purchases by individuals (2020 onwards), European Union.

TIME GEO (Labels)	2020	2021	2022	2023
European Union	53.76	56.94	56.02	58.06
Euro area	56.33	59.50	57.65	59.57
Belgium	64.64	66.13	62.60	64.97
Bulgaria	15.61	19.58	23.92	26.94
Czechia	58.75	62.74	66.35	69.07
Denmark	79.36	82.48	77.85	79.78
Germany	75.03	69.00	66.23	67.52
Estonia	56.53	61.72	59.11	62.04
Ireland	64.05	78.82	74.45	80.49
Greece	38.28	46.76	45.80	48.30
Spain	53.82	55.22	55.26	55.85
France	:	65.60	63.48	65.78
Croatia	45.81	45.71	44.40	49.93
Italy	31.42	39.78	37.28	39.19
Cyprus	31.11	43.82	33.67	50.57
Latvia	38.27	50.51	42.17	46.28
Lithuania	41.63	50.56	46.25	48.32
Luxembourg	68.94	69.74	70.33	70.27
Hungary	49.27	57.62	60.75	58.98
Malta	54.48	57.05	58.95	59.67
Netherlands	77.32	83.26	79.48	84.20
Austria	55.58	54.16	56.82	62.41
Poland	46.60	48.30	50.91	49.87
Portugal	35.25	40.44	42.67	43.95
Romania	22.11	23.05	27.09	31.72
Slovenia	51.60	58.84	50.16	53.18
Slovakia	47.87	69.07	65.18	65.84
Finland	59.66	61.96	63.47	64.39
Sweden	72.86	77.81	75.90	80.16
Iceland	61.58	69.17	:	:
Norway	70.02	80.68	80.82	78.81
Switzerland	:	70.91	:	71.24
United Kingdom	83.05	:	:	:
Bosnia and Herzegovina	17.99	20.72	:	25.52
Montenegro	15.14	16.31	18.36	18.57
North Macedonia	21.46	27.56	:	:
Albania	5.63	9.55	13.59	16.33
Serbia	28.99	35.69	39.99	45.88
Türkiye	23.93	32.37	33.59	38.02
Kosovo	35.39	:	:	:

Note: Data available here. Data Code on Eurostat: [isoc_ec_ib20$defaultview]. Annual frequency, measured as possessing a last online purchase in the previous three months, is estimated as a percentage of individuals.

In this chapter, we discuss the various dimensions of innovations influenced by the COVID-19 pandemic while considering the direct impacts and identifying key lessons. Appreciation of the criticality of innovation during the pandemic requires recognition of the underlying drivers and enablers. The role of collaboration, flexibility, and leveraging existing technologies has been among the most evident drivers in shaping innovative responses. This is a new ecosystem, one that differs from the classical friction to innovation, where innovation is relaxed or redefined, for example, by regulatory constraints or market competition. This often created an enabling environment for the pandemic period to accelerate experimentation and implementation of innovations. Finally, the pandemic brought out the theme of resilience concerning innovation. Resilient innovation is defined as the potential for resistance to and learning from shocks to be stronger.

14.2 The Impact of COVID-19 on the Global Innovation Environment

The pandemic had a profound impact on global innovation, particularly in terms of the dynamics of globalisation and the evolution of innovation. Before the pandemic, globalisation was broadly characterised by interconnected supply chains and cross-border collaboration. However, these pathways proved highly vulnerable as conditions deteriorated. The pandemic manifested as a shift in focus towards localisation and regionalisation, where a substantial reorientation of innovation dynamics has since taken place, where those who adapted most sharply garnered substantial sectoral gain or, in some cases, suffered the least from COVID-19-related slowdown. Success stories provided examples of broader pathways for corporations to adapt to the pandemic, with organisations quickly accelerating their adoption of remote technologies to maintain operations during lockdowns and the strict implementation of social distancing procedures and border closures. The pandemic also highlighted the significant role of global collaboration and open innovation when developing solutions to offset the significant challenges faced. Traditional competitive barriers were lowered as companies, research institutions, and governments collaborated to develop vaccines, treatments, and public health responses (Al-Omoush et al., 2022). Such collaboration generated a more cohesive innovation system, where shared knowledge and resources became vitally important in overcoming the crisis. However, such progress was also associated with the caveat that first-past-the-post could generate the largest gains, so those with the strongest relationships and professional trust would benefit the most from such joint research practices, as evidenced by the speed at which vaccines were developed and distributed, which broadly exemplified how collaborative efforts can lead to unprecedented innovation outcomes.

Governments also recognised the importance of startups and small and medium-sized enterprises (SMEs), necessitating substantial support and structures to restore confidence so as not to stifle any innovative progress (Caballero-Morales, 2021). Various initiatives, including financial aid packages and innovation grants, for example, were introduced, with evidence of such measures presented in Table 14.2, which broadly enable such enterprises to further advance themselves with experimentation and technology

Table 14.2: Selected global startup and SME support schemes during the COVID-19 pandemic.

Country/region	Program name	Type of initiative	Description	Date
United States	Paycheck Protection Program (PPP)	Financial Aid Package	Part of the CARES Act, the PPP provided forgivable loans to small businesses to cover payroll costs, rent, utilities, and interest on mortgages to retain employees	Mar-20
European Union	European Innovation Council (EIC) Fund	Innovation Grants	Offered financial support for innovative startups and SMEs, particularly those working on solutions related to healthcare and COVID-19 mitigation technologies	Apr-20
United Kingdom	Future Fund	Convertible Loan Scheme	Provided loans ranging from £125,000 to £5 million to startups, matched by private investment, to support innovation and R&D during the economic downturn	May-20
India	Atmanirbhar Bharat Abhiyan	Financial Aid & Incubation	A comprehensive economic stimulus package that included measures for MSMEs, such as collateral-free loans, equity infusion, and creation of an e-market linkage	May-20
Canada	Canada Emergency Business Account (CEBA)	Financial Aid Package	Offered interest-free loans of up to CAD 60,000 to small businesses and not-for-profits to help cover their operating costs during periods of reduced revenue	Apr-20
Australia	JobKeeper Payment	Wage Subsidy Program	Provided wage subsidies to businesses significantly impacted by COVID-19 to help keep employees on the payroll	Mar-20
Germany	Corona Soforthilfe	Emergency Assistance Grants	Offered direct, non-repayable grants to small businesses and freelancers to cover operating costs like rent and utility bills during the crisis	Mar-20
South Korea	K-Startup Grand Challenge	Incubation & Innovation Program	A government-sponsored startup accelerator program offering funding, office space, and mentorship to international startups in key sectors like AI and biotechnology	Jul-20
Brazil	Pronampe (National Support Program)	Low-Interest Loans	Provided low-interest loans specifically for micro and small businesses to maintain cash flow and support employment	May-20
Singapore	Startup SG Founder	Grant and Incubation Support	Enhanced grant support to startups, providing up to SGD 50,000, along with incubation and mentorship opportunities through government-accredited incubators	Apr-20

Table 14.2 (continued)

Country/region	Program name	Type of initiative	Description	Date
France	Plan de Relance (Recovery Plan)	Financial Aid & Innovation Grants	Included a specific focus on supporting SMEs and startups through grants, subsidies, and loan guarantees, particularly for those in the digital and green sectors	Sep-20
Japan	Special Measures for New Business	Subsidy and Financial Support	Provided subsidies and financial aid to SMEs, including new businesses, to cover fixed costs and support digital transformation	Apr-20
Italy	Cura Italia	Financial Aid & Loan Guarantees	Offered direct financial assistance, loan guarantees, and tax deferrals to SMEs to maintain liquidity and support continued business operations	Mar-20
South Africa	SMME Debt Relief Finance Scheme	Low-Interest Loans & Grants	Provided low-interest loans and grants to small, micro, and medium enterprises (SMMEs) affected by the COVID-19 pandemic to sustain their operations	Apr-20

Note: This table highlights various initiatives implemented worldwide to provide financial relief, foster innovation, and support the resilience of startups and SMEs during the COVID-19 pandemic. These programs played a critical role in helping businesses survive economic disruptions, adapt to new market conditions, and continue contributing to economic recovery and growth. Data sources include government publications, official announcements, and reports from international economic organisations.

Figure 14.1: Zoom share price.
Note: Data obtained from LSEG Eikon. Zoom Video Communications, Inc. provides an all-in-one intelligent collaboration platform. It provides a unified communications and collaboration platform that fundamentally changes how people interact, connecting them through frictionless and secure meetings, phone, chat, content sharing and more. Its products are grouped under various categories: Core Communications, AI, Employee Experience, Customer Experience and Developer Ecosystem. Core Communications products include Zoom Meetings, Zoom Phone, Zoom Team Chat. AI products, such as Zoom AI Companion. Employee Experience products include Zoom Rooms, Workspace Reservation, Zoom Docs and others. Customer Experience products include Zoom Contact Center, Zoom Virtual Agent, and Zoom Events. Developer Ecosystem products include Zoom Developer Platform, Zoom App Marketplace and Zoom Apps. It serves various industries, including education, entertainment/media, enterprise infrastructure, finance, etc.

to mitigate pandemic-related challenges. For example, many countries used data analytics to enact health policies, including contact tracing. Vaccine production was also supported through such policies, such as the development of the Oxford-AstraZeneca vaccine, which stemmed from concise collaboration projects. Frugal innovation was also vital in countries where cost-sensitivity relating to vaccines was of key concern. However, support enabled the production of cost-effective solutions, such as low-cost ventilators and portable diagnostic kits, that addressed local healthcare needs effectively. The effects of COVID-19 on collaboration were substantial, as travel restrictions and social distancing measures were put in place, remote collaboration tools became indispensable for researchers; evidence of such is presented in Figure 14.1, where the share price of Zoom Video Communications, Inc. displays exceptional growth in line with the expanding work-from-home policies implemented during the COVID-19 pandemic. Despite physical limitations, virtual conferences, online workshops, and digital collaboration platforms facilitated continuous R&D efforts. This shift maintained the momentum of ongoing projects and encouraged more global and inclusive participation in innovation activities.

14.3 Technological Innovations During COVID-19

Few sectors experienced as large a technological transition as that of the healthcare sector, where the pandemic rapidly transitioned technological advancements in telemedicine that had been somewhat partially planned and implemented. Virtual consultations became prominent, particularly as governments attempted to minimise population movement while shielding the most vulnerable in society. Such online meetings allowed medical practitioners to complete remote consultations while enhancing availability to somewhat remote or underserved population centres. The use of modular and temporary facilities has also become quite commonplace, adding additional floor space during high-demand periods, while also allowing for the separation of higher-risk patients. The enhancement of medical record management was also evident during the vaccination rollout, where significant numbers of the population were provided with COVID-19 vaccinations. Hospitals reorganised workflows to separate COVID-19 patients from non-infected individuals, reducing cross-infection risks and building on data management processes, but heavily built on streamlining traditional practices. Such data management technology has streamlined data sharing and coordination, which will hopefully improve the medical sector more broadly in the future.

Innovation in the retail sector saw a rapid development in e-commerce, where consumers shifted rapidly to online shopping. Such a change in dynamics necessitated the development of additional tools such as contactless delivery, curbside pickup and automated fulfilment centres, all of which were designed so that consumers could access goods safely during periods of heavy pandemic-related restrictions. From the supply side, the exceptional disruptions generated due to cross-border trade and logistical management were somewhat moderated through technological advancement, particularly that surrounding track-and-trace technology, some of which had been supported using growing blockchain technology. Supply chains that were traditionally optimised for cost-efficiency and just-in-time production proved vulnerable to disruptions caused by the pandemic. In the food and beverage industry, contactless payment and self-checkout kiosks have become commonplace, while chatbots have reduced human interaction; however, the standard of service has varied substantially worldwide.

Further, education technology experienced a rapid transformation as institutions worldwide transitioned to online learning platforms. Schools and universities adopted virtual classrooms, digital course materials, and interactive learning tools to continue operating classes during national lockdowns. Integrating such online learning systems enabled the effective delivery of educational content; however, the success of such resources was heavily reliant on broadband availability and coverage. The provision of open-source education software grew, which allowed universities with limited resources or those in regions with resource constraints to provide adequate resources to students.

The rapid development and implementation of new technological products, providing services such as video conferencing, collaboration tools, and cloud-based solutions, were vital for many organisations to maintain any semblance of cohesion during the early stages of COVID-19 restrictions, and even more so as the pandemic's damage became more apparent. The transition to remote working arrangements necessitated the implementation of associated cybersecurity measures, particularly to safeguard sensitive data transferred between non-standard channels that may not have been as secure as in an office setting. The threat of cybercriminality became an immediate secondary threat as a result of the pandemic that required substantial, immediate attention to mitigate (Pranggono and Arabo, 2021; Lallie et al., 2021; Okereafor, 2021). Further secondary effects were observed after the transition to remote working, where in several cases, it was identified that there existed a profound effect through elevated employee productivity due to factors such as reduced commuting times and the ability to create one's working arrangements (Galanti et al., 2021; Morikawa, 2022); however, this was balanced with elevated cases of reported stress and burnout, particularly instigated due to the muddied line between work and personal life.

Further, frugal innovation has been an important area of development during the pandemic, as across society, the equitable release of products such as vaccines and medicines became extremely difficult to implement. Countries with limited affordability were unable to obtain resources due to sharply elevated costs as a result of substantially elevated demand. One such example surrounded the provision and creation of ventilators as the level of patients in intensive care units as a result of COVID-19 sharply increased, where non-standard industrial corporations entered the market to produce in an attempt to provide public support while also repurposing products, such as alcohol for beverage purposes, it is used in the creation of hand sanitiser.

14.4 Innovation in Governance and Policy

The COVID-19 pandemic instigated a period of substantial innovation and significant adaptability in governance and policy, many of which would have been observed to be quite significantly outside traditional policy pathways. Governments have been central in incentivising R&D during the COVID-19 pandemic by allocating substantial scientific research funding. Additionally, governments supported remote work and digital transformation initiatives by investing in digital infrastructure, alongside the provision of tax incentives for technology adoption and implementing policies that encourage flexible work arrangements (Narayan et al., 2021; Corbet et al., 2022f) alongside international knowledge sharing (Abate et al., 2020; Ashraf, 2020a; Corbet et al., 2022a). Further, several governments launched strategic programs to boost innovation ecosystems, helping businesses and research institutions innovate at a more aggressive pace, coinciding with simplified regulatory processes and improved intellectual property protections. Public funding has been critical in de-risking R&D activities (Roper and Turner, 2020), encouraging private sector participation, and accelerating innovation.

Governments have also introduced policies to enhance internet connectivity, particularly in rural and underserved areas, to ensure a more equitable point of access to remote work opportunities. Further grants and subsidies were also made available to businesses to adopt digital tools and platforms in an attempt to facilitate continuity during the pandemic and lay the groundwork for more flexible and resilient work arrangements in the future.

Collaborative efforts in vaccine development have been a hallmark of the global response to the pandemic. Governments, international organisations, and private sector entities have joined forces to accelerate the development, production, and distribution of vaccines. Initiatives like the COVAX facility, co-led by the World Health Organisation (WHO), Gavi, and the Coalition for Epidemic Preparedness Innovations (CEPI), were instrumental in ensuring equitable vaccine distribution, particularly to low- and middle-income countries (Berkley, 2021; Usher, 2021; Eccleston-Turner and Upton, 2021). The private sector played a crucial role, with pharmaceutical companies like Pfizer-BioNTech, Moderna, and AstraZeneca, developing vaccines at record speed through partnerships with academic institutions and research organisations.

14.5 Concluding Comments

The pandemic necessitated rapid, novel solutions across multiple sectors, highlighting vulnerabilities in global supply chains and instigating a shift towards more localised and resilient production models. Innovations in digital technology facilitated the growth and development of the remote working environment, in some cases, entirely changing traditional business and educational operations. The healthcare sector witnessed unprecedented advancements, including the rapid development and deployment of medical equipment and vaccines, which served as key defensive mechanisms against the COVID-19 pandemic.

Specifically, reusing existing technologies was very helpful in some situations, especially when resources were limited. For example, the urgent need for medical supplies and equipment led to creative and cost-effective solutions, such as the use of 3D printing to create components for ventilators and personal protective equipment. This is evidenced by how resourceful and inventive people can be when faced with critical shortages and how important it is to have solutions that can be changed and scaled up. Governance and policy also played a significant role in fostering an environment conducive to innovation during the pandemic. Governments worldwide implemented measures to support research and development, providing funding and incentives for innovation in critical areas such as healthcare, digital technology, and supply chain management. The long-term implications of COVID-19 on innovation are profound and multifaceted. Businesses and organisations will likely continue investing in digital infrastructure and capabilities to enhance resilience and adaptability.

15 Concluding Comments

The COVID-19 pandemic was unprecedented in many dimensions: its scale, spread of transmission, public health response, the development and distribution of a vaccine, level of social disruption, and economic impact. In addition to challenging the public health system to its limits, the pandemic provided a stern stress test of the financial system. Initial responses were swift, with the stock market falling rapidly and precipitously, bond markets beginning to seize up, oil trading at a negative price for the first time, and cryptocurrencies demonstrating that they sometimes provided little or no hedging capacity for traditional assets. The recovery was equally swift, with stocks, commodities, and cryptocurrencies beginning a dramatic bull market less than a couple of months after the onset of the pandemic. Although the recovery was initially the result of strong monetary support, the sustained and all-encompassing nature of the subsequent performance across all asset classes highlighted strong market resilience.

Many financial lessons were learned from the pandemic. Beyond the many risks corporations face, a pandemic would have ranked among the lowest in most priority lists. The pandemic demonstrated the need to prepare for rare but impactful events. Given that a disaster such as the COVID-19 pandemic affects all companies and society more widely, should the responsibility for preparedness be underpinned by corporations or by the sovereign? In light of the subsequent defunding of several key programs relating to pandemic resilience, companies may need to consider how they can pre-empt and respond to such crises at the firm level.

The pandemic again highlighted the critical role that monetary policy plays in ensuring that markets continue to function during times of panic. Facing a liquidity crisis, especially in bond markets, the US Federal Reserve put in place a program to purchase not only Treasury and Municipal bonds but also seasoned corporate bonds. Emergency support, such as the Payroll Protection Program in the US, also helped small businesses avoid solvency issues. Finally, large-scale fiscal measures by governments globally helped to support a rapid recovery, even while doubts around the length of the pandemic persisted.

The pandemic also provided some lessons regarding market efficiency. In January and February 2020, despite evidence of a strong spread of the virus from Asia to Europe and associated excess mortalities, the market failed to price in the risks. This highlights challenges in pricing that are slowly developing but have high-impact risks. This was then followed by a swift correction, despite limited concrete economic data, suggesting the influence of emotion and uncertainty on market volatility. As highlighted above, government intervention was critical in restoring and maintaining functioning capital markets during the crisis.

COVID-19 may also have acted as a catalyst for change in financial markets. Systemic risk, often thought of as permeating from the financial sector, has now been expanded to include non-financial shocks with different triggers. Highly interconnected supply

https://doi.org/10.1515/9783111707990-015

chains resulted in just-in-time inventory failures. Market risk has been expanded to account for such operational susceptibility. Such vulnerability, in combination with significant fiscal and monetary support, also led to levels of inflationary pressure not witnessed in many decades, reawakening markets to the perils of price instability. Finally, as documented, the crisis again emphasised the critical role of government in limiting risk during crises.

The pandemic also acted as a strong catalyst for digitisation, artificial intelligence and FinTech. Digitisation was accelerated by necessity, with many workers forced to depend on collaboration tools due to remote work mandates. Similarly, banks and financial institutions moved to a digital-first model during the pandemic, with branches either closed or experiencing reduced footfall. This move to digital also helped to stimulate interest in and spur capital allocation to artificial intelligence. Direct applications to finance include credit scoring, fraud detection and algorithmic trading. Finally, COVID-19 was a major catalyst for digital payments, with sharp growth in cashless transactions evident. Decentralised platforms, such as Defi and cryptocurrency, also gained traction as an alternative to traditional centralised finance. Among the other FinTech applications that have grown rapidly, peer-to-peer lending platforms have experienced rapid growth, reaching underserved populations. Many of these COVID-19-originated changes will have a long-lasting impact on financial services.

The magnitude of the observed equity market risk premium has long been a puzzle. Rietz (1988) proposed a model where "rare events", resulting in market crashes, help to explain the size of the equity risk premium. Whether pandemic risk is a contributor to the observed equity risk premium is difficult to infer. While the magnitude of the reaction to the COVID-19 pandemic was severe, the infrequent nature of such events may not be sufficient to explain the puzzle (Julliard and Ghosh, 2012). Landier and Thesmar (2020) infer an increase of 50 basis points in the risk premium by May 2020 as a consequence of the pandemic, an increase that is offset by the reduction in interest rates. This suggests that the pandemic may serve only as a temporary catalyst for increased risk premiums, rather than explaining the associated long-run effects.

Many open research questions have emerged from the pandemic. As human-induced environmental changes increase, resulting in decreased biodiversity, this helps species that harbour pathogens transmissible to humans to thrive (Gibb et al., 2020). An associated increase in pandemic likelihood could have a substantial impact on financial markets and corporations more generally. As highlighted earlier, investors may demand a higher risk premium to compensate them for pandemic-related uncertainty. Increased tail risk may also shift the chances of excess systemic risk, resulting in financial institutions having to hold more capital. At a corporate level, concerns about pandemic vulnerability alongside associated impacts from rapid shifts in monetary policy may prompt a greater focus on risk management. At the heart of these concerns is a need to better understand, quantify and mitigate pathogens that might result in mass transmission and illness.

The market crisis emanating from the pandemic also gave rise to questions surrounding safe-haven assets. The ambiguity surrounding which assets provided safety from market turmoil stemmed from differing definitions of what constitutes a safe haven and the timing of its provision. Some research classified safe havens by including periods where the market was appreciating strongly and where no haven asset was required. Others referred to ambiguous definitions of turmoil based on measures of pandemic spread rather than focusing on what happened to financial markets. Further research is also required to understand the practical application of safe haven assets. Do such assets need to be held by investors at all times, or can occasions requiring safe havens be pre-identified, allowing changes to capital allocation over time. Furthermore, what is the tradeoff between safe havens and traditional assets in terms of performance?

Further research is also indicated on the effects of the COVID-19 pandemic on so-called “zombie firms”, companies that continue to operate based on external support even though they are unable to cover their debt costs from current earnings. During the crisis, governments globally were compelled to intervene to support companies without discrimination for their economic health. In addition to maintaining competition for healthy firms, supporting zombie firms may be a drag on productivity and economic growth, result in increased systemic risk due to non-performing loans, and reduce market competition. The consequences of the broad support of zombie firms during the pandemic are largely unknown and essential in developing a systematic response to future crises. Should policymakers put in place a strategy to discriminate between insolvent and illiquid firms during times of crisis, and if so, how is regulatory capture to be prevented?

In many regards, the pandemic acted as a natural experiment in the consumer adoption of financial technology. This provides an opportunity to test theories of habit formation and behavioural lock-in by determining whether the forced use of digital financial tools was sticky, even after the physical alternatives returned. Such research will be of particular value to policymakers as they grapple with the introduction of central bank digital currencies, and help to understand whether the pandemic improved financial access for those who were underbanked. The crisis also allows for testing whether network effects in financial technology have reached a tipping point, pushing digital finance from the early adopter stage into the mainstream. Finally, a critical and presently unanswered question is the extent to which the acceleration of financial innovations during the COVID-19 crisis affected macroeconomic and monetary channels.

Finally, the pandemic acted as a short-term wake-up call on the implications of climate change and biodiversity loss, raising public interest in sustainability more generally. This, in turn, helped to accelerate the growth of ESG investing, with substantial growth in sustainability-linked financing observed in 2020. Policymakers, in some cases, also linked recovery packages to green objectives, with programs such as the EU Green Deal. In the years following the crisis, however, interest in sustainability began to wane, in the face of challenges from inflation, excess debt and recessionary risks. The unprovoked attack by Russia on Ukraine also created an energy crisis, with a fall-back on fossil fuels. Furthermore, greenwashing concerns made it more difficult for investors to allocate capital to credible sustainability projects. Much further research is warranted to understand how finance can support the transition, including demonstrating long-term value from sustainability investments, understanding the real change made in companies adopting sustainability-linked funding, managing financial risks associated with climate change, and producing data which provides accurate measurement and accountability for sustainability and associated investments globally.

It is difficult to overstate the impact COVID-19 had on global finance. Some of the effects were immediate and obvious—extreme market swings, sudden policy interventions—while others are still playing out. The crisis forced both the private and public sectors to react to a form of risk that had rarely been taken seriously. Whether those reactions lead to lasting change is still uncertain. What is clear, however, is that finance can no longer afford to treat events like the COVID-19 pandemic as remote possibilities. There is still much to learn about risk, resilience, and how financial systems respond when the unexpected becomes reality.

Bibliography

Abate, M., Christidis, P., Purwanto, A. J. (2020). Government support to airlines in the aftermath of the COVID-19 pandemic. *Journal of Air Transport Management* **89**, 101931.

Abouk, R., Heydari, B. (2021). The immediate effect of COVID-19 policies on social-distancing behavior in the United States. *Public Health Reports* **136**(2), 245–252.

Aburto, J. M., Schöley, J., Kashnitsky, I., Zhang, L., Rahal, C., Missov, T. I., Mills, M. C., Dowd, J. B., Kashyap, R. (2022). Quantifying impacts of the COVID-19 pandemic through life-expectancy losses: A population-level study of 29 countries. *International Journal of Epidemiology* **51**(1), 63–74.

Acharya, V. V., Steffen, S. (2020). The risk of being a fallen angel and the corporate dash for cash in the midst of COVID. *The Review of Corporate Finance Studies* **9**(3), 430–471.

Acharya, V. V., Thakor, A. V. (2016). The dark side of liquidity creation: Leverage and systemic risk. *Journal of Financial Intermediation* **28**, 4–21.

Adcock, C., Bessler, W., Conlon, T. (2022). Characteristic-sorted portfolios and macroeconomic risks—an orthogonal decomposition. *Journal of Empirical Finance* **65**, 24–50.

Adedoyin, O. B., Soykan, E. (2023). COVID-19 pandemic and online learning: the challenges and opportunities. *Interactive Learning Environments* **31**(2), 863–875.

Adrian, T., Fleming, M., Shachar, O., Vogt, E. (2017). Market liquidity after the financial crisis. *Annual Review of Financial Economics* **9**(1), 43–83.

Aguiar-Conraria, L., Soares, M. J. (2014). The continuous wavelet transform: Moving beyond uni-and bivariate analysis. *Journal of Economic Surveys* **28**(2), 344–375.

Agur, I., Ari, A., Dell'Ariccia, G. (2022). Designing central bank digital currencies. *Journal of Monetary Economics* **125**, 62–79.

Ahmed, R., Borio, C., Disyatat, P., Hofmann, B. (2024). Losing traction? The real effects of monetary policy when interest rates are low. *Journal of International Money and Finance* **141**, 102999.

Ahonen, E., Corbet, S., Goodell, J. W., Günay, S., Larkin, C. (2022). Are carbon futures prices stable? New evidence during negative oil. *Finance Research Letters* **47**, 102723.

Aizenman, J., Ito, H., Pasricha, G. K. (2022). Central bank swap arrangements in the COVID-19 crisis. *Journal of International Money and Finance* **122**, 102555.

Akhtaruzzaman, M., Boubaker, S., Lucey, B. M., Sensoy, A. (2021). Is gold a hedge or a safe-haven asset in the COVID-19 crisis? *Economic Modelling* **102**, 105588.

Akyildirim, E., Corbet, S., Sensoy, A., Yarovaya, L. (2020). The impact of blockchain-related name changes on corporate performance. *Journal of Corporate Finance* **65**, 101759.

Akyildirim, E., Corbet, S., Hou, G., Hu, Y., Oxley, L. (2022). Another iceberg ahead: Are corporate reputational catastrophes treated differently during recessions? Available at SSRN 4230956.

Akyildirim, E., Corbet, S., Ongena, S., Oxley, L. (2023). Greenwashing: Do investors, markets and boards really care? Swiss Finance Institute Research Paper (23-90).

Akyildirim, E., Conlon, T., Corbet, S., Oxley, L. (2024a). 'Take Back Control': The implications of Brexit uncertainty on investor perception of ESG reputational events. *European Financial Management* **31**(1), 72–114.

Akyildirim, E., Corbet, S., Ongena, S., Staunton, D. (2024b). Examining the relationship between bank reputational disaster and sponsored money market fund flows. Available at SSRN 4773381.

Al Farooque, O., Baghdadi, G., Trinh, H. H., Khandaker, S. (2023). Stock liquidity during COVID-19 crisis: A cross-country analysis of developed and emerging economies, and economic policy uncertainty. *Emerging Markets Review* **55**, 101025.

Al-Khawaja, H. A., Yamin, I., Alshehadeh, A. (2023). The COVID-19 pandemic's effects on fintech in banking sector. *Review of Economics and Finance* **21**(1), 316–322.

Al-Omoush, K. S., Ribeiro-Navarrete, S., Lassala, C., Skare, M. (2022). Networking and knowledge creation: Social capital and collaborative innovation in responding to the COVID-19 crisis. *Journal of Innovation & Knowledge* **7**(2), 100181.

https://doi.org/10.1515/9783111707990-016

Alabi, M. O., Ngwenyama, O. (2023). Food security and disruptions of the global food supply chains during COVID-19: Building smarter food supply chains for post COVID-19 era. *British Food Journal* **125**(1), 167–185.

Alaoui Mdaghri, A., Raghibi, A., Thanh, C. N., Oubdi, L. (2021). Stock market liquidity, the great lockdown and the COVID-19 global pandemic nexus in MENA countries. *Review of Behavioral Finance* **13**(1), 51–68.

Albani, V., Loria, J., Massad, E., Zubelli, J. (2021). COVID-19 underreporting and its impact on vaccination strategies. *BMC Infectious Diseases* **21**, 1–13.

Albuquerque, R., Koskinen, Y., Yang, S., Zhang, C. (2020). Resiliency of environmental and social stocks: An analysis of the exogenous COVID-19 market crash. *The Review of Corporate Finance Studies* **9**(3), 593–621.

Alessandrini, F., Jondeau, E. (2020). Optimal strategies for ESG portfolios. *Swiss Finance Institute Research Paper*, 20–21.

Almeida, F., Duarte Santos, J., Monteiro, J. A. (2020). The challenges and opportunities in the digitalization of companies in a post-COVID-19 world. *IEEE Engineering Management Review* **48**(3), 97–103.

Aloui, D., Benkraiem, R., Guesmi, K., Vigne, S. (2023). The European Central Bank and green finance: How would the green quantitative easing affect the investors' behavior during times of crisis? *International Review of Financial Analysis* **85**, 102464.

Alshrari, A. S., Hudu, S. A., Imran, M., Asdaq, S. M. B., Ali, A. M., Rabbani, S. I. (2022). Innovations and development of COVID-19 vaccines: A patent review. *Journal of Infection and Public Health* **15**(1), 123–131.

Amankwah-Amoah, J. (2020). Note: Mayday, mayday, mayday! Responding to environmental shocks: Insights on global airlines' responses to COVID-19. *Transportation Research. Part E, Logistics and Transportation Review* **143**, 102098.

Amankwah-Amoah, J., Khan, Z., Wood, G., Knight, G. (2021). COVID-19 and digitalization: The great acceleration. *Journal of Business Research* **136**, 602–611.

Amiti, M., Heise, S., Karahan, F., Şahin, A. (2024). Inflation strikes back: The role of import competition and the labor market. *NBER Macroeconomics Annual* **38**(1), 71–131.

Andreff, W. (2011). Some comparative economics of the organization of sports: Competition and regulation in North American vs. European professional team sports leagues. *The European Journal of Comparative Economics* **8**(1), 3–27.

Andrijevic, M., Schleussner, C.-F., Gidden, M. J., McCollum, D. L., Rogelj, J. (2020). COVID-19 recovery funds dwarf clean energy investment needs. *Science* **370**(6514), 298–300.

Ang, A., Bekaert, G. (2004). How regimes affect asset allocation. *Financial Analysts Journal* **60**(2), 86–99.

Apergis, N., Lau, C. K., Xu, B. (2023). The impact of COVID-19 on stock market liquidity: Fresh evidence on listed Chinese firms. *International Review of Financial Analysis* **90**, 102847.

Apostolakis, G. N., Floros, C., Gkillas, K., Wohar, M. (2021). Political uncertainty, COVID-19 pandemic and stock market volatility transmission. *Journal of International Financial Markets, Institutions & Money* **74**, 101383.

Aragon, F., Bernal, N., Bosch, M., Molina, O. (2024). COVID-19 and economic preferences: Evidence from a panel of cab drivers. *Journal of Behavioral and Experimental Economics* **112**, 102257.

Aretz, K., Bartram, S. M., Pope, P. F. (2010). Macroeconomic risks and characteristic-based factor models. *Journal of Banking & Finance* **34**(6), 1383–1399.

Ashraf, B. N. (2020a). Economic impact of government interventions during the COVID-19 pandemic: International evidence from financial markets. *Journal of Behavioral and Experimental Finance* **27**, 100371.

Ashraf, B. N. (2020b). Stock markets' reaction to COVID-19: Cases or fatalities? *Research in International Business and Finance* **54**, 101249.

Attig, N., Sy, O. (2023). Diversification during hard times. *Financial Analysts Journal* **79**(2), 45–64.

Autor, D., Cho, D., Crane, L. D., Goldar, M., Lutz, B., Montes, J., Peterman, W. B., Ratner, D., Villar, D., Yildirmaz, A. (2022). The $800 billion paycheck protection program: Where did the money go and why did it go there? *The Journal of Economic Perspectives* **36**(2), 55–80.

Azizah, A., Arsawan, W. E., Diah, A. M. (2024). Investigating risk management toward sustainable performance: Evidence from emerging market. *Management and Accounting Review* **23**(1), 573–600.
Bachas, N., Ganong, P., Noel, P. J., Vavra, J. S., Wong, A., Farrell, D., Greig, F. E. (2020). Initial impacts of the pandemic on consumer behavior: Evidence from linked income, spending, and savings data.
Badr, H. S., Du, H., Marshall, M., Dong, E., Squire, M. M., Gardner, L. M. (2020). Association between mobility patterns and COVID-19 transmission in the USA: A mathematical modelling study. *Lancet. Infectious Diseases* **20**(11), 1247–1254.
Bae, K.-H., El Ghoul, S., Gong, Z. J., Guedhami, O. (2021). Does CSR matter in times of crisis? Evidence from the COVID-19 pandemic. *Journal of Corporate Finance* **67**, 101876.
Bai, M., Zhang, Y., Yu, C.-F. J. (2024). Do firms gamble for resurrection from COVID-19? *Economics Letters* **241**, 111835.
Bailey, C., Brody, R., Sokolowski, M. (2022). Fraudulent loans and the United States Paycheck Protection program. *Journal of Financial Crime* **29**(2), 519–532.
Baker, S. R., Bloom, N., Davis, S. J., Kost, K., Sammon, M., Viratyosin, T. (2020). The unprecedented stock market reaction to COVID-19. *The Review of Asset Pricing Studies* **10**(4), 742–758.
Baláž, V., Chen, J., Williams, A., Li, G. (2024). Stability of risk and uncertainty preferences in tourism. *Annals of Tourism Research* **105**, 103726.
Bao, Z., Huang, D. (2021). Shadow banking in a crisis: Evidence from FinTech during COVID-19. *Journal of Financial and Quantitative Analysis* **56**(7), 2320–2355.
Barbier, E. B. (2020). Greening the post-pandemic recovery in the G20. *Environmental & Resource Economics* **76**(4), 685–703.
Barrdear, J., Kumhof, M. (2022). The macroeconomics of central bank digital currencies. *Journal of Economic Dynamics and Control* **142**, 104148.
Barrett, C. B. (2020). Actions now can curb food systems fallout from COVID-19. *Nature Food* **1**(6), 319–320.
Bartram, S. M., Bodnar, G. M. (2009). No place to hide: The global crisis in equity markets in 2008/2009. *Journal of International Money and Finance* **28**(8), 1246–1292.
Bas, T., Malki, I., Sivaprasad, S. (2024). Connectedness between central bank digital currency index, financial stability and digital assets. *Journal of International Financial Markets, Institutions & Money* **92**, 101981.
Basten, C. (2020). Higher bank capital requirements and mortgage pricing: Evidence from the counter-cyclical capital buffer. *Review of Finance* **24**(2), 453–495.
Baumgartner, R. J., Ebner, D. (2010). Corporate sustainability strategies: sustainability profiles and maturity levels. *Sustainable Development* **18**(2), 76–89.
Baur, D. G., Lucey, B. M. (2010). Is gold a hedge or a safe haven? An analysis of stocks, bonds and gold. *Financial Review* **45**(2), 217–229.
Baur, D. G., McDermott, T. K. (2010). Is gold a safe haven? International evidence. *Journal of Banking & Finance* **34**(8), 1886–1898.
Beber, A., Brandt, M. W., Kavajecz, K. A. (2009). Flight-to-quality or flight-to-liquidity? Evidence from the Euro-area bond market. *The Review of Financial Studies* **22**(3), 925–957.
Beck, M. J., Hensher, D. A. (2020). Insights into the impact of COVID-19 on household travel and activities in Australia—the early days of easing restrictions. *Transport Policy* **99**, 95–119.
Bei, Z., Lin, J., Zhou, Y. (2024). No safe haven, only diversification and contagion—Intraday evidence around the COVID-19 pandemic. *Journal of International Money and Finance* **143**, 103069.
Belhadi, A., Kamble, S., Jabbour, C. J. C., Gunasekaran, A., Ndubisi, N. O., Venkatesh, M. (2021). Manufacturing and service supply chain resilience to the COVID-19 outbreak: Lessons learned from the automobile and airline industries. *Technological Forecasting & Social Change* **163**, 120447.
Benbouzid, N., Kumar, A., Mallick, S. K., Sousa, R. M., Stojanovic, A. (2022). Bank credit risk and macro-prudential policies: Role of counter-cyclical capital buffer. *Journal of Financial Stability* **63**, 101084.
Bentes, S. R., Gubareva, M., Teplova, T. (2022). The impact of COVID-19 on gold seasonality. *Applied Economics* **54**(40), 4700–4710.

Berger, A. N., Demirgüç-Kunt, A. (2021). Banking research in the time of COVID-19. *Journal of Financial Stability* **57**, 100939.

Berger, A. N., Demirgüç-Kunt, A., Moshirian, F., Saunders, A. (2021). The way forward for banks during the COVID-19 crisis and beyond: Government and central bank responses, threats to the global banking industry. *Journal of Banking & Finance* **133**, 106303.

Berkley, S. (2021). COVAX: More than a beautiful idea. *The Lancet* **398**(10298), 388.

Berkman, H., Malloch, H. (2023). Stock valuation during the COVID-19 pandemic: An explanation using option-based discount rates. *Journal of Banking & Finance* **147**, 106386.

Bernanke, B. S. (2020). The new tools of monetary policy. *American Economic Review* **110**(4), 943–983.

Bernstein, S., Townsend, R. R., Xu, T. (2024). Flight to safety: How economic downturns affect talent flows to startups. *The Review of Financial Studies* **37**(3), 837–881.

Bessler, W., Wolff, D. (2015). Do commodities add value in multi-asset portfolios? An out-of-sample analysis for different investment strategies. *Journal of Banking & Finance* **60**, 1–20.

Bessler, W., Opfer, H., Wolff, D. (2017). Multi-asset portfolio optimization and out-of-sample performance: An evaluation of Black–Litterman, mean-variance, and naïve diversification approaches. *European Journal of Finance* **23**(1), 1–30.

Bessler, W., Conlon, T., Huan, X. (2019). Does corporate hedging enhance shareholder value? A meta-analysis. *International Review of Financial Analysis* **61**, 222–232.

Bessler, W., Taushanov, G., Wolff, D. (2021). Optimal asset allocation strategies for international equity portfolios: A comparison of country versus industry optimization. *Journal of International Financial Markets, Institutions & Money* **72**, 101343.

Bhargava, V., Weeks, H. S. (2022). Short-term REIT performance under pandemic conditions. *The Journal of Real Estate Portfolio Management* **28**(1), 62–77.

Bhattacharyay, B. N. (2021). Managing climate-related financial risk: Prospects and challenges. *Contributions to Conflict Management, Peace Economics and Development* **29**, 39–56.

Bianchi, F., Bianchi, G., Song, D. (2023). The long-term impact of the COVID-19 unemployment shock on life expectancy and mortality rates. *Journal of Economic Dynamics and Control* **146**, 104581.

Bick, A., Blandin, A., Mertens, K. et al. (2020). Work from home after the COVID-19 outbreak. *Federal Reserve Bank of Dallas Research, 2017.*

Blanchard, O. J., Bernanke, B. S. (2023). What caused the US pandemic-era inflation? *National Bureau of Economic Research.*

Blau, B. M., Griffith, T. G., Whitby, R. J. (2021). Inflation and Bitcoin: A descriptive time-series analysis. *Economics Letters* **203**, 109848.

Blitz, D., Vidojevic, M. (2019). The characteristics of factor investing. *The Journal of Portfolio Management* **45**(3), 69–86.

Blitz, D., Baltussen, G., van Vliet, P. (2020). When equity factors drop their shorts. *Financial Analysts Journal* **76**(4), 73–99.

Blustein, D. L., Duffy, R., Ferreira, J. A., Cohen-Scali, V., Cinamon, R. G., Allan, B. A. (2020). Unemployment in the time of COVID-19: A research agenda. *Journal of Vocational Behaviour* **119**, 103436.

Bollaert, H., Lopez-de Silanes, F., Schwienbacher, A. (2021). Fintech and access to finance. *Journal of Corporate Finance* **68**, 101941.

Bolton, P., Santos, T., Scheinkman, J. A. (2011). Outside and inside liquidity. *The Quarterly Journal of Economics* **126**(1), 259–321.

Boserup, B., McKenney, M., Elkbuli, A. (2020). Alarming trends in US domestic violence during the COVID-19 pandemic. *The American Journal of Emergency Medicine* **38**(12), 2753.

Boucher, C., Tokpavi, S. (2019). Stocks and bonds: Flight-to-safety for ever? *Journal of International Money and Finance* **95**, 27–43.

Bouri, E., Molnár, P., Azzi, G., Roubaud, D., Hagfors, L. I. (2017). On the hedge and safe haven properties of bitcoin: Is it really more than a diversifier? *Finance Research Letters* **20**, 192–198.

Bowes, A., Lomax, L., Piasecki, J. (2021). A losing battle? Women's sport pre-and post-COVID-19. *European Sport Management Quarterly* **21**(3), 443–461.
Bowes, A., Lomax, L., Piasecki, J. (2022). The impact of the COVID-19 lockdown on elite sportswomen. *Managing Sport and Leisure* **27**(6), 513–529.
Brada, J. C., Gajewski, P., Kutan, A. M. (2021). Economic resiliency and recovery, lessons from the financial crisis for the COVID-19 pandemic: A regional perspective from Central and Eastern Europe. *International Review of Financial Analysis* **74**, 101658.
Bredin, D., Conlon, T., Potì, V. (2015). Does gold glitter in the long-run? Gold as a hedge and safe haven across time and investment horizon. *International Review of Financial Analysis* **41**, 320–328.
Bredin, D., Conlon, T., Potì, V. (2017). The price of shelter-Downside risk reduction with precious metals. *International Review of Financial Analysis* **49**, 48–58.
Breugem, M., Corvino, R., Marfè, R., Schönleber, L. (2024). Pandemic tail risk. *Journal of Banking & Finance* **167**, 107257.
Brodeur, A., Gray, D., Islam, A., Bhuiyan, S. (2021). A literature review of the economics of COVID-19. *Journal of Economic Surveys* **35**(4), 1007–1044.
Buckman, S. R., Shapiro, A. H., Sudhof, M., Wilson, D. J. et al. (2020). News sentiment in the time of COVID-19. *FRBSF Economic Letter* **8**(1), 5–10.
Buheji, M., da Costa Cunha, K., Beka, G., Mavric, B., De Souza, Y., da Costa Silva, S. S., Hanafi, M., Yein, T. C. (2020). The extent of COVID-19 pandemic socio-economic impact on global poverty. A global integrative multidisciplinary review. *American Journal of Economics* **10**(4), 213–224.
Butler, K. C., Joaquin, D. C. (2002). Are the gains from international portfolio diversification exaggerated? The influence of downside risk in bear markets. *Journal of International Money and Finance* **21**(7), 981–1011.
Caballero, R., Simsek, A. (2021). A model of endogenous risk intolerance and LSAPs: Asset prices and aggregate demand in a "COVID-19" shock. *The Review of Financial Studies* **34**(11), 5522–5580.
Caballero-Morales, S.-O. (2021). Innovation as recovery strategy for SMEs in emerging economies during the COVID-19 pandemic. *Research in International Business and Finance* **57**, 101396.
Campbell, R., Koedijk, K., Kofman, P. (2002). Increased correlation in bear markets. *Financial Analysts Journal* **58**(1), 87–94.
Caporale, G. M., Kang, W.-Y., Spagnolo, F., Spagnolo, N. (2022). The COVID-19 pandemic, policy responses and stock markets in the G20. *International Economics* **172**, 77–90.
Carroll, R., Conlon, T., Cotter, J., Salvador, E. (2017). Asset allocation with correlation: A composite trade-off. *European Journal of Operational Research* **262**(3), 1164–1180.
Cepel, M., Gavurova, B., Dvorsky, J., Belas, J. (2020). The impact of the COVID-19 crisis on the perception of business risk in the same segment. *Journal of International Studies* **13**(3), 248–263.
Chabi-Yo, F., Huggenberger, M., Weigert, F. (2022). Multivariate crash risk. *Journal of Financial Economics* **145**(1), 129–153.
Chae, B. K., Sheu, C., Park, E. O. (2024). The value of data, machine learning, and deep learning in restaurant demand forecasting: Insights and lessons learned from a large restaurant chain. *Decision Support Systems* **184**, 114291.
Chan, K., Yang, J., Zhou, Y. (2018). Conditional co-skewness and safe-haven currencies: A regime switching approach. *Journal of Empirical Finance* **48**, 58–80.
Chang, H.-Y., Tang, W., Hatef, E., Kitchen, C., Weiner, J. P., Kharrazi, H. (2021). Differential impact of mitigation policies and socioeconomic status on COVID-19 prevalence and social distancing in the United States. *BMC Public Health* **21**(1), 1140.
Chang, L., Gan, X., Mohsin, M. (2022). Studying corporate liquidity and regulatory responses for economic recovery in COVID-19 crises. *Economic Analysis and Policy* **76**, 211–225.
Cheema, M. A., Faff, R., Szulczyk, K. R. (2022). The 2008 global financial crisis and COVID-19 pandemic: How safe are the safe haven assets? *International Review of Financial Analysis* **83**, 102316.

Chen, S.-S. (2009). Predicting the bear stock market: Macroeconomic variables as leading indicators. *Journal of Banking & Finance* **33**(2), 211–223.

Chen, Z., Jiang, K. (2024). Digitalization and corporate investment efficiency: Evidence from China. *Journal of International Financial Markets, Institutions & Money* **91**, 101915.

Chen, H., Siklos, P. L. (2022). Central bank digital currency: A review and some macro-financial implications. *Journal of Financial Stability* **60**, 100985.

Chen, A. Y., Zimmermann, T. (2021). Open source cross-sectional asset pricing. *Critical Finance Review*, forthcoming.

Cheng, I.-H. (2020). Volatility markets underreacted to the early stages of the COVID-19 pandemic. *The Review of Asset Pricing Studies* **10**(4), 635–668.

Cho, D., Han, H. (2021). The tail behavior of safe haven currencies: A cross-quantilogram analysis. *Journal of International Financial Markets, Institutions & Money* **70**, 101257.

Choi, S.-Y. (2022). Credit risk interdependence in global financial markets: Evidence from three regions using multiple and partial wavelet approaches. *Journal of International Financial Markets, Institutions & Money* **80**, 101636.

Chong, J., Phillips, G. M. (2016). ESG investing: A simple approach. *The Journal of Wealth Management* **19**(2), 73.

Chowell, G., Mizumoto, K. (2020). The COVID-19 pandemic in the USA: What might we expect? *Lancet* **395**(10230), 1093.

Christensen, J. H., Gillan, J. M. (2022). Does quantitative easing affect market liquidity? *Journal of Banking & Finance* **134**, 106349.

Christoffersen, P., Langlois, H. (2013). The joint dynamics of equity market factors. *Journal of Financial and Quantitative Analysis* **48**(5), 1371–1404.

Ciner, C., Gurdgiev, C., Lucey, B. M. (2013). Hedges and safe havens: An examination of stocks, bonds, gold, oil and exchange rates. *International Review of Financial Analysis* **29**, 202–211.

Cioroianu, I., Conlon, T., Corbet, S., Larkin, C., Oxley, L., Taffler, R. (2024). The influence of social media emotions: Evidence from the kodak manic episode. *Journal of Behavioral Finance*, 1–28.

Cirelli, F., Gertler, M. (2022). Economic winners versus losers and the unequal pandemic recession.

Cirera, X., Cruz, M., Davies, E., Grover, A., Iacovone, L., Cordova, J. E. L., Medvedev, D., Maduko, F. O., Nayyar, G., Reyes Ortega, S. et al. (2021). Policies to support businesses through the COVID-19 shock: A firm level perspective. *The World Bank Research Observer* **36**(1), 41–66.

Coibion, O., Gorodnichenko, Y., Weber, M. (2020). The cost of the COVID-19 crisis: Lockdowns, macroeconomic expectations, and consumer spending.

Çolak, G., Öztekin, Ö. (2021). The impact of COVID-19 pandemic on bank lending around the world. *Journal of Banking & Finance* **133**, 106207.

Conlon, T., Corbet, S. (2023). The problem with NFTs. Available at SSRN 4640796.

Conlon, T., Cotter, J. (2012). An empirical analysis of dynamic multiscale hedging using wavelet decomposition. *The Journal of Futures Markets* **32**(3), 272–299.

Conlon, T., Cotter, J. (2013). Downside risk and the energy hedger's horizon. *Energy Economics* **36**, 371–379.

Conlon, T., McGee, R. (2020a). Safe haven or risky hazard? Bitcoin during the COVID-19 bear market. *Finance Research Letters* **35**, 101607.

Conlon, T., McGee, R. J. (2020b). Betting on Bitcoin: Does gambling volume on the blockchain explain bitcoin price changes? *Economics Letters* **191**, 108727.

Conlon, T., McGee, R. (2021). ICO fraud and regulation. In: *Batten–Corbet–Lucey Handbooks in Alternative Investments*. De Gruyter.

Conlon, T., Ruskin, H. J., Crane, M. (2007). Random matrix theory and fund of funds portfolio optimisation. *Physica A: Statistical Mechanics and Its Applications* **382**(2), 565–576.

Conlon, T., Crane, M., Ruskin, H. J. (2008). Wavelet multiscale analysis for hedge funds: Scaling and strategies. *Physica A: Statistical Mechanics and its Applications* **387**(21), 5197–5204.

Conlon, T., Ruskin, H. J., Crane, M. (2009a). Multiscaled cross-correlation dynamics in financial time-series. *Advances in Complex Systems* **12**(04n05), 439–454.

Conlon, T., Ruskin, H. J., Crane, M. (2009b). Seizure characterisation using frequency-dependent multivariate dynamics. *Computers in Biology and Medicine* **39**(9), 760–767.

Conlon, T., Cotter, J., Gencay, R. (2018a). Long-run wavelet-based correlation for financial time series. *European Journal of Operational Research* **271**(2), 676–696.

Conlon, T., Lucey, B. M., Uddin, G. S. (2018b). Is gold a hedge against inflation? A wavelet time-scale perspective. *Review of Quantitative Finance and Accounting* **51**(2), 317–345.

Conlon, T., Corbet, S., McGee, R. J. (2020). Are cryptocurrencies a safe haven for equity markets? An international perspective from the COVID-19 pandemic. *Research in International Business and Finance* **54**, 101248.

Conlon, T., Corbet, S., McGee, R. J. (2021). Inflation and cryptocurrencies revisited: A time-scale analysis. *Economics Letters* **206**, 109996.

Conlon, T., Corbet, S., Hou, G., Hu, Y., Oxley, L. (2022). Beyond the noise: Information discovery in Bitcoin revisited. Available at SSRN 4649154.

Conlon, T., Corbet, S., Hu, Y. (2023a). The collapse of the FTX exchange: The end of cryptocurrency's age of innocence. *The British Accounting Review*, 101277.

Conlon, T., Corbet, S., Hu, Y. (2023b). Understanding the contagion effects of the FTX exchange collapse. Available at SSRN 4640797.

Conlon, T., Cotter, J., Kovalenko, I., Post, T. (2023c). A financial modeling approach to industry exchange-traded funds selection. *Journal of Empirical Finance* **74**, 101441.

Conlon, T., Corbet, S., Hou, Y. G., Hu, Y., Oxley, L. (2024a). Bitcoin forks: What drives the branches? *Research in International Business and Finance* **69**, 102261.

Conlon, T., Corbet, S., Hou, Y. G., Hu, Y., Oxley, L. (2024b). Seeking a shock haven: Hedging extreme upward oil price changes. *International Review of Financial Analysis* **94**, 103245.

Conlon, T., Corbet, S., Hou, Y. G. (2024c). Contagion effects of permissionless, worthless cryptocurrency tokens: Evidence from the collapse of FTX. *Journal of International Financial Markets, Institutions & Money* **91**, 101940.

Conlon, T., Corbet, S., McGee, R. (2024d). Enduring relief or fleeting respite? Bitcoin as a hedge and safe haven for the US dollar. *Annals of Operations Research* **337**, 45–73.

Conlon, T., Corbet, S., Hou, G., Hu, Y., Larkin, C. J., Oxley, L. (2024e). Understanding sentiment shifts in central bank digital currencies. *Journal of Behavioral and Experimental Finance* **44**, 100988.

Conlon, T., Corbet, S., McGee, R. J. (2024f). The Bitcoin volume-volatility relationship: A high frequency analysis of futures and spot exchanges. *International Review of Financial Analysis* **91**, 103013.

Conlon, T., Corbet, S., Oxley, L. (2024g). Investor sentiment, unexpected inflation and bitcoin basis risk. *The Journal of Futures Markets* **44**(11), 1807–1831.

Conlon, T., Cotter, J., Eyiah-Donkor, E. (2024h). Forecasting the price of oil: A cautionary note. *Journal of Commodity Markets* **33**, 100378.

Conlon, T., Cotter, J., Ropotos, I. (2024i). Diversification with globally integrated US stocks. *Journal of International Financial Markets, Institutions & Money* **90**, 101889.

Connor, J., Madhavan, S., Mokashi, M., Amanuel, H., Johnson, N. R., Pace, L. E., Bartz, D. (2020). Health risks and outcomes that disproportionately affect women during the COVID-19 pandemic: A review. *Social Science & Medicine* **266**, 113364.

Corbet, S., Gurdgiev, C. (2019). What the hack: Systematic risk contagion from cyber events. *International Review of Financial Analysis* **65**, 101386.

Corbet, S., Gurdgiev, C. (2020). An incentives-based mechanism for corporate cyber governance enforcement and regulation. In: *Ecological, Societal, and Technological Risks and the Financial Sector*, pp. 281–307.

Corbet, S., Larkin, C. (2024). *Themes in Alternative Investments*, Volume 1. Walter de Gruyter GmbH & Co KG.

Corbet, S., Oxley, L. (2023). Investigating the academic response to cryptocurrencies: Insights from research diversification as separated by journal ranking. *Review of Corporate Finance* **3**(4), 487–528.
Corbet, S., Cumming, D. J., Lucey, B. M., Peat, M., Vigne, S. A. (2020a). The destabilising effects of cryptocurrency cybercriminality. *Economics Letters* **191**, 108741.
Corbet, S., Goodell, J. W., Günay, S. (2020b). Co-movements and spillovers of oil and renewable firms under extreme conditions: New evidence from negative WTI prices during COVID-19. *Energy Economics* **92**, 104978.
Corbet, S., Hou, Y. G., Hu, Y., Larkin, C., Oxley, L. (2020c). Any port in a storm: Cryptocurrency safe-havens during the COVID-19 pandemic. *Economics Letters* **194**, 109377.
Corbet, S., Hou, Y., Hu, Y., Oxley, L. (2020d). The influence of the COVID-19 pandemic on asset-price discovery: Testing the case of Chinese informational asymmetry. *International Review of Financial Analysis* **72**, 101560.
Corbet, S., Larkin, C., Lucey, B. (2020e). The contagion effects of the COVID-19 pandemic: Evidence from gold and cryptocurrencies. *Finance Research Letters* **35**, 101554.
Corbet, S., Hou, Y. G., Hu, Y., Oxley, L. (2021a). An analysis of investor behaviour and information flows surrounding the negative WTI oil price futures event. *Energy Economics* **104**, 105589.
Corbet, S., Hou, Y. G., Hu, Y., Oxley, L. (2021b). Volatility spillovers during market supply shocks: The case of negative oil prices. *Resources Policy* **74**, 102357.
Corbet, S., Hou, Y. G., Hu, Y., Oxley, L., Xu, D. (2021). Pandemic-related financial market volatility spillovers: Evidence from the Chinese COVID-19 epicentre. *International Review of Economics & Finance* **71**, 55–81.
Corbet, S., Hou, Y., Hu, Y., Oxley, L. (2022). Did COVID-19 tourism sector supports alleviate investor fear? *Annals of Tourism Research* **95**, 103434.
Corbet, S., Hou, Y., Hu, Y., Oxley, L. (2022b). Financial contagion among COVID-19 concept-related stocks in China. *Applied Economics* **54**(21), 2439–2452.
Corbet, S., Hou, Y., Hu, Y., Oxley, L. (2022c). The growth of oil futures in China: Evidence of market maturity through global crises. *Energy Economics* **114**, 106243.
Corbet, S., Hou, Y. G., Hu, Y., Oxley, L. (2022d). The influence of the COVID-19 pandemic on the hedging functionality of Chinese financial markets. *Research in International Business and Finance* **59**, 101510.
Corbet, S., Hou, Y. G., Hu, Y., Oxley, L. (2022e). We Reddit in a forum: The influence of message boards on firm stability. *Review of Corporate Finance* **2**(1), 151–190.
Corbet, S., Cumming, D. J., Hou, Y. G., Hu, Y., Oxley, L. (2022f). Have crisis-induced banking supports influenced European bank performance, resilience and price discovery? *Journal of International Financial Markets, Institutions & Money* **78**, 101566.
Corbet, S., Nicolau, J. L., Oxley, L. (2023). Spillover effects of sanctions on airlines. *Journal of Travel Research* **64**(1), 74–89. https://doi.org/10.1177/00472875231210977.
Corbet, S., Hou, Y., Hu, Y., Oxley, L. (2024). Time varying risk aversion and its connectedness: Evidence from cryptocurrencies. *Annals of Operations Research* **338**, 879–923.
Cordeiro, M. C., Santos, L., Angelo, A. C. M., Marujo, L. G. (2022). Research directions for supply chain management in facing pandemics: An assessment based on bibliometric analysis and systematic literature review. *International Journal of Logistics Research and Applications* **25**(10), 1313–1333.
Couch, K. A., Fairlie, R. W., Xu, H. (2020). Early evidence of the impacts of COVID-19 on minority unemployment. *Journal of Public Economics* **192**, 104287.
Courtemanche, C., Garuccio, J., Le, A., Pinkston, J., Yelowitz, A. (2020). Strong social distancing measures in the United States reduced the COVID-19 growth rate: Study evaluates the impact of social distancing measures on the growth rate of confirmed COVID-19 cases across the United States. *Health Affairs* **39**(7), 1237–1246.
Cox, J., Greenwald, D. L., Ludvigson, S. C. (2020). What explains the COVID-19 stock market? *National Bureau of Economic Research*.
Cui, T., Suleman, M. T., Zhang, H. (2022). Do the green bonds overreact to the COVID-19 pandemic? *Finance Research Letters* **49**, 103095.

Cui, L., Wu, H., Wu, L., Kumar, A., Tan, K. H. (2023). Investigating the relationship between digital technologies, supply chain integration and firm resilience in the context of COVID-19. *Annals of Operations Research* **327**(2), 825–853.
Cukierman, A. (2013). Monetary policy and institutions before, during, and after the global financial crisis. *Journal of Financial Stability* **9**(3), 373–384.
Dafermos, Y., Nikolaidi, M., Galanis, G. (2018). Climate change, financial stability and monetary policy. *Ecological Economics* **152**, 219–234.
Daly, M. C., Buckman, S. R., Seitelman, L. M. (2020). The unequal impact of COVID-19: Why education matters. *FRBSF Economic Letter* **17**(5), 1–5.
Daniel, K., Moskowitz, T. J. (2016). Momentum crashes. *Journal of Financial Economics* **122**(2), 221–247.
Daragmeh, A., Lentner, C., Sági, J. (2021). FinTech payments in the era of COVID-19: Factors influencing behavioral intentions of "Generation X" in Hungary to use mobile payment. *Journal of Behavioral and Experimental Finance* **32**, 100574.
Davoodalhosseini, S. M. (2022). Central bank digital currency and monetary policy. *Journal of Economic Dynamics and Control* **142**, 104150.
de Souza, W. M., Buss, L. F., Candido, D. d.S., Carrera, J.-P., Li, S., Zarebski, A. E., Pereira, R. H. M., Prete, C. A. Jr., de Souza-Santos, A. A., Parag, K. V. et al. (2020). Epidemiological and clinical characteristics of the COVID-19 epidemic in Brazil. *Nature Human Behaviour* **4**(8), 856–865.
DeAngelo, H., Stulz, R. M. (2015). Liquid-claim production, risk management, and bank capital structure: Why high leverage is optimal for banks. *Journal of Financial Economics* **116**(2), 219–236.
Dell'Ariccia, G., Ratnovski, L. (2019). Bailouts and systemic insurance. *Journal of Banking & Finance* **105**, 166–177.
Deloitte Sports Business Group (2020). Understanding the Impact of COVID-19 on the Sports Industry. Accessed: 2024-08-19.
DeLuca, S., Papageorge, N., Kalish, E. (2020). The unequal cost of social distancing. *Johns Hopkins Coronavirus Resource Center.*
Demers, E., Hendrikse, J., Joos, P., Lev, B. (2021). ESG did not immunize stocks during the COVID-19 crisis, but investments in intangible assets did. *Journal of Business Finance & Accounting* **48**(3–4), 433–462.
Demirgüç-Kunt, A., Pedraza, A., Ruiz-Ortega, C. (2021). Banking sector performance during the COVID-19 crisis. *Journal of Banking & Finance* **133**, 106305.
Deslandes, A., Berti, V., Tandjaoui-Lambotte, Y., Alloui, C., Carbonnelle, E., Zahar, J. R., Brichler, S., Cohen, Y. (2020). SARS-CoV-2 was already spreading in France in late December 2019. *International Journal of Antimicrobial Agents* **55**(6), 106006.
Dhawan, S. (2020). Online learning: A panacea in the time of COVID-19 crisis. *Journal of Educational Technology Systems* **49**(1), 5–22.
Dichtl, H., Drobetz, W., Lohre, H., Rother, C., Vosskamp, P. (2019). Optimal timing and tilting of equity factors. *Financial Analysts Journal* **75**(4), 84–102.
Didier, T., Huneeus, F., Larrain, M., Schmukler, S. L. (2021). Financing firms in hibernation during the COVID-19 pandemic. *Journal of Financial Stability* **53**, 100837.
Ding, W., Levine, R., Lin, C., Xie, W. (2021). Corporate immunity to the COVID-19 pandemic. *Journal of Financial Economics* **141**(2), 802–830.
Dingil, A. E., Esztergár-Kiss, D. (2021). The influence of the COVID-19 pandemic on mobility patterns: The first Wave's results. *Transportation Letters* **13**(5–6), 434–446.
Dionysopoulos, L., Marra, M., Urquhart, A. (2023). Central bank digital currencies: A critical review. *International Review of Financial Analysis* **91**, 103031.
Divakaruni, A., Zimmerman, P. (2024). Uncovering retail trading in bitcoin: The impact of COVID-19 stimulus checks. *Management Science* **70**(4), 2066–2085.
D'Lima, W., Lopez, L. A., Pradhan, A. (2022). COVID-19 and housing market effects: Evidence from US shutdown orders. *Real Estate Economics* **50**(2), 303–339.

Dobrucali, E., Sadikoglu, E., Demirkesen, S., Zhang, C., Tezel, A. (2022). Exploring the impact of COVID-19 on the United States construction industry: Challenges and opportunities. *IEEE Transactions on Engineering Management* **71**, 1245–1257.

Dube, K., Nhamo, G., Chikodzi, D. (2021). COVID-19 cripples global restaurant and hospitality industry. *Current Issues in Tourism* **24**(11), 1487–1490.

Duffie, D., Pan, J. (1997). An overview of value at risk. *The Journal of Derivatives* **4**(3), 7–49.

Duncan, E., Horvath, A., Iercosan, D., Loudis, B., Maddrey, A., Martinez, F., Mooney, T., Ranish, B., Wang, K., Warusawitharana, M. et al. (2022). COVID-19 as a stress test: Assessing the bank regulatory framework. *Journal of Financial Stability* **61**, 101016.

Dunz, N., Essenfelder, A. H., Mazzocchetti, A., Monasterolo, I., Raberto, M. (2023). Compounding COVID-19 and climate risks: The interplay of banks' lending and government's policy in the shock recovery. *Journal of Banking & Finance* **152**, 106306.

Dyba, W., Di Maria, E. (2024). Assessment and support of the digitalization of businesses in Europe during and after the COVID-19 pandemic. *Regional Science Policy and Practice* **16**(1), 12717.

Early, J., Hernandez, A. (2021). Digital disenfranchisement and COVID-19: Broadband internet access as a social determinant of health. *Health Promotion Practice* **22**(5), 605–610.

Eccles, N., Viviers, S. (2011). The origins and meanings of names describing investment practices that integrate a consideration of ESG issues in the academic literature. *Journal of Business Ethics* **104**, 389–402.

Eccleston-Turner, M., Upton, H. (2021). International collaboration to ensure equitable access to vaccines for COVID-19: The ACT-Accelerator and the COVAX facility. *The Milbank Quarterly* **99**(2), 426–449.

Eiling, E., Gerard, B., Hillion, P., de Roon, F. A. (2012). International portfolio diversification: Currency, industry and country effects revisited. *Journal of International Money and Finance* **31**(5), 1249–1278.

Eisenkopf, J., Juranek, S., Walz, U. (2023). Responsible investment and stock market shocks: Short-term insurance without persistence. *British Journal of Management* **34**(3), 1420–1439.

Elsayed, A. H., Naifar, N., Nasreen, S., Tiwari, A. K. (2022). Dependence structure and dynamic connectedness between green bonds and financial markets: Fresh insights from time-frequency analysis before and during COVID-19 pandemic. *Energy Economics* **107**, 105842.

Engle, R. (2002). Dynamic conditional correlation: A simple class of multivariate generalized autoregressive conditional heteroskedasticity models. *Journal of Business & Economic Statistics* **20**(3), 339–350.

Engle, R. F., Campos-Martins, S. (2023). What are the events that shake our world? Measuring and hedging global COVOL. *Journal of Financial Economics* **147**(1), 221–242.

Enilov, M., Mensi, W., Stankov, P. (2023). Does safe haven exist? Tail risks of commodity markets during COVID-19 pandemic. *Journal of Commodity Markets* **29**, 100307.

Erb, C. B., Harvey, C. R. (2013). The golden dilemma. *Financial Analysts Journal* **69**(4), 10–42.

Erel, I., Liebersohn, J. (2022). Can FinTech reduce disparities in access to finance? Evidence from the Paycheck Protection Program. *Journal of Financial Economics* **146**(1), 90–118.

Esparcia, C., Jareño, F., Umar, Z. (2022). Revisiting the safe haven role of Gold across time and frequencies during the COVID-19 pandemic. *North American Journal of Economics and Finance* **61**, 101677.

European Commission (2020). Mapping study on measuring the economic impact of COVID-19 on the sport sector in the EU.

European Parliament (2021). Resolution on the impact of COVID-19 on youth and on sport. Technical Report 2020/2646(RSP), European Parliament, Brussels.

Evans, M. L., Lindauer, M., Farrell, M. E. (2020). A pandemic within a pandemic—intimate partner violence during COVID-19. *The New England Journal of Medicine* **383**(24), 2302–2304.

Ewertowski, T., Butlewski, M. (2022). Managerial perception of risk in an organization in a post-COVID-19 work environment. *International Journal of Environmental Research and Public Health* **19**(22), 14978.

Fahlenbrach, R., Rageth, K., Stulz, R. M. (2021). How valuable is financial flexibility when revenue stops? Evidence from the COVID-19 crisis. *The Review of Financial Studies* **34**(11), 5474–5521.

Fama, E. F., French, K. R. (1992). The cross-section of expected stock returns. *The Journal of Finance* **47**(2), 427–465.
Fatani, M., Shamayleh, A., Alshraideh, H. (2024). Assessing the disruption impact on healthcare delivery. *Journal of Primary Care and Community Health*, 15.
Fatica, S., Panzica, R. (2024). Sustainable investing in times of crisis: Evidence from bond holdings and the COVID-19 pandemic. *Journal of Banking & Finance* **166**, 107238.
Fatum, R., Yamamoto, Y. (2016). Intra-safe haven currency behavior during the global financial crisis. *Journal of International Money and Finance* **66**, 49–64.
Favre, L., Galeano, J.-A. (2002). Mean-modified value-at-risk optimization with hedge funds. *The Journal of Alternative Investments* **5**(2), 21–25.
Fernandez-Perez, A., Gilbert, A., Indriawan, I., Nguyen, N. H. (2021). COVID-19 pandemic and stock market response: A culture effect. *Journal of Behavioral and Experimental Finance* **29**, 100454.
Fernandez-Perez, A., Fuertes, A.-M., Miffre, J. (2023). The negative pricing of the May 2020 WTI contract. *The Energy Journal* **44**(1), 119–142.
Fethi, M. D., Pasiouras, F. (2010). Assessing bank efficiency and performance with operational research and artificial intelligence techniques: A survey. *European Journal of Operational Research* **204**(2), 189–198.
Fischer, S. (2021). *Comparing the monetary policy responses of major central banks to the great financial crisis and the COVID-19 pandemic*. Technical report, Working Paper. MA, USA: MIT Management Sloan School, Cambridge.
Flath, L., Kemmerzell, J., Knodt, M. (2023). Hydrogen governance in Germany: A challenge for federal coordination. *Regional & Federal Studies* **34**(5), 757–779.
Flavin, T. J., Morley, C. E., Panopoulou, E. (2014). Identifying safe haven assets for equity investors through an analysis of the stability of shock transmission. *Journal of International Financial Markets, Institutions & Money* **33**, 137–154.
Fletcher, E., Larkin, C., Corbet, S. (2021). Countering money laundering and terrorist financing: A case for bitcoin regulation. *Research in International Business and Finance* **56**, 101387.
Florio, C., Brotto, L. (2024). Enterprise risk management and resilience in SMEs during COVID-19 pandemic: The case of Italian dealerships. *Management for Professionals, Part F* **2445**, 249–277.
Foley, S., Karlsen, J. R., Putniņš, T. J. (2019). Sex, drugs, and bitcoin: How much illegal activity is financed through cryptocurrencies? *The Review of Financial Studies* **32**(5), 1798–1853.
Foroni, C., Marcellino, M., Stevanovic, D. (2022). Forecasting the COVID-19 recession and recovery: Lessons from the financial crisis. *International Journal of Forecasting* **38**(2), 596–612.
Fu, J., Mishra, M. (2022). Fintech in the time of COVID-19: Technological adoption during crises. *Journal of Financial Intermediation* **50**, 100945.
Fu, X., Qiang, Y., Liu, X., Jiang, Y., Cui, Z., Zhang, D., Wang, J. (2022). Will multi-industry supply chains' resilience under the impact of COVID-19 pandemic be different? A perspective from China's highway freight transport. *Transport Policy* **118**, 165–178.
Gabryelczyk, R. (2020). Has COVID-19 accelerated digital transformation? Initial lessons learned for public administrations. *Information Systems Management* **37**(4), 303–309.
Galaitsi, S. E., Cegan, J. C., Volk, K., Joyner, M., Trump, B. D., Linkov, I. (2021). The challenges of data usage for the United States' COVID-19 response. *International Journal of Information Management* **59**, 102352.
Galanti, T., Guidetti, G., Mazzei, E., Zappalà, S., Toscano, F. (2021). Work from home during the COVID-19 outbreak: The impact on employees' remote work productivity, engagement, and stress. *Journal of Occupational and Environmental Medicine* **63**(7), e426–e432.
Gamal, A., Abdel-Basset, M., Chakrabortty, R. K. (2022). Intelligent model for contemporary supply chain barriers in manufacturing sectors under the impact of the COVID-19 pandemic. *Expert Systems with Applications* **205**, 117711.
Garcia-Garcia, B., James, M., Koller, D., Lindholm, J., Mavromati, D., Parrish, R., Rodenberg, R. (2020). The impact of COVID-19 on sports: A mid-way assessment. *The International Sports Law Journal* **20**(3–4), 115–119.

Garel, A., Petit-Romec, A. (2021). Investor rewards to environmental responsibility: Evidence from the COVID-19 crisis. *Journal of Corporate Finance* **68**, 101948.

Gençay, R., Selçuk, F., Whitcher, B. J. (2001). *An Introduction to Wavelets and Other Filtering Methods in Finance and Economics*. Elsevier.

Gençay, R., Selçuk, F., Whitcher, B. (2003). Systematic risk and timescales. *Quantitative Finance* **3**(2), 108.

Georgarakos, D., Kenny, G. (2022). Household spending and fiscal support during the COVID-19 pandemic: Insights from a new consumer survey. *Journal of Monetary Economics* **129**, S1–S14.

Gianfrate, G., Rubin, M., Ruzzi, D., van Dijk, M. (2024). On the resilience of ESG firms during the COVID-19 crisis: Evidence across countries and asset classes. *Journal of International Business Studies* **55**, 1069–1084.

Gibb, R., Redding, D. W., Chin, K. Q., Donnelly, C. A., Blackburn, T. M., Newbold, T., Jones, K. E. (2020). Zoonotic host diversity increases in human-dominated ecosystems. *Nature* **584**(7821), 398–402.

Glennerster, R., Snyder, C. M., Tan, B. J. (2022). Calculating the costs and benefits of advance preparations for the next pandemic. *IMF Economic Review*.

Gomis-Porqueras, P., Shi, S., Tan, D. (2022). Gold as a financial instrument. *Journal of Commodity Markets* **27**, 100218.

Gonzalez, L., Powell, J. G., Shi, J., Wilson, A. (2005). Two centuries of bull and bear market cycles. *International Review of Economics & Finance* **14**(4), 469–486.

González-Serrano, M. H., Dos Santos, M. A., Sendra-Garcia, J., Calabuig, F. (2023). Sports entrepreneurship during COVID-19: Technology as an ally to maintain the competitiveness of small businesses. *Technological Forecasting and Social Change* **187**, 122256.

Goodell, J. W., Corbet, S. (2024). The evolving landscape of energy finance: challenges and opportunities during global uncertainty. In: *Handbook of Financial Integration*, 172–191.

Goodell, J. W., Corbet, S., Yadav, M. P., Kumar, S., Sharma, S., Malik, K. (2022). Time and frequency connectedness of green equity indices: Uncovering a socially important link to Bitcoin. *International Review of Financial Analysis* **84**, 102379.

Goodell, J. W., Corbet, S., Hou, Y. G., Hu, Y., Oxley, L. (2024). Isolating defensive corporate ESG effects: Evidence from purely domestic anti-COVID-19 measures. *Journal of Financial Stability* **71**, 101220.

Gormsen, N. J., Koijen, R. S. (2023). Financial markets and the COVID-19 pandemic. *Annual Review of Financial Economics* **15**(1), 69–89.

Gorton, G. (2017). The history and economics of safe assets. *Annual Review of Economics* **9**(1), 547–586.

Grantz, K. H., Meredith, H. R., Cummings, D. A., Metcalf, C. J. E., Grenfell, B. T., Giles, J. R., Mehta, S., Solomon, S., Labrique, A., Kishore, N. et al. (2020). The use of mobile phone data to inform analysis of COVID-19 pandemic epidemiology. *Nature Communications* **11**(1), 4961.

Grasselli, M. R. (2022). Monetary policy responses to COVID-19: A comparison with the 2008 crisis and implications for the future of central banking. *Review of Political Economy* **34**(3), 420–445.

Grimm, J. (2021). Securing the remote workforce in the new normal. *Computer Fraud and Security* **2021**(2), 8–11.

Grisse, C., Nitschka, T. (2015). On financial risk and the safe haven characteristics of Swiss franc exchange rates. *Journal of Empirical Finance* **32**, 153–164.

Guimarães, D. S., Nascimento, A. M., de Albuquerque Rodrigues, G. P., dos Santos, L. O. C., Batista, M. G. R. (2022). Forced digital transformation during the COVID-19 pandemic. *International Journal of Entrepreneurship and Innovation Management* **26**(5–6), 381–396.

Gultekin, B., Demir, S., Gunduz, M. A., Cura, F., Ozer, L. (2022). The logistics service providers during the COVID-19 pandemic: The prominence and the cause-effect structure of uncertainties and risks. *Computers & Industrial Engineering* **165**, 107950.

Gupta, P., Kumar, S., Suman, R. R., Kumar, V. (2020). Sentiment analysis of lockdown in India during COVID-19: A case study on Twitter. *IEEE Transactions on Computational Social Systems* **8**(4), 992–1002.

Gupta, A., Zhu, H., Doan, M. K., Michuda, A., Majumder, B. (2021a). Economic impacts of the COVID-19 lockdown in a remittance-dependent region. *American Journal of Agricultural Economics* **103**(2), 466–485.

Gupta, J., Bavinck, M., Ros-Tonen, M., Asubonteng, K., Bosch, H., van Ewijk, E., Hordijk, M., Van Leynseele, Y., Cardozo, M. L., Miedema, E. et al. (2021b). COVID-19, poverty and inclusive development. *World Development* **145**, 105527.

Gursoy, D., Chi, C. G., Chi, O. H. (2021). Effects of COVID-19 pandemic on restaurant and hotel customers' sentiments towards dining out, travelling to a destination and staying at hotels. *Journal of Hospitality* **3**(1), 1–17.

Haas, J., Neely, C. J., Emmons, W. R. (2020). Responses of international central banks to the COVID-19 crisis. *FRB of St. Louis Working Paper*, forthcoming.

Haase, F., Neuenkirch, M. (2023). Predictability of bull and bear markets: A new look at forecasting stock market regimes (and returns) in the us. *International Journal of Forecasting* **39**(2), 587–605.

Hackethal, A., Hanspal, T., Lammer, D. M., Rink, K. (2022). The characteristics and portfolio behavior of bitcoin investors: Evidence from indirect cryptocurrency investments. *Review of Finance* **26**(4), 855–898.

Hameiri, S. (2021). COVID-19: Is this the end of globalization? *International Journal* **76**(1), 30–41.

Hamilton, J. D. (2009). Causes and consequences of the oil shock of 2007–08. *National Bureau of Economic Research*.

Hammerschmidt, J., Durst, S., Kraus, S., Puumalainen, K. (2021). Professional football clubs and empirical evidence from the COVID-19 crisis: Time for sport entrepreneurship? *Technological Forecasting & Social Change* **165**, 120572.

Harjoto, M. A., Rossi, F., Lee, R., Sergi, B. S. (2021). How do equity markets react to COVID-19? Evidence from emerging and developed countries. *Journal of Economics and Business* **115**, 105966.

Hasbrouck, J. (2018). High-frequency quoting: Short-term volatility in bids and offers. *Journal of Financial and Quantitative Analysis* **53**(2), 613–641.

Hassan, T. A., Hollander, S., Van Lent, L., Schwedeler, M., Tahoun, A. (2023). Firm-level exposure to epidemic diseases: COVID-19, SARS, and H1N1. *The Review of Financial Studies* **36**(12), 4919–4964.

He, Z., O'Connor, F., Thijssen, J. (2018). Is gold a sometime safe haven or an always hedge for equity investors? A Markov-switching CAPM approach for US and UK stock indices. *International Review of Financial Analysis* **60**, 30–37.

He, Z., Nagel, S., Song, Z. (2022). Treasury inconvenience yields during the COVID-19 crisis. *Journal of Financial Economics* **143**(1), 57–79.

Heiniger, S., Koeniger, W., Lechner, M. (2024). The heterogeneous response of real estate prices during the COVID-19 pandemic. *Journal of the Royal Statistical Society Series A: Statistics in Society*, qnae078.

Henry, R. (2020). Innovations in agriculture and food supply in response to the COVID-19 pandemic. *Molecular Plant* **13**(8), 1095–1097.

Heo, W., Grable, J., Rabbani, A. (2021a). A test of the association between the initial surge in COVID-19 cases and subsequent changes in financial risk tolerance. *Review of Behavioral Finance* **13**(1), 3–19.

Heo, W., Rabbani, A., Grable, J. (2021b). An evaluation of the effect of the COVID-19 pandemic on the risk tolerance of financial decision makers. *Finance Research Letters* **41**, 101842.

Hepburn, C., O'Callaghan, B., Stern, N., Stiglitz, J., Zenghelis, D. (2020). Will COVID-19 fiscal recovery packages accelerate or retard progress on climate change? *Oxford Review of Economic Policy* **36**(Supplement_1), S359–S381.

Heyden, K. J., Heyden, T. (2021). Market reactions to the arrival and containment of COVID-19: An event study. *Finance Research Letters* **38**, 101745.

Hillier, D., Draper, P., Faff, R. (2006). Do precious metals shine? An investment perspective. *Financial Analysts Journal* **62**(2), 98–106.

Hiziroglu, O. A., Aydin, A. E., Van Isacker, K., Milis, G., Sirashki, H., Tsoris, P. (2024). The role of digital transformation for SMEs during a health crisis: Lessons learnt from COVID-19 epidemic. *CEUR Workshop Proceedings* **3698**, 11–22.

Hoang, K., Arif, M., Nguyen, C. (2022a). Corporate investment and government policy during the COVID-19 crisis. *International Review of Economics & Finance* **80**, 677–696.

Hoang, K., Nguyen, C., Tran, D. V., Phan, A. (2022b). International corporate cash holdings and firm-level exposure to COVID-19: Do cultural dimensions matter? *Journal of Risk and Financial Management* **15**(6), 262.

Hodbod, A., Hommes, C., Huber, S. J., Salle, I. (2021). The COVID-19 consumption game-changer: Evidence from a large-scale multi-country survey. *European Economic Review* **140**, 103953.

Holshue, M. L., DeBolt, C., Lindquist, S., Lofy, K. H., Wiesman, J., Bruce, H., Spitters, C., Ericson, K., Wilkerson, S., Tural, A. et al. (2020). First case of 2019 novel coronavirus in the United States. *The New England Journal of Medicine* **382**(10), 929–936.

Hossain, M. M., Tasnim, S., Sultana, A., Faizah, F., Mazumder, H., Zou, L., McKyer, E. L. J., Ahmed, H. U., Ma, P. (2020). Epidemiology of mental health problems in COVID-19: A review. *F1000Research* **9**, 636.

Hossfeld, O., MacDonald, R. (2015). Carry funding and safe haven currencies: A threshold regression approach. *Journal of International Money and Finance* **59**, 185–202.

Howard, G., Liebersohn, J., Ozimek, A. (2023). The short-and long-run effects of remote work on US housing markets. *Journal of Financial Economics* **150**(1), 166–184.

Hsu, T.-J., Huang, A. Y. (2024). On the resilience of US ESG stocks: Evidence from the COVID-19 market crashes. *Economics Letters* **235**, 111532.

Hsu, C.-C., Chau, K. Y., Chien, F. (2023). Natural resource volatility and financial development during COVID-19: Implications for economic recovery. *Resources Policy* **81**, 103343.

Hu, Y., Lang, C., Corbet, S., Wang, J. (2024). The impact of COVID-19 on the volatility connectedness of the Chinese tourism sector. *Research in International Business and Finance* **68**, 102192.

Huang, B., Wang, B., Chen, Z. (2024). Individual investment adaptations to COVID-19 lockdowns. *North American Journal of Economics and Finance* **70**, 102071.

Hubbard, R. G., Strain, M. R. (2020). *Has the paycheck protection program succeeded?* Technical report, National Bureau of Economic Research.

Hunjra, A. I., Kijkasiwat, P., Arunachalam, M., Hammami, H. (2021). COVID-19 health policy intervention and volatility of Asian capital markets. *Technological Forecasting & Social Change* **169**, 120840.

Huynh, T. L. D., Foglia, M., Nasir, M. A., Angelini, E. (2021). Feverish sentiment and global equity markets during the COVID-19 pandemic. *Journal of Economic Behavior & Organization* **188**, 1088–1108.

In, F., Kim, S. (2006). The hedge ratio and the empirical relationship between the stock and futures markets: A new approach using wavelet analysis. *The Journal of Business* **79**(2), 799–820.

Islam, M. A. (2021). Investor sentiment in the equity market and investments in corporate-bond funds. *International Review of Financial Analysis* **78**, 101898.

Ivanov, D. (2024). Exiting the COVID-19 pandemic: After-shock risks and avoidance of disruption tails in supply chains. *Annals of Operations Research* **335**(3), 1627–1644.

Izzeldin, M., Muradoğlu, Y. G., Pappas, V., Sivaprasad, S. (2021). The impact of COVID-19 on G7 stock markets volatility: Evidence from a ST-HAR model. *International Review of Financial Analysis* **74**, 101671.

Jackwerth, J. (2020). What do index options teach us about COVID-19? *The Review of Asset Pricing Studies* **10**(4), 618–634.

Jaffe, J. F. (1989). Gold and gold stocks as investments for institutional portfolios. *Financial Analysts Journal* **45**(2), 53–59.

Jain, K., Conlon, T., Cotter, J. (2024). Are the diversification benefits of Emerging and Frontier markets retained in the long-run? Available at SSRN 4767036.

Jiang, Y., Wen, J. (2020). Effects of COVID-19 on hotel marketing and management: A perspective article. *International Journal of Contemporary Hospitality Management* **32**(8), 2563–2573.

Jiang, P., Van Fan, Y., Klemeš, J. J. (2021). Impacts of COVID-19 on energy demand and consumption: Challenges, lessons and emerging opportunities. *Applied Energy* **285**, 116441.

Jiang, K., Du, X., Chen, Z. (2022). Firms' digitalization and stock price crash risk. *International Review of Financial Analysis* **82**, 102196.

Jiang, K., Zhou, M., Chen, Z. (2025). Digitalization and firms' systematic risk in China. *International Journal of Finance & Economics* **30**(1), 522–551.

John, K., Li, J. (2021). COVID-19, volatility dynamics, and sentiment trading. *Journal of Banking & Finance* **133**, 106162.

Jordan, K., Adams, P., Jaramillo, P., Muller, N. (2023). Closing the gap: Achieving US climate goals beyond the inflation reduction act. *Renewable and Sustainable Energy Transition* **4**, 100065.

Jordà, Ò., Singh, S. R., Taylor, A. M. (2022). Longer-run economic consequences of pandemics. *Review of Economics and Statistics* **104**(1), 166–175.

Julliard, C., Ghosh, A. (2012). Can rare events explain the equity premium puzzle? *The Review of Financial Studies* **25**(10), 3037–3076.

Kahneman, D., Tversky, A. (1979). Prospect theory: An analysis of decision under risk. *Econometrica* **47**(2), 363–391.

Kantamneni, N. (2020). The impact of the COVID-19 pandemic on marginalized populations in the United States: A research agenda. *Journal of Vocational Behavior* **119**, 103439.

Kapetanios, G., Mumtaz, H., Stevens, I., Theodoridis, K. (2012). Assessing the economy-wide effects of quantitative easing. *The Economic Journal* **122**(564), F316–F347.

Kargar, M., Lester, B., Lindsay, D., Liu, S., Weill, P.-O., Zúñiga, D. (2021). Corporate bond liquidity during the COVID-19 crisis. *The Review of Financial Studies* **34**(11), 5352–5401.

Keister, T., Monnet, C. (2022). Central bank digital currency: Stability and information. *Journal of Economic Dynamics and Control* **142**, 104501.

Khan, S. U. (2022). Financing constraints and firm-level responses to the COVID-19 pandemic: International evidence. *Research in International Business and Finance* **59**, 101545.

Khan, M. A., Riaz, H., Ahmed, M., Saeed, A. (2022). Does green finance really deliver what is expected? An empirical perspective. *Borsa Istanbul Review* **22**(3), 586–593.

Khan, S. A. R., Piprani, A. Z., Yu, Z. (2023). Supply chain analytics and post-pandemic performance: mediating role of triple-A supply chain strategies. *International Journal of Emerging Markets* **18**(6), 1330–1354.

Kim, R. Y. (2020). The impact of COVID-19 on consumers: Preparing for digital sales. *IEEE Engineering Management Review* **48**(3), 212–218.

Kim, S. In, F. (2005). The relationship between stock returns and inflation: New evidence from wavelet analysis. *Journal of Empirical Finance* **12**(3), 435–444.

Kim, Y., Liu, A. (2022). Social distancing, trust and post-COVID-19 recovery. *Tourism Management* **88**, 104416.

Klöckner, M., Schmidt, C. G., Wagner, S. M., Swink, M. (2023). Firms' responses to the COVID-19 pandemic. *Journal of Business Research* **158**, 113664.

Koch, J., Frommeyer, B., Schewe, G. (2020). Online shopping motives during the COVID-19 pandemic—lessons from the crisis. *Sustainability* **12**(24), 10247.

Kofman, Y. B., Garfin, D. R. (2020). Home is not always a haven: The domestic violence crisis amid the COVID-19 pandemic. *Psychological Trauma: Theory, Research, Practice, and Policy* **12**(S1), S199.

Kogan, S., Makarov, I., Niessner, M., Schoar, A. (2024). Are cryptos different? Evidence from retail trading. *Journal of Financial Economics* **159**, 103897.

Kohl, M., Habl, A., Kallali, K., Puff, J., Fottner, J., Oger, R., Lauras, M., Li, J. (2022). Managing supply chains during the COVID-19 crisis: Synthesis of academic and practitioner visions and recommendations for the future. *International Journal of Logistics Management* **33**(4), 1386–1407.

Kole, E., Van Dijk, D. (2017). How to identify and forecast bull and bear markets? *Journal of Applied Econometrics* **32**(1), 120–139.

Konstantakis, K. N., Xidonas, P., Michaelides, P. G., Goutte, S. (2023). Gold and COVID-19: Uncovering the safe haven hypothesis with dynamic msr modeling. *International Review of Financial Analysis* **89**, 102858.

Korkmaz, Ö., Erer, E., Erer, D. (2022). Internet access and its role on educational inequality during the COVID-19 pandemic. *Telecommunications Policy* **46**(5), 102353.

Kozak, S. (2022). Dynamics of bond and stock returns. *Journal of Monetary Economics* **126**, 188–209.

Kucher, O., Kurov, A., Wolfe, M. H. (2023). A shot in the arm: The effect of COVID-19 vaccine news on financial and commodity markets. *Financial Review* **58**(3), 575–596.

Kuester, K., Mittnik, S., Paolella, M. S. (2006). Value-at-risk prediction: A comparison of alternative strategies. *Journal of Financial Econometrics* **4**(1), 53–89.

Kurniasih, D., Akbar, F. (2021). E-commerce pandemic COVID-19 home industries and SMEs. *International Journal of Research and Applied Technology* **1**(1), 70–75.

Kusumahadi, T. A., Permana, F. C. (2021). Impact of COVID-19 on global stock market volatility. *Journal of Economic Integration* **36**(1), 20–45.

Kutnjak, A. (2021). COVID-19 accelerates digital transformation in industries: Challenges, issues, barriers and problems in transformation. *IEEE Access* **9**, 79373–79388.

Kuznyetsova, A., Sydorchenko, T., Zadvorna, O., Nikonenko, U., Khalina, O. (2021). Assessment of aspects of the COVID-19 crisis in the context of ensuring economic security. *International Journal of Safety and Security Engineering* **11**(6), 615–622.

Kyriazis, N., Corbet, S. (2024). Evaluating the dynamic connectedness of financial assets and bank indices during black-swan events: A Quantile-VAR approach. *Energy Economics* **131**, 107329.

Kyriazis, N., Papadamou, S., Tzeremes, P., Corbet, S. (2023). The differential influence of social media sentiment on cryptocurrency returns and volatility during COVID-19. *The Quarterly Review of Economics and Finance* **89**, 307–317.

La Rosa, G., Iaconelli, M., Mancini, P., Ferraro, G. B., Veneri, C., Bonadonna, L., Lucentini, L., Suffredini, E. (2020). First detection of SARS-CoV-2 in untreated wastewaters in Italy. *Science of the Total Environment* **736**, 139652.

Laborde, D., Martin, W., Swinnen, J., Vos, R. (2020). COVID-19 risks to global food security. *Science* **369**(6503), 500–502.

Laeven, L. (2022). Pandemics, intermediate goods, and corporate valuation. *Journal of International Money and Finance* **120**, 102505.

Lallie, H. S., Shepherd, L. A., Nurse, J. R., Erola, A., Epiphaniou, G., Maple, C., Bellekens, X. (2021). Cyber security in the age of COVID-19: A timeline and analysis of cyber-crime and cyber-attacks during the pandemic. *Computers & Security* **105**, 102248.

Landier, A., Thesmar, D. (2020). Earnings expectations during the COVID-19 crisis. *The Review of Asset Pricing Studies* **10**(4), 598–617.

Lane, P. R. (2020). *The market stabilisation role of the pandemic emergency purchase programme*. Yale School of Management, EliScholar, European Central Bank (ECB).

Lang, C., Hu, Y., Corbet, S., Hou, Y. G. (2024). Tail risk connectedness in G7 stock markets: Understanding the impact of COVID-19 and related variants. *Journal of Behavioral and Experimental Finance* **41**, 100889.

Lau, H., Khosrawipour, T., Kocbach, P., Ichii, H., Bania, J., Khosrawipour, V. (2021). Evaluating the massive underreporting and undertesting of COVID-19 cases in multiple global epicenters. *Pulmonology* **27**(2), 110–115.

Le Billon, P., Lujala, P., Singh, D., Culbert, V., Kristoffersen, B. (2021). Fossil fuels, climate change, and the COVID-19 crisis: Pathways for a just and green post-pandemic recovery. *Climate Policy* **21**(10), 1347–1356.

Lee, C.-C., Li, X., Yu, C.-H., Zhao, J. (2021a). Does fintech innovation improve bank efficiency? Evidence from China's banking industry. *International Review of Economics & Finance* **74**, 468–483.

Lee, S. Y. T., Park, M., Shin, Y. (2021b). *Hit harder, recover slower? Unequal employment effects of the COVID-19 shock*. Technical report, National Bureau of Economic Research.

Lee, C.-C., Ni, W., Zhang, X. (2023). FinTech development and commercial bank efficiency in China. *Global Finance Journal* **57**, 100850.

Leng, A., Sun, Y. (2024). The impact mechanism and breakthrough path of COVID-19 on enterprise financial distress: Evidence from China. *Economic Analysis and Policy* **82**, 16–31.

Li, L., Miu, P. (2023). Are cryptocurrencies a safe haven for stock investors? A regime-switching approach. *Journal of Empirical Finance* **70**, 367–385.

Li, H., Yu, L., He, W. (2019). The impact of GDPR on global technology development. *Journal of Global Information Technology Management* **22**(1), 1–6.

Li, L., Strahan, P. E., Zhang, S. (2020). Banks as lenders of first resort: Evidence from the COVID-19 crisis. *The Review of Corporate Finance Studies* **9**(3), 472–500.

Li, G., Li, N., Sethi, S. P. (2021a). Does CSR reduce idiosyncratic risk? Roles of operational efficiency and AI innovation. *Production and Operations Management* **30**(7), 2027–2045.

Li, K., Liu, X., Mai, F., Zhang, T. (2021b). The role of corporate culture in bad times: Evidence from the COVID-19 pandemic. *Journal of Financial and Quantitative Analysis* **56**(7), 2545–2583.

Liguori, E. W., Pittz, T. G. (2020). Strategies for small business: Surviving and thriving in the era of COVID-19. *Journal of the International Council for Small Business* **1**(2), 106–110.

Ling, D. C., Wang, C., Zhou, T. (2020). A first look at the impact of COVID-19 on commercial real estate prices: Asset-level evidence. *The Review of Asset Pricing Studies* **10**(4), 669–704.

Liu, Z., Huynh, T. L. D., Dai, P.-F. (2021a). The impact of COVID-19 on the stock market crash risk in China. *Research in International Business and Finance* **57**, 101419.

Liu, A., Kim, Y. R., O'Connell, J. F. (2021b). COVID-19 and the aviation industry: The interrelationship between the spread of the COVID-19 pandemic and the frequency of flights on the EU market. *Annals of Tourism Research* **91**, 103298.

Liu, C., Zhang, X., Zhou, Z. (2023). Are commodity futures a hedge against inflation? A markov-switching approach. *International Review of Financial Analysis* **86**, 102492.

Long, H., Chang, C.-P., Jegajeevan, S., Tang, K. (2022). Can Central Bank mitigate the effects of the COVID-19 pandemic on the macroeconomy? *Emerging Markets Finance & Trade* **58**(9), 2652–2669.

Long, H., Chiah, M., Cakici, N., Zaremba, A., Bilgin, M. H. (2024). ESG investing in good and bad times: An international study. *Journal of International Financial Markets, Institutions & Money* **91**, 101916.

Madhav, N. K., Oppenheim, B., Stephenson, N., Badker, R., Jamison, D. T., Lam, C., Meadows, A. (2023). *Estimated future mortality from pathogens of epidemic and pandemic potential.* Technical report, Center for Global Development.

Maheu, J. M., McCurdy, T. H. (2000). Identifying bull and bear markets in stock returns. *Journal of Business & Economic Statistics* **18**(1), 100–112.

Mammaev, R. A., Idziev, G. I., Ismailova, F. N., Magomedov, R. M., Omarova, N. G. (2023). Sustainable development of Industry 4.0 as a pioneering line of industry in the post-pandemic period. *Advances in Science, Technology and Innovation, Part F* **1**, 391–394.

Marcelo, J. L. M., Quirós, J. L. M., Martins, J. L. (2013). The role of country and industry factors during volatile times. *Journal of International Financial Markets, Institutions & Money* **26**, 273–290.

Mariana, C. D., Ekaputra, I. A., Husodo, Z. A. (2021). Are Bitcoin and Ethereum safe-havens for stocks during the COVID-19 pandemic? *Finance Research Letters* **38**, 101798.

Martinez, M. M., Feijoo-Cid, M., Fernandez-Cano, M., Llorens-Serrano, C., Navarro-Gine, A. (2024). Psychosocial risk in healthcare workers after one year of COVID-19. *Occupational Medicine* **74**(1), 37–44.

Mayer, T., Schnabl, G. (2021). COVID-19 and the euthanasia of interest rates: A critical assessment of central bank policy in our times. *Journal of Policy Modeling* **43**(6), 1241–1258.

Mazur, M., Dang, M., Vega, M. (2021). COVID-19 and the March 2020 stock market crash. Evidence from S&P1500. *Finance Research Letters* **38**, 101690.

McGrail, D. J., Dai, J., McAndrews, K. M., Kalluri, R. (2020). Enacting national social distancing policies corresponds with dramatic reduction in COVID-19 infection rates. *PLoS ONE* **15**(7), e0236619.

Meehan, D., Corbet, S. (2023). Comparing the resilience of socially responsible and SIN investment during the COVID-19 pandemic. Available at SSRN 4710761.

Menkir, T. F., Chin, T., Hay, J. A., Surface, E. D., De Salazar, P. M., Buckee, C. O., Watts, A., Khan, K., Sherbo, R., Yan, A. W. et al. (2021). Estimating internationally imported cases during the early COVID-19 pandemic. *Nature Communications* **12**(1), 311.

Meric, I., Ratner, M., Meric, G. (2008). Co-movements of sector index returns in the world's major stock markets in bull and bear markets: Portfolio diversification implications. *International Review of Financial Analysis* **17**(1), 156–177.

Mhlanga, D. (2022). The role of financial inclusion and FinTech in addressing climate-related challenges in the Industry 4.0: Lessons for Sustainable Development Goals. *Frontiers in Climate* **4**, 949178.

Miller, M., Weller, P., Zhang, L. (2002). Moral hazard and the us stock market: Analysing the 'Greenspan put'. *The Economic Journal* **112**(478), C171–C186.

Minesso, M. F., Mehl, A., Stracca, L. (2022). Central bank digital currency in an open economy. *Journal of Monetary Economics* **127**, 54–68.

Moerman, G. A. (2008). Diversification in euro area stock markets: Country versus industry. *Journal of International Money and Finance* **27**(7), 1122–1134.

Monasterolo, I. (2020). Climate change and the financial system. *Annual Review of Resource Economics* **12**, 299–320.

Moosavi, J., Fathollahi-Fard, A. M., Dulebenets, M. A. (2022). Supply chain disruption during the COVID-19 pandemic: Recognizing potential disruption management strategies. *International Journal of Disaster Risk Reduction* **75**, 102983.

Morikawa, M. (2022). Work-from-home productivity during the COVID-19 pandemic: Evidence from Japan. *Economic Inquiry* **60**(2), 508–527.

Muthuppalaniappan, M., Stevenson, K. (2021). Healthcare cyber-attacks and the COVID-19 pandemic: An urgent threat to global health. *International Journal for Quality in Health Care* **33**(1), mzaa117.

Naeem, M. A., Conlon, T., Cotter, J. (2022). Green bonds and other assets: Evidence from extreme risk transmission. *Journal of Environmental Management* **305**, 114358.

Nahm, J. M., Miller, S. M., Urpelainen, J. (2022). G20's US$14-trillion economic stimulus reneges on emissions pledges. *Nature* **603**(7899), 28–31.

Narayan, P. K., Phan, D. H. B., Liu, G. (2021). COVID-19 lockdowns, stimulus packages, travel bans, and stock returns. *Finance Research Letters* **38**, 101732.

Nasir, M. A., Le, T. N. L., Ghabri, Y., Huynh, L. D. T. (2023). Sovereign bonds and flight to safety: Implications of the COVID-19 crisis for sovereign debt markets in the G-7 and E-7 economies. *International Review of Financial Analysis* **86**, 102548.

Nauright, J., Zipp, S., Kim, Y. H. (2020). The sports world in the era of COVID-19. *Sport in Society* **23**, 1703–1706.

Nguyen, A. B., Do, D. T., Le, H. A. (2024). The impact of the COVID-19 pandemic exposure on the corporate cash policy of Vietnam-listed enterprises. *Economics and Finance Letters* **11**(1), 45–56.

Nicola, M., Alsafi, Z., Sohrabi, C., Kerwan, A., Al-Jabir, A., Iosifidis, C., Agha, M., Agha, R. (2020). The socio-economic implications of the coronavirus pandemic (COVID-19): A review. *International Journal of Surgery* **78**, 185–193.

Nouvellet, P., Bhatia, S., Cori, A., Ainslie, K. E., Baguelin, M., Bhatt, S., Boonyasiri, A., Brazeau, N. F., Cattarino, L., Cooper, L. V. et al. (2021). Reduction in mobility and COVID-19 transmission. *Nature Communications* **12**(1), 1–9.

Nozawa, Y., Qiu, Y. (2021). Corporate bond market reactions to quantitative easing during the COVID-19 pandemic. *Journal of Banking & Finance* **133**, 106153.

Nyberg, H. (2013). Predicting bear and bull stock markets with dynamic binary time series models. *Journal of Banking & Finance* **37**(9), 3351–3363.

Ogunnusi, M., Hamma-Adama, M., Salman, H., Kouider, T. (2020). COVID-19 pandemic: The effects and prospects in the construction industry. *International Journal of Real Estate Studies* **14**(Special Issue 2), 120–128.

Ogunnusi, M., Omotayo, T., Hamma-Adama, M., Awuzie, B. O., Egbelakin, T. (2021). Lessons learned from the impact of COVID-19 on the global construction industry. *Journal of Engineering, Design and Technology* **20**(1), 299–320.

O'Hara, M., Zhou, X. A. (2021). Anatomy of a liquidity crisis: Corporate bonds in the COVID-19 crisis. *Journal of Financial Economics* **142**(1), 46–68.

Okereafor, K. (2021). *Cybersecurity in the COVID-19 Pandemic*. CRC Press.

Ozdemir, D., Sharma, M., Dhir, A., Daim, T. (2022). Supply chain resilience during the COVID-19 pandemic. *Technology in Society* **68**, 101847.

Pagan, A. R., Sossounov, K. A. (2003). A simple framework for analysing bull and bear markets. *Journal of Applied Econometrics* **18**(1), 23–46.

Pagnottoni, P., Spelta, A., Pecora, N., Flori, A., Pammolli, F. (2021). Financial earthquakes: SARS-CoV-2 news shock propagation in stock and sovereign bond markets. *Physica A: Statistical Mechanics and its Applications* **582**, 126240.

Papadamou, S., Fassas, A. P., Kenourgios, D., Dimitriou, D. (2021). Flight-to-quality between global stock and bond markets in the COVID era. *Finance Research Letters* **38**, 101852.

Park, M. Lim, J. T., Cook, A. R., Dickens, B. L. et al. (2021). Urban-rural disparities for COVID-19: Evidence from 10 countries and areas in the Western Pacific. *Health Data Science* **2021**, 9790275.

Paudel, P. (2021). Online education: Benefits, challenges and strategies during and after COVID-19 in higher education. *International Journal on Studies in Education* **3**(2), 70–85.

Pekar, J., Worobey, M., Moshiri, N., Scheffler, K., Wertheim, J. O. (2021). Timing the SARS-CoV-2 index case in Hubei province. *Science* **372**(6540), 412–417.

Petrosky-Nadeau, N., Valletta, R. G. et al. (2020). An unemployment crisis after the onset of COVID-19. *FRBSF Economic Letter* **12**(1), 1–5.

Pham, S. D., Nguyen, T. T. T., Do, H. X., Vo, X. V. (2023). Portfolio diversification during the COVID-19 pandemic: Do vaccinations matter? *Journal of Financial Stability* **65**, 101118.

Pranggono, B., Arabo, A. (2021). COVID-19 pandemic cybersecurity issues. *Internet Technology Letters* **4**(2), e247.

Qin, X., Huang, G., Shen, H., Fu, M. (2020). COVID-19 pandemic and firm-level cash holding—moderating effect of Goodwill and Goodwill impairment. *Emerging Markets Finance & Trade* **56**(10), 2243–2258.

Qin, M., Zhang, X., Li, Y., Badarcea, R. M. (2023). Blockchain market and green finance: The enablers of carbon neutrality in China. *Energy Economics* **118**, 106501.

Rafaï, I., Blayac, T., Dubois, D., Duchêne, S., Nguyen-Van, P., Ventelou, B., Willinger, M. (2023). Stated preferences outperform elicited preferences for predicting reported compliance with COVID-19 prophylactic measures. *Journal of Behavioral and Experimental Economics* **107**, 102089.

Rajkumar, R. P. (2020). COVID-19 and mental health: A review of the existing literature. *Asian Journal of Psychiatry* **52**, 102066.

Ramelli, S., Wagner, A. (2020). Feverish stock price reactions to COVID-19. *The Review of Corporate Finance Studies* **9**, 622–655.

Ranaldo, A., Söderlind, P. (2010). Safe haven currencies. *Review of Finance* **14**(3), 385–407.

Ratten, V., da Silva Braga, V. L., da Encarnação Marques, C. S. (2021). Sport entrepreneurship and value co-creation in times of crisis: The COVID-19 pandemic. *Journal of Business Research* **133**, 265–274.

Reboredo, J. C. (2013a). Is gold a hedge or safe haven against oil price movements? *Resources Policy* **38**(2), 130–137.

Reboredo, J. C. (2013b). Is gold a safe haven or a hedge for the US dollar? Implications for risk management. *Journal of Banking & Finance* **37**(8), 2665–2676.

Rietz, T. A. (1988). The equity risk premium: a solution. *Journal of Monetary Economics* **22**(1), 117–131.

Rodnyansky, A., Darmouni, O. M. (2017). The effects of quantitative easing on bank lending behavior. *The Review of Financial Studies* **30**(11), 3858–3887.

Roper, S., Turner, J. (2020). R&D and innovation after COVID-19: What can we expect? A review of prior research and data trends after the great financial crisis. *International Small Business Journal: Researching Entrepreneurship* **38**(6), 504–514.

Rua, A., Nunes, L. C. (2009). International comovement of stock market returns: A wavelet analysis. *Journal of Empirical Finance* **16**(4), 632–639.

Rubbaniy, G., Khalid, A. A., Syriopoulos, K., Samitas, A. (2022). Safe-haven properties of soft commodities during times of COVID-19. *Journal of Commodity Markets* **27**, 100223.

Ruiz-Martínez, I., Esparcia, J. (2020). Internet access in rural areas: Brake or stimulus as post-COVID-19 opportunity? *Sustainability* **12**(22), 9619.

Ryan, M., Corbet, S., Oxley, L. (2024). Is gold always a safe haven? *Finance Research Letters* **64**, 105438.

Rösch, D. M., Subrahmanyam, A., Van Dijk, M. A. (2017). The dynamics of market efficiency. *The Review of Financial Studies* **30**(4), 1151–1187.

Salisu, A. A., Raheem, I. D., Vo, X. V. (2021). Assessing the safe haven property of the gold market during COVID-19 pandemic. *International Review of Financial Analysis* **74**, 101666.

Samitas, A., Kampouris, E., Polyzos, S. (2022). COVID-19 pandemic and spillover effects in stock markets: A financial network approach. *International Review of Financial Analysis* **80**, 102005.

Scherf, M., Matschke, X., Rieger, M. O. (2022). Stock market reactions to COVID-19 lockdown: A global analysis. *Finance Research Letters* **45**, 102245.

Scrimgeour, F., Corbet, S., Akyildirim, E. (2024). Understanding the impact of ESG incidents on agricultural corporations. Available at SSRN 4870499.

Seshadri, U., Kumar, P. (2023). A novel approach to conducting business research after COVID-19: Incorporating crisis elements in the study frameworks. *International Journal of Law and Management* **65**(1), 88–103.

Shachat, J., Walker, M., Wei, L. (2021). How the onset of the COVID-19 pandemic impacted pro-social behaviour and individual preferences: Experimental evidence from China. *Journal of Economic Behavior & Organization* **190**, 480–494.

Shahed, K. S., Azeem, A., Ali, S. M., Moktadir, M. A. (2021). A supply chain disruption risk mitigation model to manage COVID-19 pandemic risk. *Environmental Science and Pollution Research*, 1–16.

Shahzad, S. J. H., Bouri, E., Roubaud, D., Kristoufek, L., Lucey, B. (2019). Is Bitcoin a better safe-haven investment than gold and commodities? *International Review of Financial Analysis* **63**, 322–330.

Shao, X., Liu, S., Ran, R., Liu, Y. (2022). Environmental regulation, market demand, and green innovation: Spatial perspective evidence from China. *Environmental Science and Pollution Research* **29**(42), 63859–63885.

Sharma, A., Nicolau, J. L. (2020). An open market valuation of the effects of COVID-19 on the travel and tourism industry. *Annals of Tourism Research* **83**, 102990.

Sharma, A. K., Rai, S. K. (2024). COVID-19 and sectoral employment in India: Impact and implications. *Indian Journal of Labour Economics* **67**(1), 177–196.

Sharma, G. D., Tiwari, A. K., Talan, G., Jain, M. (2021). Revisiting the sustainable versus conventional investment dilemma in COVID-19 times. *Energy Policy* **156**, 112467.

Shaw, N., Eschenbrenner, B., Baier, D. (2022). Online shopping continuance after COVID-19: A comparison of Canada, Germany and the United States. *Journal of Retailing and Consumer Services* **69**, 103100.

Sheehan, N. T., Vaidyanathan, G., Fox, K. A., Klassen, M. (2023). Making the invisible, visible: Overcoming barriers to ESG performance with an ESG mindset. *Business Horizons* **66**(2), 265–276.

Shen, H., Fu, M., Pan, H., Yu, Z., Chen, Y. (2020). The impact of the COVID-19 pandemic on firm performance. *Emerging Markets Finance & Trade* **56**(10), 2213–2230.

Siedner, M. J., Harling, G., Reynolds, Z., Gilbert, R. F., Haneuse, S., Venkataramani, A. S., Tsai, A. C. (2020). Social distancing to slow the US COVID-19 epidemic: Longitudinal pretest–posttest comparison group study. *PLoS Medicine* **17**(8), e1003244.

Singh, S., McNab, C., Olson, R. M., Bristol, N., Nolan, C., Bergstrøm, E., Bartos, M., Mabuchi, S., Panjabi, R., Karan, A. et al. (2021). How an outbreak became a pandemic: A chronological analysis of crucial junctures and international obligations in the early months of the COVID-19 pandemic. *The Lancet* **398**(10316), 2109–2124.

Smales, L. A. (2024). Stock market liquidity during crisis periods: Australian evidence. *Accounting and Finance* **64**(2), 1849–1878.

Soto-Acosta, P. (2020). COVID-19 pandemic: Shifting digital transformation to a high-speed gear. *Information Systems Management* **37**(4), 260–266.

Soto-Acosta, P. (2024). Navigating uncertainty: Post-pandemic issues on digital transformation. *Information Systems Management* **41**(1), 20–26.
Spatt, C. S. (2020). A tale of two crises: The 2008 mortgage meltdown and the 2020 COVID-19 crisis. *The Review of Asset Pricing Studies* **10**(4), 759–790.
Spelta, A., Pecora, N., Flori, A., Giudici, P. (2023). The impact of the SARS-CoV-2 pandemic on financial markets: A seismologic approach. *Annals of Operations Research* **330**(1), 639–664.
Suardi, S., Xu, C., Zhou, Z. I. (2022). COVID-19 pandemic and liquidity commonality. *Journal of International Financial Markets, Institutions & Money* **78**, 101572.
Sukharev, O. S. (2020). Economic crisis as a consequence COVID-19 virus attack: Risk and damage assessment. *Quantitative Finance and Economics* **4**(2), 274–293.
Sun, X., Wandelt, S., Zheng, C., Zhang, A. (2021). COVID-19 pandemic and air transportation: Successfully navigating the paper hurricane. *Journal of Air Transport Management* **94**, 102062.
Sun, X., Wandelt, S., Zhang, A. (2022). STARTUPS: Founding airlines during COVID-19—A hopeless endeavor or an ample opportunity for a better aviation system? *Transport Policy* **118**, 10–19.
Suthar, A. B., Wang, J., Seffren, V., Wiegand, R. E., Griffing, S., Zell, E. (2022). Public health impact of COVID-19 vaccines in the US: Observational study. *BMJ* **377**, e069317.
Symons, K., Breitbarth, T., Zubcevic-Basic, N., Wilson, K., Sherry, E., Karg, A. (2022). The (un) level playing field: Sport media during COVID-19. *European Sport Management Quarterly* **22**(1), 55–71.
Szczygielski, J. J., Charteris, A., Bwanya, P. R., Brzeszczyński, J. (2022). The impact and role of COVID-19 uncertainty: A global industry analysis. *International Review of Financial Analysis* **80**, 101837.
Szczygielski, J. J., Charteris, A., Bwanya, P. R., Brzeszczyński, J. (2023). Which COVID-19 information really impacts stock markets? *Journal of International Financial Markets, Institutions & Money* **84**, 101592.
Taleb, N. N. (2007). Black swans and the domains of statistics. *The American Statistician* **61**(3), 198–200.
Tanin, T. I., Sarker, A., Brooks, R., Do, H. X. (2022). Does oil impact gold during COVID-19 and three other recent crises? *Energy Economics* **108**, 105938.
Tawiah, B., O'Connor Keefe, M. (2022). Cash holdings and corporate investment: Evidence from COVID-19. *Review of Corporate Finance*.
Taylor, L. (2022). COVID-19: True global death toll from pandemic is almost 15 million, says WHO. *BMJ: British Medical Journal* **377**, o1144.
Thu, T. P. B., Ngoc, P. N. H., Hai, N. M. et al. (2020). Effect of the social distancing measures on the spread of COVID-19 in 10 highly infected countries. *Science of the Total Environment* **742**, 140430.
Todorov, K. (2020). Quantify the quantitative easing: Impact on bonds and corporate debt issuance. *Journal of Financial Economics* **135**(2), 340–358.
Topcu, M., Gulal, O. S. (2020). The impact of COVID-19 on emerging stock markets. *Finance Research Letters* **36**, 101691.
Torero, M. (2020). Without food, there can be no exit from the pandemic. *Nature* **580**(7805), 588–589.
Torrence, C., Compo, G. P. (1998). A practical guide to wavelet analysis. *Bulletin of the American Meteorological Society* **79**(1), 61–78.
Tufail, S., Alvi, S., Hoang, V.-N., Wilson, C. (2024). The effects of conventional and unconventional monetary policies of the US, EU, and China on global green investment. *Energy Economics* **134**, 107549.
Tuna, G., Tuna, V. E. (2022). Are effects of COVID-19 pandemic on financial markets permanent or temporary? Evidence from gold, oil and stock markets. *Resources Policy* **76**, 102637.
Tut, D. (2023). FinTech and the COVID-19 pandemic: Evidence from electronic payment systems. *Emerging Markets Review* **54**, 100999.
Urquhart, A., Zhang, H. (2019). Is Bitcoin a hedge or safe haven for currencies? An intraday analysis. *International Review of Financial Analysis* **63**, 49–57.
Usher, A. D. (2021). A beautiful idea: How COVAX has fallen short. *The Lancet* **397**(10292), 2322–2325.
Vacha, L., Barunik, J. (2012). Co-movement of energy commodities revisited: Evidence from wavelet coherence analysis. *Energy Economics* **34**(1), 241–247.

Vale, M. M., Berenguer, E., de Menezes, M. A., de Castro, E. B. V., de Siqueira, L. P., Rita de Cássia, Q. P. (2021). The COVID-19 pandemic as an opportunity to weaken environmental protection in Brazil. *Biological Conservation* **255**, 108994.

Van Duuren, E., Plantinga, A., Scholtens, B. (2016). ESG integration and the investment management process: Fundamental investing reinvented. *Journal of Business Ethics* **138**, 525–533.

Van Nieuwerburgh, S. (2023). The remote work revolution: Impact on real estate values and the urban environment: 2023 AREUEA Presidential Address. *Real Estate Economics* **51**(1), 7–48.

Velde, F. R. (2022). What happened to the US economy during the 1918 influenza pandemic? A view through high-frequency data. *The Journal of Economic History* **82**(1), 284–326.

Vissing-Jorgensen, A. (2021). The Treasury market in Spring 2020 and the response of the Federal Reserve. *Journal of Monetary Economics* **124**, 19–47.

Wang, P., Zhang, W., Li, X., Shen, D. (2019). Is cryptocurrency a hedge or a safe haven for international indices? A comprehensive and dynamic perspective. *Finance Research Letters* **31**, 1–18.

Wellenius, G. A., Vispute, S., Espinosa, V., Fabrikant, A., Tsai, T. C., Hennessy, J., Dai, A., Williams, B., Gadepalli, K., Boulanger, A. et al. (2021). Impacts of social distancing policies on mobility and COVID-19 case growth in the US. *Nature Communications* **12**(1), 3118.

Wen, F., Tong, X., Ren, X. (2022). Gold or Bitcoin, which is the safe haven during the COVID-19 pandemic? *International Review of Financial Analysis* **81**, 102121.

Weston, M. A. (2020). COVID-19's lasting impact on the sports industry: Financial, legal, and innovation. *Santa Clara Law Review* **61**, 121.

Williams, A., Chen, J., Li, G., Baláž, V. (2022). Risk, uncertainty and ambiguity amid COVID-19: A multi-national analysis of international travel intentions. *Annals of Tourism Research* **92**, 103346.

Williamson, S. D. (2012). Liquidity, monetary policy, and the financial crisis: A new monetarist approach. *American Economic Review* **102**(6), 2570–2605.

Wong, A. Y.-T., Fong, T. P. W. (2018). Safehavenness of currencies. *The European Journal of Finance* **24**(4), 300–332.

Wright, J. H. (2022). The extent and consequences of Federal Reserve balance sheet shrinkage. *Brookings Papers on Economic Activity* **53(2 (Fall))**, 259–275.

Xiong, J., Lipsitz, O., Nasri, F., Lui, L. M., Gill, H., Phan, L., Chen-Li, D., Iacobucci, M., Ho, R., Majeed, A. et al. (2020). Impact of COVID-19 pandemic on mental health in the general population: A systematic review. *Journal of Affective Disorders* **277**, 55–64.

Xu, Z., Elomri, A., Kerbache, L., El Omri, A. (2020). Impacts of COVID-19 on global supply chains: Facts and perspectives. *IEEE Engineering Management Review* **48**(3), 153–166.

Xu, J., She, S., Gao, P., Sun, Y. (2023). Role of green finance in resource efficiency and green economic growth. *Resources Policy* **81**, 103349.

Xu, D., Hu, Y., Corbet, S., Lang, C. (2024). Return connectedness of green bonds and financial investment channels in China: Implications for hedging and regulation. *Research in International Business and Finance* **70**, 102329.

Yan, C., Zhang, Z., Feng, Y. (2023). COVID-19 pandemic, corporate investment and the real option value. *Emerging Markets Finance & Trade* **59**(13), 3842–3865.

Yang, Y., Zhang, C. X., Rickly, J. M. (2021). A review of early COVID-19 research in tourism: Launching the Annals of Tourism Research's Curated Collection on coronavirus and tourism. *Annals of Tourism Research* **91**, 103313.

Yin, X., Xu, Z. (2022). An empirical analysis of the coupling and coordinative development of China's green finance and economic growth. *Resources Policy* **75**, 102476.

You, L., Daigler, R. T. (2010). Is international diversification really beneficial? *Journal of Banking & Finance* **34**(1), 163–173.

Yousaf, I., Suleman, M. T., Demirer, R. (2022). Green investments: A luxury good or a financial necessity? *Energy Economics* **105**, 105745.

Yu, C.-H., Wu, X., Zhang, D., Chen, S., Zhao, J. (2021). Demand for green finance: Resolving financing constraints on green innovation in China. *Energy Policy* **153**, 112255.

Zaerpour, N., Gharehgozli, A., Siddique, S., Dung, P. (2023). Impacts of pandemics on supply chains: Lessons learned, transition, and future. *International Journal of Advanced Operations Management* **15**(3), 224–247.

Zhang, D., Sogn-Grundvåg, G. (2022). Credit constraints and the severity of COVID-19 impact: Empirical evidence from enterprise surveys. *Economic Analysis and Policy* **74**, 337–349.

Zhang, D., Hu, M., Ji, Q. (2020). Financial markets under the global pandemic of COVID-19. *Finance Research Letters* **36**, 101528.

Zhang, L., Darzi, A., Ghader, S., Pack, M. L., Xiong, C., Yang, M., Sun, Q., Kabiri, A., Hu, S. (2023). Interactive COVID-19 mobility impact and social distancing analysis platform. *Transportation Research Record* **2677**(4), 168–180.

Zhao, L., Zhang, Y., Sadiq, M., Hieu, V. M., Ngo, T. Q. (2023). Testing green fiscal policies for green investment, innovation and green productivity amid the COVID-19 era. *Economic Change and Restructuring* **56**(5), 2943–2964.

Zheng, M. (2022). Is cash the panacea of the COVID-19 pandemic: Evidence from corporate performance. *Finance Research Letters* **45**, 102151.

Zheng, M., Huang, R., Wang, X., Li, X. (2023). Do firms adopting cloud computing technology exhibit higher future performance? A textual analysis approach. *International Review of Financial Analysis* **90**, 102866.

Zhou, H., Liu, J. (2023). Digitalization of the economy and resource efficiency for meeting the ESG goals. *Resources Policy* **86**, 104199.

Zhou, S., Meng, X. (2023). Are government bonds still safe havens in the context of COVID-19? *Applied Economics Letters* **30**(1), 14–18.

Zhou, G., Zhu, J., Luo, S. (2022). The impact of fintech innovation on green growth in China: Mediating effect of green finance. *Ecological Economics* **193**, 107308.

Zhu, Q., Ma, D., He, X. (2023). Digital transformation and firms' pollution emissions. *Technological Forecasting & Social Change* **197**, 122910.

Zhuang, Q., Luo, W., Li, Y. (2023). How does COVID-19 affect corporate research and development? Evidence from China. *Emerging Markets Finance & Trade* **59**(9), 3011–3023.

List of Tables

https://doi.org/10.1515/9783111707990-017

List of Figures

https://doi.org/10.1515/9783111707990-018

Index

https://doi.org/10.1515/9783111707990-019